Resisting Manchukuo

Contemporary Chinese Studies

This series, a joint initiative of UBC Press and the UBC Institute of Asian Research, Centre for Chinese Research, seeks to make available the best scholarly work on contemporary China. Volumes cover a wide range of subjects related to China, Taiwan, and the overseas Chinese world.

Glen Peterson, *The Power of Words: Literacy and Revolution in South China, 1949-95*

Wing Chung Ng, *The Chinese in Vancouver: The Pursuit of Power and Identity, 1945-80*

Yijiang Ding, *Chinese Democracy after Tiananmen*

Diana Lary and Stephen MacKinnon, eds., *Scars of War: The Impact of Warfare on Modern China*

Eliza W.Y. Lee, ed., *Gender and Change in Hong Kong: Globalization, Postcolonialism, and Chinese Patriarchy*

Christopher A. Reed, *Gutenberg in Shanghai: Chinese Print Capitalism, 1876-1937*

James A. Flath, *The Cult of Happiness: Nianhua, Art, and History in Rural North China*

Erika E.S. Evasdottir, *Obedient Autonomy: Chinese Intellectuals and the Achievement of Orderly Life*

Hsiao-ting Lin, *Tibet and Nationalist China's Frontier: Intrigues and Ethnopolitics, 1928-49*

Xiaoping Cong, *Teachers' Schools in the Making of the Modern Chinese Nation-State, 1897-1937*

Diana Lary, ed., *The Chinese State at the Borders*

Resisting Manchukuo:
Chinese Women Writers and the Japanese Occupation

Norman Smith

UBCPress · Vancouver · Toronto

16 15 14 13 12 11 10 09 08 07   5 4 3 2 1

Printed in Canada on ancient-forest-free paper (100% post-consumer recycled) that is processed chlorine- and acid-free, with vegetable-based inks.

Library and Archives Canada Cataloguing in Publication

Smith, Norman (Norman Dennis)
Resisting Manchukuo : Chinese women writers and the Japanese occupation / Norman Smith.

(Contemporary Chinese studies, ISSN 1206-9523)
Includes bibliographical references and index.
ISBN 978-0-7748-1335-8

1. Women authors, Chinese – China – Manchuria – Biography. 2. Women authors, Chinese – 20th century – Biography. 3. Chinese literature – Women authors – History and criticism. 4. Women and literature – China – Manchuria – History – 20th century. 5. Sino-Japanese Conflict, 1937-1945 – Women – China – Manchuria. 6. Manchuria (China) – History – 1931-1945. I. Title.

PL2278.S65 2007   895.1'51099287   C2006-906304-4

Canada

UBC Press gratefully acknowledges the financial support for our publishing program of the Government of Canada through the Book Publishing Industry Development Program (BPIDP), and of the Canada Council for the Arts, and the British Columbia Arts Council.

This book has been published with the help of a grant from the Canadian Federation for the Humanities and Social Sciences, through the Aid to Scholarly Publications Programme, using funds provided by the Social Sciences and Humanities Research Council of Canada, and with the help of the K.D. Srivastava Fund.

Cover art: The calligraphy on the cover was done by Li Zhengzhong and reads, "Fankang Manzhouguo" (Resist Manchukuo). The full text appears on p. 2.

UBC Press
The University of British Columbia
2029 West Mall
Vancouver, BC V6T 1Z2
604-822-5959 / Fax: 604-822-6083
www.ubcpress.ca

Contents

Illustrations

Acknowledgments

This project has been the subject of a great deal of critical and kind attention from a group of people whom I greatly admire. The few words here can never express the extent of my gratitude for their impact on this study and on my life. I thank Glen Peterson, who is an outstanding source of guidance and encouragement. His scholarly direction influences me in countless ways. Thanks also to Diana Lary for her inspiration and for enthusiastic support of this project from the beginning. She is an ideal mentor. I particularly treasure having had the opportunity to work closely with Catherine Swatek on several of the key texts. Her zest for literary work is truly inspiring. I thank all of my friends, colleagues, and the librarians at the University of British Columbia, whose help was instrumental in bringing this work to fruition. Timothy Cheek and Bill Wray offered useful criticisms and insights. Tracy Eso, Kelly Lautt, and Bill Sewell provided thoughtful commentary as chapters developed.

This book was conceived and assumed its present structure at the University of British Columbia, but it was greatly enriched during postdoctoral studies at the Institute for Chinese Studies at Oxford and at the Project for Critical Asian Studies at the University of Washington. I thank Tani Barlow, Madeleine Yue Dong, Rana Mitter, and Junko Nakajima for all of their help. I finished the writing in the collegial atmosphere of History and Women's Studies at the University of Guelph. I am grateful to all of my colleagues, friends, and students for their enthusiastic support; I am particularly thankful for Sheena Marti's assistance with photograph reproduction. I also thank the anonymous readers for the journals in which articles from this work were published; their comments were more valuable than they'll ever know.

At UBC Press, Emily Andrew has provided constant support and encouragement. Her choice of readers contributed much to this project. Camilla Blakeley has been an ideal motivator, carefully guiding me through the publication process. Thanks are also due her husband, Gary Blakeley, for suggesting the title. I acknowledge with the greatest of appreciation the editing skills of Barbara Tessman. The cover of this volume was conceived and executed by David Drummond. I thank him for a wonderfully evocative contribution.

I am especially grateful to a group of people in Changchun without whom this project would have been unimaginable. Chang Guizhi, formerly of the Women's Federation, and her husband, editor Li Jianqun, warmly opened many doors for me. I will be forever grateful to them. Their daughter, Li Ruomu, helped me through many of those doors and into places I could never have anticipated – including the study of Pan Wu, a scholar who writes under the pen name of Shangguan Ying. I thank Pan Wu for sharing both his keen interest in Manchukuo literature and his collection of rare materials, most of which is now permanently housed at Changchun Municipal Library. Discussions in Pan Wu's study proved essential to the development of this project at several key points. I am also grateful for the friendship and assistance of Manchukuo literature scholars Li Chunyan and Lü Qinwen. The friendship of Jilin University's Ren Yuhua, and of her entire family, made Changchun feel like home. Yao Wei and his family similarly made Shenyang a place worth living in.

The libraries in Changchun are invaluable resources, which to date have been far too underutilized. At Jilin Provincial Library, director Zhao Shuqin has been tremendously generous and supportive. At the Changchun Municipal Library, I thank director Liu Huijuan, a fellow scholar of Manchukuo, for her unwavering support. Ms Liu and Ms Zhao are surrounded by a dedicated and professional staff who truly made my work at their institutions a delightful experience. In particular, I note the help of Fu Jun, Jie Lijuan, Li Wanchun, Liu Yanan, Song Li, Wei Fengying, and Zhang Yinghua.

In Beijing, Feng Shehui of Beijing University provided helpful insight into twentieth-century Chinese literature and helped me to locate difficult to obtain resources. At the Beijing Municipal College of Social Sciences, Zhang Quan has been a friend and mentor for many years. In Harbin, during a wonderful week in 2004, the writer Chen Ti generously shared his memories of life in Manchukuo. In Dalian, Li Xiaojiang and Liu Jinghui provided thoughtful reflection on my work.

I am indebted to the four surviving women of this study, and their respective spouses: Lan Ling, Mei Niang, Yang Xu and Zhang Hong'en, and Zhu Ti and Li Zhengzhong. It has been a privilege to listen to their life stories, and to know them and their families. I am deeply saddened that Lan Ling and Yang Xu were not able to see publication of this work. Huge thanks are due Mei Niang's daughter, Liu Qing, for bringing us together – and for her constant encouragement and insightful comments along the way, in Vancouver and Beijing. Lan Ling's daughter Zhu Huimei has generously provided biographical information, photographs, and her friendship. Zhu Ti and Li Zhengzhong's family have provided great friendship and support in Dalian and in Shenyang.

I am delighted to acknowledge the following sources of funding: a Chiang Ching-Kuo doctoral fellowship; a Social Sciences and Humanities Research Council of Canada (SSHRC) grant for doctoral research at the University of British Columbia; and a SSHRC grant for postdoctoral research.

Material for portions of this work appeared originally in: "Disrupting Narratives," *Modern China* 30, 3 (2004): 295-325, reprinted by permission of Sage Publishers Inc.; "Regulating Chinese Women's Sexuality during the Japanese Occupations of Manchuria: Between the Lines of Wu Ying's 'Lu' (Lust) and Yang Xu's *Wo de Riji* (*My Diary*)," from the *Journal of the History of Sexuality* 13, 3: 49-70, copyright ©2004 by the University of Texas Press, all rights reserved; "Taming Wild Horses: The Banning of Yang Xu's Diary and the Construction of Womanhood in Japanese-Occupied Manchuria," *Views from the Edge, Occasional Working Papers in Women's Studies and Gender Relations* 10, 2 (2001), 26-36; "'Only Women Can Change This World into Heaven': Mei Niang, Male Chauvinist Society, and the Japanese Cultural Agenda in North China, 1939-1941," *Modern Asian Studies* 40, 1 (2006): 81-107; "Disguising Resistance in Manchukuo: Feminism as Anti-Colonialism in the Collected Works of Zhu Ti," *International History Review* 28, 3 (2006): 515-36; "The Difficulties of Despair: Dan Di and Chinese Cultural Production in Manchukuo," *Journal of Women's History* 18, 1 (2006): 71-100; and "'I Am an Ordinary Woman': Yang Xu and the Articulation of Chinese Ideals of Womanhood in Japanese Occupied Manchuria," *Asian Journal of Women's Studies* 8, 3 (2002): 35-54. All material has been revised for the purposes of the current book.

I remain most deeply appreciative of all my family and friends for tolerating the absences that this project demanded and for making the time we did have together so wonderful. I thank them all and, especially Barbara and Danial Bertrand and family, Don Smith, Lorraine and Mike King and family, and Richard Cheng. This work is dedicated to a woman whose life-long optimism and perseverance have inspired those who know her: my mother, Margaret Arseneau.

Introduction

In early November 1944, Mei Niang (b. 1920),[1] the pre-eminent woman writer in north China, travelled from her home in Beijing to Nanjing, the capital of Japan's conquests in south China and the site of notorious wartime atrocities, to attend the third and final Greater East Asia Writers' Congress (*Dadongya wenxuezhe dahui/Daitōa bungakusha taikai*). At the congress, one of Japan's most prominent colonial institutions, Mei Niang's novella *Xie* (*Crabs*) was acclaimed novel of the year, and she was fêted for her achievements as a writer, editor, and translator. Her work attracted audiences across East Asia: just the previous year, in the fall of 1943, her fame was celebrated as bookstores in Beijing and Shanghai, both occupied by the Japanese, conducted polls to determine the most beloved contemporary Chinese woman writer.[2] The results linked her name with that of Shanghai's Zhang Ailing (1920-95) in the catchphrase, "nan Ling, bei Mei" (the south has Zhang Ailing, the north has Mei Niang). The two women were widely acclaimed for career accomplishments in territories under Japanese domination, contexts radically different from the post-occupation period, which subsequently spawned highly politicized evaluations of their legacies.

Mei Niang solidified her position as a critic of patriarchy in China's literary world of the late 1930s, in the Japanese colonial state of Manchukuo (1932-45).[3] Her work was featured in Japanese-owned, Chinese-language publications for much of the occupation; she published in Beijing, Manchukuo, and Japan. Unfortunately for her, recognition of *Xie* as novel of the year by the Greater East Asia Writers' Congress came at the most inopportune time for the ambitious twenty-four year old. By 1944, Japan had been mortally weakened by war against China and the Western Allies. As the Japanese Empire tottered into its final year and colonial officials guarded against any signs of sedition, Mei Niang's attendance at the high-profile Nanjing Congress was all but mandatory, despite any personal misgivings she may have had. Less than a year after her reception, however, Japan was defeated, stripped of its colonial possessions, and those Chinese who had achieved any success under Japanese dominion were tarred for their "colonial" careers. Mei Niang, whose name was publicly linked with the congress, paid a heavy price for her youthful ambitions.

A photograph survives from the Nanjing Congress (Figure I.1). It vividly illustrates the prominence accorded Mei Niang, a lone woman surrounded by men who also played key roles in the Japanese Empire's literary world. The group of writers, editors, and publishers is shadowed by a soldier, suggesting the dangers attendant to colonial cultural work. The photograph attests to Mei Niang's attendance at the congress, where she received her award and the substantial prize of twenty thousand yen.[4] Notably absent is her husband, Liu Longguang (1920-49) who, although the most prominent Chinese editor in north China, was wary of association with the congress. In the photograph, Mei Niang appears confident and self-assured, unaware that she was standing at the pinnacle of her career. Sporting a stylish leopard skin coat and a short, modern permanent wave hairstyle, she stands out among the men who surround her. But the centrality the congress photograph accorded her belies the high profiles achieved by her female peers in Manchukuo's literary world, as their male counterparts were forced into silence, exile, or the grave. Mei Niang's career successes garnered her undeniable fame, but there were other highly regarded Chinese women writers in Manchukuo: Dan Di (1916-92),[5] Lan Ling (1918-2003),[6] Wu Ying (1915-61),[7] Yang Xu (1918-2004),[8] Zhu Ti (b. 1923),[9] and Zuo Di (1920-76).[10] These seven women forged long-forgotten legacies that are

I.1 Mei Niang at the 1944 Greater East Asia Writers' Congress in Nanjing, at which *Xie* (*Crabs*) was acclaimed novel of the year. Mei Niang is standing behind Wang Jieren and Hou Shaojun, both kneeling.

integral to understanding Chinese cultural production in the Japanese colonial milieu.

This book interrogates the nature of Manchukuo's Chinese-language literary production at the high point of Japanese rule, focusing on the legacies of the most prolific Chinese women writers. I have two aims. The first is to paint in broad strokes the framework of Manchukuo's Chinese-language literary world. Three questions guided this endeavour: What factors induced Chinese writers to cooperate with the Japanese to work within colonial institutions in Manchukuo? How was the literature produced by Chinese writers influenced by the increasingly ponderous regulatory framework that cultural functionaries designed to control Manchukuo culture? Why were Chinese careers in that literary world subject to so much official persecution, both during and after the occupation? This study examines the specificities of literary production in Manchukuo and reflects on more universal characteristics of cultural production in colonial spaces.

The second overriding aim of this book is to contextualize the activities of the most prolific Chinese women writers in Manchukuo. How is it that Mei Niang, a woman born in Vladivostok and raised in one of the most northerly regions of China, was awarded the Japanese Empire's most prestigious literary prize in 1944? What forces propelled Mei Niang from the "backwaters" of Manchukuo to the forefront of the East Asian literary world? Were Mei Niang and her peers pressured by colonial officials to trumpet officially sanctioned ideals in their writings? Why did they pursue such high-profile careers in an unquestionably controversial context? What factors drove them to it? Their legacies were achieved at great personal cost and constitute a virtually forgotten vantage point from which to reflect on Chinese life in the Japanese colony of Manchukuo, from a women-centred perspective.

Canadian author Margaret Atwood has suggested that "literature is not only a mirror, it is also a map, a geography of the mind."[11] This study contextualizes the work of Manchukuo's Chinese women writers to offer a reconfigured, women-centred cultural geography of Manchukuo. These writers worked within a weighty regulatory framework to map out careers, which ultimately undermined the state that staked claim to their allegiance and sought to contour their self-identities. Restoring the women to a position that reflects their contemporary status will afford a deeper understanding of their lives and the context in which over thirty million Chinese lived in Manchukuo.

Format and Sources

This book comprises eight chapters. Chapter 1 provides an introduction, and Chapter 2 outlines the foundations of Japanese colonial rule in Manchukuo, emphasizing the debate over ideals of womanhood that erupted in the warlord era and radiated through occupation society. As will be shown, progressive gendered ideals of modernity, as articulated with reference to May Fourth notions of women's individual emancipation, inspired young Chinese women in Manchukuo to take advantage of the opportunities offered them by the Japanese colonial state. Chapter 3 sketches Manchukuo's literary world, outlining the boom in Chinese-language literature that followed a brief collapse of cultural production in the wake of the Japanese invasion. Contrary to popular belief, in the late 1930s and early 1940s Manchukuo was the site of a vibrant Chinese-language popular culture, which bound local writers with Chinese elsewhere, despite the shifting boundaries that accompanied the Japanese Empire's expansive growth. The endurance of May Fourth ideals attests to a cultural vitality in the Republic of China far greater than that state's contemporary economic, military, or political status suggests.

Chapter 4 recounts the lives of Dan Di, Lan Ling, Mei Niang, Wu Ying, Yang Xu, Zhu Ti, and Zuo Di. Their family backgrounds, early childhoods and education, and career paths during the occupation are reconstructed to illustrate how their legacies can enhance the understanding of Chinese life in Manchukuo. Chapters 5 and 6 introduce the main themes in their written work. Chapter 5 examines the women's critiques of Manchukuo's patriarchal foundations through the tropes of "patience and endurance"; love, marriage, and childbirth; and sexuality. This chapter highlights the feminist discourses that informed their work. Chapter 6 details the women's ambitions to "expose the reality" of Chinese lives under Japanese occupation, underlining the oppositional stances that they adopted towards what they perceived to be Manchukuo's retrogressive cultural agenda. Chapters 5 and 6 together argue the relevance of these writers' long-forgotten legacies to assessing Chinese lives under Japanese occupation.

Chapter 7 recounts the final stage of Japanese rule and the women's post-occupation lives, underlining the devastating ramifications of the writers' youthful ambitions. During the last year of the occupation, most of the women experienced official censure or worse. After the occupation, they were persecuted for presumed traitorous collaboration with the ruling Japanese. The final chapter suggests the value of pursuing Chinese women-centred perspectives in the study of Chinese lives under Japanese occupation.

The primary literature that is the focus of this study was authored by women and written in Chinese. Secondary sources, written by women and men in Chinese and English, have been used to contextualize their legacies. Japanese sources translated into Chinese or English, including collections of colonial statutes, intelligence reports, and scholarly work, have also been consulted. The accumulated work of the seven women writers constitutes a rich Chinese-language commentary on the Japanese occupation. The volume and breadth of their collective written legacy are staggering. Works include hundreds of novellas, short stories, poems, essays, jottings (*biji*), and one play, published in major contemporary journals, newspapers, and books. These materials were published in Manchukuo, Beijing, and Japan. During the Japanese occupation, five of the authors published collected works and two published more than one volume: Dan Di's *Andi he Mahua* (*Andi and Mahua*) (1944); Mei Niang's *Xiaojie ji* (*Young Lady's Collection*) (1936), *Di'er dai* (*The Second Generation*) (1940), *Yu* (*Fish*) (1943), and *Xie* (*Crabs*) (1944); Wu Ying's *Liang ji* (*Two Extremes*) (1939); Yang Xu's *Luoying ji* (*Collection of Fallen Petals*) (1943), and *Wo de riji* (*My Diary*) (1944); and Zhu Ti's *Ying* (*Cherry*) (1945). The region's tumultuous history has taken a heavy toll on these volumes, which were typically published in quantities of two to three thousand but are now extremely rare. Currently, no copies of Mei Niang's *Xiaojie ji* are known to exist.[12] One copy each of Dan Di's *Andi he Mahua* and Yang Xu's *Wo de riji* are held in Chinese libraries.

The primary sources used in this study are located in Changchun Municipal Library, Heilongjiang Provincial Library, Jilin Provincial Library, Liaoning Provincial Library, Shenyang Municipal Library, and the University of British Columbia's Asian library. In addition, original writings by Dan Di, Lan Ling, Mei Niang, Wu Ying, Yang Xu, and Zhu Ti have been made available to me by the authors themselves and by private collectors. Li Zhengzong and Zhu Ti provided me with a copy of Dan Di's still unpublished memoir, "San ru lianyu" (Thrice into Purgatory), and I am especially indebted for access to the private collection of Pan Wu. All translations are my own unless otherwise noted.

Resisting Manchukuo

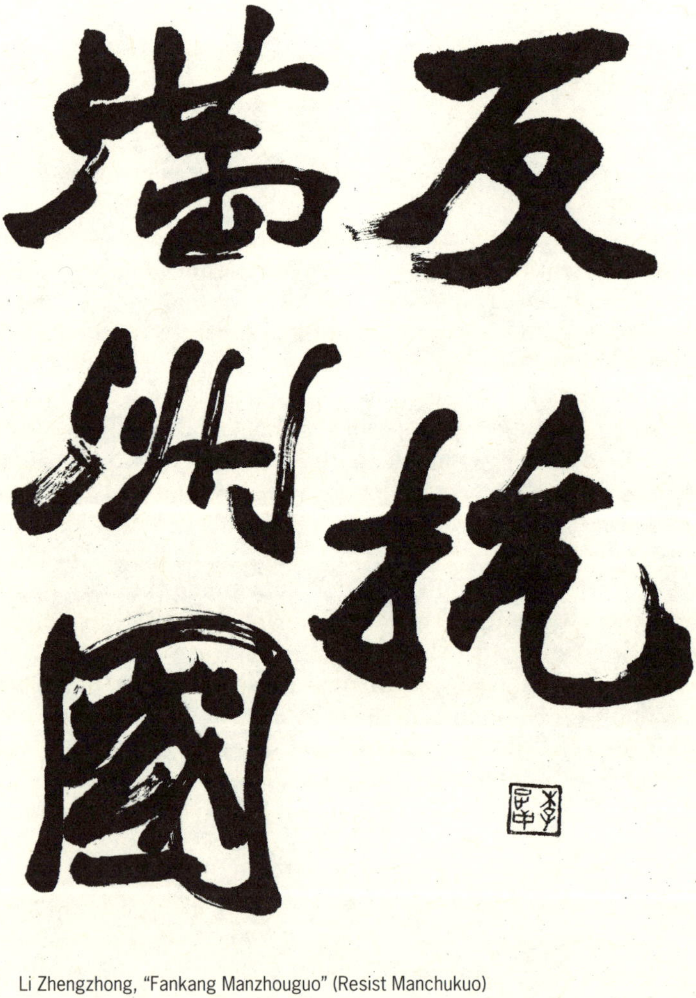

Li Zhengzhong, “Fankang Manzhouguo” (Resist Manchukuo)

1

Chinese Women and Cultural Production in a Japanese Colonial Context

The Japanese occupation of Manchuria began on 18 September 1931, when rogue officers of the Japanese Guandong army blew up a railway track outside of the regional centre, Fengtian.[1] That explosion precipitated an invasion that within months brought virtually all of Manchuria under Japanese dominion. The region, long considered outside the borders of "China proper," constituted "the Three Eastern Provinces" or the land that lay "beyond the pass" of the Great Wall. But with the founding of the Manchu Qing dynasty (1644-1912), the homeland of the Manchu peoples was solidly fixed within the Chinese imperium. The collapse of the imperial order resulted in a warlord regime that in many ways perpetuated late Qing development among the diverse population of Chinese, Japanese, Koreans, Manchus, Mongols, and Russians. With the Japanese invasion, these inhabitants saw the political context in which they lived their lives dramatically transform. Japan's rapid seizure of the region was capped by the formal establishment of Manchukuo (literally, "country of the Manchus") on 1 March 1932. The long-term, informal participation of Japan in developing the "pioneering" Manchu homeland was supplanted by a brutal military regime driven by Japanese dreams of empire. Despite the trappings of statehood and the 1934 coronation of the Qing dynasty's last Manchu emperor, Henry Aixin-Gioro Puyi (1908-67), Manchukuo's independence was a sham – it was in fact a Japanese colonial enterprise. For fourteen years, more than thirty million Chinese people from all walks of life lived in Manchukuo under Japanese colonial rule. All levels of local society were forced to reconcile momentous international events with their individual lives.

Perceptions of Manchukuo have always stressed the colony's Japanese identity. Japanese-owned media, the film and popular music industries, and official Manchukuo publications mythologized a paternal, inherently hierarchical relationship between Manchukuo and Japan; the emperor Puyi even submitted to an honorific position within the Japanese imperial family. Manchukuo was propped up by a ponderous Japanese military presence and therefore became to Chinese nationalists an intolerable symbol of Republican

China's military and political impotence and what Yamamuro Shin'ichi has recently suggested might properly be considered "an Auschwitz state or a concentration-camp state, more than just a puppet state."[2] The regime's racist policies privileged high-ranking Japanese and subordinated all other ethnic groups, to the extent of mandating race-based restrictions – on access to rice, wheat flour, sugar, milk products, cooking oil, matches, salt, and cotton cloth – that underlined Chinese national impotence and exacerbated contempt for Puyi's fledgling regime.[3] Officials attempted to superimpose upon the region's diverse ethnic makeup a Manchukuo identity from which a modern citizenry would emerge; the bureaucracy even dictated reference to the Han Chinese majority and their language as Manchukuoan.[4] The new terminology reflected officialdom's professed ambitions for the region, but it was not embraced by the disaffected public.

Manchukuo's instant disappearance following Japan's defeat in 1945 did little to enhance interpretations of Chinese life in the occupied territory, which were thereafter constructed on the basis of presumed loyalty to the Chinese nation-state: Chinese who fought or fled from the Japanese did so for strictly patriotic reasons, while those who remained and achieved any success under Japanese rule were tarred with epithets ranging from *kuilei* (puppet) and *pao gou* (running dog) to the ultimate condemnation, *Hanjian* (Chinese traitor). These labels contrast markedly with the term *hezuo* (to work together), that Timothy Brook has shown was used in contemporary references to Sino-Japanese cooperation in occupied south China (1937-45). Regardless of the seemingly less judgmental terminology, Brook stresses that collaboration of any sort was widely considered a "moral failure," even if it related to the performance of mundane tasks, such as supplying food, organizing transport, and arranging security.[5] Brook provides an important reminder that "collaboration happened when individual people in real places were forced to deal with each other."[6] In the south of China, many viewed the Japanese presence as a "provisional" circumstance requiring practical adaptation.[7] If their immediate survival hinged on "parroting the hyperboles of Japanese propaganda," they viewed this cost as minimal.[8] The long-term consequences of collaboration, however, were magnified for Manchuria, where the Japanese occupation lasted far longer and the populace harboured more serious doubts about the return of Chinese sovereignty. After 1949, the Maoist state (1949-76) moved to control historical narratives, restricting access to primary materials that shed any but the dimmest light on that era. Individuals who had lived through the occupation were also eager to put the dangerous ambiguity of their colonial past behind them. Understanding the Chinese *experience* of Japanese imperialism was supplanted by the imperative of demonstrating Chinese nationalist *resistance* to it. The contempt with which the entire period was treated is illustrated by the customary, and still prevalent, addition of the prefix *wei* (bogus) to all references to the Manchukuo period, for example *wei Manzhouguo* (bogus Manchukuo).

Chinese renunciation of Manchukuo mirrors English-language studies, which have tended to limit any praise for Japanese domination of the region to the area of economic development; Manchukuo has been dismissed as a cultural wasteland. To date, most work on the occupation era not only dismisses the very idea of Chinese culture in Manchukuo but silences the Chinese majority by focusing on Japanese-language sources or by depicting the Chinese as drones of Japanese economic policies, hapless puppets, or duplicitous traitors. Critics assume that no cultural achievements of any value can be attributed to Manchukuo, certainly none involving any self-respecting Chinese. Even Ronald Suleski's authoritative *The Modernization of Manchuria: An Annotated Bibliography* (1994) contains few entries on Chinese culture, and not one reference to women's experiences in particular. The same silence regarding cultural production and women's experiences characterizes most scholarly work on other occupied areas of China. Only recently have historians begun to direct attention to the "conflicting motives, tactical concessions, sheer helplessness, and all the other existential uncertainties that characterized" Chinese lives during Japanese occupation.[9]

In their volume on collaboration in wartime China, *Chinese Collaboration with Japan, 1937-45: The Limits of Accommodation*, David Barrett and Larry Shyu challenge "the moralistic framework in which wartime history is viewed," championing the extension of scholarly inquiry to subjects ranging from political activism to the movie industry, from northern China to its southern extremes.[10] Barrett argues the relevance of analyses of Vichy France (1940-4) to understanding colonial societies, underlining the value of distinguishing between the terms *collaboration* and *collaborationism*. This is an important distinction. He suggests that the latter term should properly be reserved for those French fascist groups that shared a "committed, ideological identification" with Germany's National Socialist program.[11] In Vichy France sympathy existed for the Nazi agenda, but Barrett cites a "virtual absence of [Chinese] ideological identification with Japan."[12] Japanese colonial propaganda, stressing a "shared race and shared culture" (*tongzhong tongwen*), rang hollow for the Chinese, who faced a brutal Japanese invasion without adequate military support from the Chinese government. Abandoned by the state, the population was forced to come to terms with the occupiers if they entertained any chance of survival; "for the great mass of the population in occupied China, there was no alternative to living with the enemy."[13] Yet the Chinese term *Hanjian*, once applied wholesale to the women who will be considered in this volume, and to many other Chinese as well, reflects more accurately collaborationism than collaboration. It thus has a far narrower application than has been the case. "Collaboration" may have been widespread in Japanese occupied territories, but "collaborationism" was far more rare, at least partly because the brutality of Japanese rule gave little cause for Chinese support.

As with interpretations of Nazi-occupied Europe, existing scholarship on Manchukuo (with few notable exceptions) is dominated by a Manichaean division between collaboration and resistance. In Europe, postwar disavowal of life under the Nazis is exemplified by the appropriation of the surname of Norway's puppet ruler Vidkun Quisling as a synonym for treason while staggering numbers of French have claimed membership in that country's underground resistance. But blanket condemnation of colonial society has been problematized by the revelation of what Nicholas Dirks has identified as the "parallel mutualities of colonizers and colonized."[14] Focus on the culture in which colonizers and colonized were mutually embedded – as individuals and as members of communities – allows the conflicted relationships that inevitably developed between them to become more readily apparent. As the cultural milieux of colonial societies are brought to light, once strictly drawn divisions between collaboration and resistance blur.

Not surprisingly, a highly contested middle ground lies between the two extremes of collaborationism and resistance. Werner Rings's pioneering study of life in Europe under German occupation is particularly germane, for it raises a once unthinkable question, "Could not collaboration itself be a form of resistance?"[15] Rings examines Nazi control over Europe from the late 1930s, identifying four degrees of "collaboration" and five degrees of "resistance." According to Rings, collaboration in Nazi-occupied Europe ranged from neutrality, in order to secure basic needs for survival, to unconditional, conditional, and tactical collaboration, the last characterized by a hostile stance towards the invader.[16] Resistance was similarly multi-faceted: symbolic (expressing pride in native culture), polemic (fomenting protest), defensive (protecting the needy), offensive (engaging in physical combat), or enchained (continuing activities while imprisoned).[17] Rings assigns these stances a permeability that destabilizes the essentializing nature of post-occupation narratives: individuals could simultaneously engage in seemingly contradictory behaviour. Rings also points to a counter-intuitive representation of responses to German occupation: as German troops advanced, the "resisters" fled with whatever possessions they could muster while the "collaborators" remained to face an unknown future under the occupying forces. As a degree of normalcy developed within the colonial regimes, those who had fled came to be praised for their adversarial positions while those who had remained to cope with the new reality were condemned by the expatriates as traitors.

Keith Schoppa has compared the Vichy experience to the Japanese occupation of Shaoxing County in south China, where, he argues, "the major division [of collaboration and resistance] masked other [differences] that sometimes ran deeper still."[18] In Shaoxing, "collaboration was not necessarily summed up by the word betrayal; resistance did not necessarily connote nationalism."[19] Schoppa demonstrates how "a host of reasons shaped by personal aims and existential needs and pressures" structured elite responses to Japanese dominion.[20] Local desire for stability and order on the heels of calamitous Republican mismanagement "likely made Japanese collaborationist control seem less a shift in kind than of degree."[21] Life in wartorn China forced difficult decisions, and "as people grappled with the often brutal realities, and as the community turned inward, it is not so much that nationalism was absent or tenuous as that it was temporarily subordinated to an array of more primordial loyalties and identities."[22] Although people's supposed degree of patriotism has dominated subsequent assessment of wartime behaviour, the necessities of day-to-day survival weighed more heavily on those Chinese who found themselves surrounded by the soldiers of imperial Japan. Survival necessitated an array of accommodation with the occupying foreigners, regardless of one's affection for the Chinese nation.

Analysis of the colonial experience as it was lived raises awareness of the layers of influences that structured individual lives. John Boyle's study of Wang Jingwei, the most famous Chinese collaborator, provides an explanatory framework for Wang's high-profile departure from the Republic: individuals could be swayed to work with Japan for distinctly personal career objectives or by a desire to see China freed "from Western imperialist domination and from the specter of Bolshevization."[23] Boyle reveals that individual decisions could be based on incentives ranging from greed to altruism, or any combination in between. Lo Jiu-jung has cautioned, however, that "for ordinary people, collaboration was seldom a matter of choice. It was lack of choice which ruled their lives."[24] Lo reasons that harsh Republican rule in the 1930s, and widespread poverty, left ordinary people with little option but to stay and hope for the best as the Japanese foisted colonial regimes upon them. Both Boyle and Lo stress that perceptions of "the enemy" and experience of Republican rule were crucial determinants of personal behaviour in a colonial context. For many, foreign rule could be preferable to native rule. Boyle cites historian Lin Han-sheng's observation that "in the historical experience of China ... collaboration with alien enemies has always been a common phenomenon, it has actually enriched China's culture and enlarged her territory and influence."[25] Lin's view of historical collaboration reminds us that in the past "alien enemies" lived alongside Chinese populations that stood their ground against the ebb and flow of political borders. In *Creating a Chinese Harbin*, James Carter argues that foreign presences – Russian and Japanese – were key to the development of the city of Harbin: "Chinese nationalism in Harbin grew out of simultaneous opposition to and cooperation with the large foreign presence."[26] Carter demonstrates how "Harbin's early nationalists ... sought to enhance their city's Chinese identity – in opposition to foreigners – while at the same time modernizing it – in cooperation with foreigners."[27] Thus, foreigners inspired varied reactions, on individual, regional and national levels.

Studies on Manchuria are beginning to reveal the complex interaction of Japanese, Chinese Republican, and Russian influences during the 1920s that eventuated in Japanese domination. Japanese economic and military expansionism overwhelmed the Chinese and Russians, fostering a plurality of responses to the Japanese presence, which itself was also deeply factionalized. Rana Mitter has deconstructed the "Manchurian myth" – that a spontaneous anti-Japanese resistance met the Japanese invasion – to show that in Manchukuo "collaborators with the Japanese, nationalist exiles from the occupation who promoted resistance, and resistance fighters on the ground in the occupied zone" were swayed by various individual, but *rarely nationalist,* agendas.[28] Nationalist sentiments were not the sole driving force that determined one's position towards China, Japan, or Manchukuo. The Chinese population's varied responses that Mitter has documented contradict long-held assumptions of an immediate, outraged backlash of Chinese patriotic resistance in the face of expanding Japanese imperialism. Mitter traces "the development of the narrative of resistance to the occupation" that played, and continues to play, a central role in the creation of regional identity.[29] He argues that the occupation bore several dimensions, both the long-stressed negativity of imperialist occupation *and* a more positive aspect that enabled Chinese political activists to pinpoint Japan as an imperialist aggressor against whom they could fashion an essential "nationalism of necessity" for China.[30] To this end, the occupation of Manchuria was used as a trope around which individuals espousing nationalist rhetoric could fashion new, grand myths to propel the masses, and themselves, towards future prosperity. Prasenjit Duara's *Sovereignty and Authenticity: Manchukuo and the East Asian Modern* problematizes the "facile clarity" through which the Manchurian myth and Manchukuo were long understood.[31] He "de-composes" the regime's sovereignty claims, via notions of Asianism, citizenship, ideal womanhood, and native-place literature, to argue that Manchukuo was a manifestation of the "East Asian modern."[32] Duara demonstrates how socio-cultural discourses were transformed by "historical, local, and regional practices and conceptions, vocabulary and symbols" to produce what supporters deemed Asia's most modern, multi-ethnic state, blending the best of the West and the East.[33]

There appears to be a growing consensus among revisionist scholars that singular focus on the state in a colonial context erases the complexities that characterized contemporary life. Recent scholarship suggests that, in China and Vichy France at least, individual lives within colonial regimes were influenced by circumstances that bore little relation to one's sense of patriotism. A myriad of pressures acted to deflect the rigid categorization that developed in postwar narratives.

Colonial Culture and Manchukuo

Nowhere does the complexity of colonial life manifest itself more than in the arena of cultural production. Michael Adas, in his examination of colonial southeast Asia, has demonstrated how colonizers there refused to tolerate religious sects or banditry but lacked the essential language skills or appreciation for the political intent of writers to control the "cultural expression of the colonized."[34] Arguing against perceptions that colonial culture serves only to legitimize the colonizing state, Adas stresses that the contradictory, interdependent relationships between the colonizers and the colonized enabled local theatre, satire, and other vehicles for ridicule of the rulers to persist despite an often overbearing colonial presence. In France, Henri Michel, "the doyen of Resistance historians," has similarly argued that any meaningful evaluation of the colonial legacy must situate it within its contemporary context. He proposes that "any action or writing that violates the 1940 armistice between France and Germany" must be viewed as resistance regardless of its production within a colonial framework.[35] Michel argues that writers in Vichy France who produced literature that denigrated German cultural or political ideals were an integral element of the French resistance against Nazi rule. Margaret Atack has also asserted that literature does not reflect resistance, but is part of it.[36] The present study reveals the contradictory relationships that developed within the nexus of colonialism, cultural production, and ideals of womanhood in Manchukuo.

The problem with received interpretations of colonial cultural production is superbly illustrated in Poshek Fu's examination of the moral and political responses of Shanghai's writing community to Japanese occupation from 1937 to 1945. Fu identifies three types of responses by intellectuals to Japanese occupation: passivity, resistance, and collaboration. Fu cites May Fourth literary influences that revolutionized concepts of individual autonomy in the 1920s and 1930s, enabling a "culture of criticism" to survive foreign occupation.[37] He highlights how the complex colonial environment could empower intellectuals to pursue the "cherished tradition of using literature as a political medium."[38] His documentation of intensifying levels of censorship and oppression after the 1937 crackdown on publishing, and of the "dark world" (*hei'an shijie*) of Shanghai from 8 December 1941, provides significant parallels with the "dark era" (*hei'an shiqi*) of Manchukuo. More recently, Fu has further challenged the "moral binarism" that informs interpretations of colonial life, demonstrating how Shanghai filmmakers engaged in both "passive collaboration and indirect resistance."[39] He compellingly argues that although "Shanghai cinema constituted an institutional part of the occupying power, it did not articulate an ideological position to legitimate that power."[40] Fu cites Japanese entrepreneur Kawakita Nagamasa who "opted for co-operation [with Chinese in the film industry] – not domination – because he was concerned that if the reorganization went too far all the major stars and directors would flee to the unoccupied interior."[41]

Fu brings light to a condition previously neglected by scholars: collaboration and resistance within the same institutional space. The Japanese colonial agenda in Shanghai required the participation of Chinese, which in turn necessitated their accommodation. Fu asks, "was filming any more 'traitorous' than, say, removing garbage or fighting fires as a profession? Of course, whether there was a difference depends on the extent to which their films participated, as cultural and social practices, *in the legitimizing discourse of the enemy*" (emphasis added).[42] Fu underlines an important distinction between working with or for and *proselytizing for* the colonial state. For the vast majority of the population, work was necessary for survival. Thus, conduct should be judged "traitorous" not according to the work engaged in but rather according to whether that work legitimized the occupying power. The cinematic world of occupied Shanghai "was an institutional part of the Japanese propaganda machine, but by almost exclusively making entertainment films it resisted legitimating the occupying power. It did not participate in the legitimizing discourse of the occupation, yet it did contribute to the normalization of the banality of occupied life."[43] Contemporary artists and audiences were attuned to artistic nuances that are only beginning to be incorporated into studies of colonial life. The differentiation between intellectuals who occupied colonial institutional spaces and intellectuals whose cultural productions served to legitimize Japanese colonialism points to a diverse positionality possible in colonial societies.

Analysis of the relationships within colonial cultural production highlights how writers operated through regulatory regimes constructed by officials who could be blind, sympathetic, or hostile to their activities. Through their work, writers were able to engage their audiences in reflections on contemporary life and, by association, on the colonial regime. In occupied France, writer Edith Thomas famously declared in 1942 that "not to speak the truth was to be an accomplice"; similarly, in 1939 in Manchukuo, Liang Shanding advocated "exposing reality" (*baolu zhenshi*).[44] Writers such as Thomas and Liang engaged with colonial institutions in order to communicate their alienation to a receptive readership. Max Adereth, describing the work of the celebrated couple Elsa Triolet and Louis Aragon, argues that "in none of these short stories is there any mention of the Resistance, all that they describe is the hopeless, heartbreaking everyday life of the time ... 'Woe unto us' ... said the author, and this is how his readers-cum-accomplices took it."[45] Ironically, the writers forged successful colonial careers by fashioning bleak, pessimistic portraits of contemporary society. Life's "heartbreaking" nature emerged as a dominant trope in both the literature of Vichy France and Japanese-occupied China, to reflect negatively on those colonial regimes.

Path-breaking works on the Chinese literary worlds of Japanese-occupied Beijing and Shanghai reveal that "occupation literature shows very little cultural identification with the Japanese."[46] Edward Gunn, Jr. has critically appraised the literature produced in Beijing and Shanghai from 1937 to 1945, situating it within the mainstream of modern Chinese literary history and criticism. He argues that writers remained under foreign occupation because of economic necessity or ties to the city or region: "regional affiliation was decisive in their decisions" to remain under Japanese rule.[47] Gunn identifies a variety of Chinese responses to the Japanese, most often characterized by "resistance, dissent, or disengagement."[48] The negativity of local Chinese literature testifies to the alienation most writers felt towards Japanese colonial rule. Although colonial officials attempted to rein in such negativity, they were for the most part unsuccessful: "The failure of functionaries to inject writers with a sense of joy, confidence, and militant mission is evident not only from a perusal of the contents of the literature, but from explicit statements by Japanese critics themselves."[49] Colonial officials sponsored Chinese literary production in order to legitimate their rule, but they could not completely control writers who were influenced not only by censors and state directives but also by their own agendas and audiences.

The conflicted nature of colonial cultural production is also revealed in the "triangulation between colonial Taiwan, imperial Japan, and nationalist China" that informs perceptions of Taiwanese history and identity.[50] Leo Ching notes how popular fiction from the Japanese-occupation era, long condemned as "enslaving literature" (*nuli hua de wenxue*), began to attract public and academic attention in the 1990s as Taiwan's socio-political climate became more open to discussion of its colonial history; Hoshina Hironobu argues that since then the public and academic attention has "spread like a little boom."[51] Ching argues that in light of Taiwan's occupation by Manchu (1683-1895), Japanese (1895-1945), and mainland Chinese (1945-) forces, alternate readings of "collaboration" with imperial Japan must be accommodated. Ching demonstrates that in *kōmin* (imperial peoples) literature of the early 1940s in Taiwan, "the struggle over identity emerges as the dominant discourse for the colonized," a "necessary internalization of politics into the personal."[52] The resultant, often dire, criticism of colonial society was similar to that in work by Japanese leftists. Ching cites Japanese author Hayama Yoshiki's praise for the novel *Papaiya no aru machi* (*A Town of Papaya Trees*, 1937) by Taiwanese author Lung Yingtsung (Japanese pen name Ryu Ei-so). Hayama lauds Lung's work for voicing "not only the cry of the Taiwanese, but also the cries of all the oppressed classes. It is in the spirit of Pushkin, Gorki, and Lu Hsün; it [has much] in common with Japanese proletarian work. It fully embodies the highest literary principles."[53] Thus, this "enslaving literature" did not legitimize Japanese colonial rule but was fixed within an international context of cultural criticism. The interpretive frameworks advanced by Ching, Gunn, and Fu have valuable application to Manchukuo, where writers similarly suffered post-liberation censure for their colonial activities.

For decades after the collapse of Manchukuo, all literary production from within the colony was dismissed as the work of *Hanjian*, with the exception of the early work of those who had fled by 1935, the "exiled faction" (*liuwang pai*). Manchukuo's "literature of the enemy occupation" (*lunxian wenxue*) was condemned wholesale for the writers' presumed collaboration with the Japanese. During the Maoist era, Manchukuo's writers were variously censured, imprisoned, or otherwise silenced. Ironically, the success that they attained by painting the Manchukuo period as one of unremitting bleakness contributed to their subsequent downfall. Specifically, their portraits of contemporary life made it possible, perhaps even likely, for subsequent critics to interpret that period as one in which only the most sycophantic traitors would have managed to survive. Thus from the mid-1950s to the end of the 1970s, the writers were condemned as traitors and their legacies "frozen at the bottom of history" (*fengdong zai lishi diceng*).[54]

Shangguan Ying, an avid consumer of Manchukuo literature as a child, has identified two dominant reactions to it in the Maoist era: condemnation (rejection of it as the work of traitors) and disregard (total denial of its existence).[55] Arguing that both stances distort the writers' original intent as well as their impact on contemporary readers, Shangguan emphasizes that their work must be evaluated within the context of the regulatory regime in which they lived and wrote, a reading he insists highlights their insight and courage. Zhang Quan has paralleled the trauma of Japanese occupation with that of the Cultural Revolution, claiming that literati in both periods "endured humiliation in order to carry out an important mission" (*ren ru fu zhong*).[56] Zhang believes that their work reveals the writers' "suffering souls and bodies" (*ling yu rou de monan zhong*) as they struggled to survive desperate circumstances.[57] Shangguan and Zhang represent the sea change in China regarding that country's colonial literary legacy. However, Zhang warns that the 1996 condemnation of the immensely popular woman writer Zhang Ailing in the Chinese press as a "traitor to China" for her activities during the Japanese occupation of Shanghai illustrates continued polarization of the field.[58]

Post-Mao liberalization is freeing scholars to reassess received interpretations of Manchukuo's Chinese-language literature. The first steps towards a more objective understanding of life and literature in Manchukuo were taken in China after Mao Zedong's death, at the Third Plenary Session of the Eleventh Central Committee of the Communist Party in 1978. At that meeting, the political verdict on Manchukuo literature was officially reversed, restoring the writers' reputations and clearing the way for reassessment of their legacies. Political liberalization, increasing access to primary materials, and a resurgence in regional pride have since piqued scholarly interest in Manchukuo writers, as reflected in their presence in compendia and other major literary works. Their work was featured in two journals established in the 1980s, *Dongbei wenxue yanjiu shiliao* (*Historical Research Materials of Northeastern Literature*) and *Dongbei xiandai wenxue shiliao* (*Historical Materials of Modern Northeastern Literature*), which meld rare archival materials from the early twentieth century with later work by authors of the Northeast as well as scholarly articles. In the late 1980s two volumes of Manchukuo-era short fiction were published. The first of these, *Changye yinghuo* (*Fireflies of the Long Night*) (1986), a collection of women's writings, went through two printings. The second is a volume of men's fiction, *Zhuxin ji* (*Candlewick Collection*) (1989). Significantly, both collections feature work from, and do not distinguish between, the exiled faction and other Manchukuo writers. Individual volumes of collected works by Mei Niang and Zuo Di, as well as by male writers (most prominently Gu Ding and Liang Shanding), have also been published.[59]

The resurgence of interest in Manchukuo literature was sparked by the writers who survived the decades of Maoist persecution. In 1986, Liang Shanding was among the first in China to denounce the politicized division of Manchukuo writers into two artificial camps, a division from which he personally suffered. During the Maoist era, Liang was imprisoned for his Manchukuo career, instigating a political divorce from his wife, Zuo Di (who was sentenced to labour reform for her work and died while Liang was in jail), and alienating his children, from whom he remained estranged till his death. Liang criticized the arbitrary persecution of those who had remained in Manchukuo, arguing that the long-standing preoccupation with the exiled faction's literary legacy offers only partial, distorted perceptions of what life was really like for the thirty million Chinese who had lived under Japanese rule.[60] In Liang's view, the nature of Japanese imperialism and Chinese lives within it are incomprehensible as long as the voices and experiences of those who actually lived through it are ignored.

In 1991, Manchukuo literature was the subject of a scholarly conference in Shenyang, attended by Liang and many of his surviving peers, including Dan Di, Lan Ling, Li Zhengzhong (b. 1920), Mei Niang, Wang Qiuying (1913-96), Yang Xu, and Zhu Ti, among others. This event was the culmination of more than a decade of work to restore their work and names and has spurred an unprecedented range of critical analyses, unimaginable during the Maoist era.[61] Scholars have begun to reassess Manchukuo's Chinese-language literature, promoting its literary and historical significance and resituating it in regional, national, and international historical narratives. Since the 1990s, revisionist Chinese interpretations have been transforming perceptions of this literature from singularly treasonous to a form of patriotic resistance against Japanese oppression. Yet Prasenjit Duara has cautioned that this wholesale rehabilitation of the authors militates against accurate interpretation of their work. Specifically, he argues that Liang Shanding's acclaimed novel *Lüse de gu* (*The Green Valley*) does not promote nationalist discourses but rather the "conflict between capital and community."[62] Duara objects that Liang's stance should not be interpreted as anti-Japanese but rather as opposition to the particular political environment within which it was produced. Duara's work underlines the importance of contextualization and the ongoing politicization of Manchukuo's Chinese-language literature.

Imperialism and Ideals of Womanhood

The collaboration/resistance dichotomy that structured post-colonial understandings of wartime activities in the 1930s and 1940s was bolstered by a truism: armed forces played pivotal, deservedly celebrated, roles in the termination of those colonial regimes. The praise accorded the military, however, had an unfortunate consequence: it downplayed less obvious ways in which individuals could disregard, or undermine the legitimacy of, a colonial state. Margaret Atack and Paula Schwartz have questioned depictions of the French resistance that focus on combat or formal groups – foci that they argue necessarily result in the occultation of women.[63] They argue that colonial societies cannot be understood by focusing on institutions in which women played a minor role and which continue to eclipse women's historical experience. Most studies of early-twentieth-century colonial societies have silenced voices that exerted considerable contemporary influence, including "new women" who advocated women's dominion over their bodies, relationships, and careers. Feminist and revisionist studies are providing important new insight into the legacies of women long silenced in the historical record. Women may not have played dominant roles in the military or in politics, but that fact did not exclude them from colonial life: men and women were variously incorporated into colonial regimes "for different symbolic purposes."[64] Colonial states have, as an essential element of their legitimation, assigned great significance to dictating ideals of womanhood.

Significant parallels exist between women's experiences in the "dark era" of Manchukuo and those of the "dark years" (*années noires*) of German-occupied France.[65] In both states, colonial officials actively sought to structure popular culture and ideals of womanhood to bolster reformulated conservative agendas. In Vichy France, rejection of the triptych "Liberty, Equality, Fraternity" in favour of "Work, Family, Fatherland" reflected that state's relationship with its German overlords, who themselves touted the slogan "Children, Church, Kitchen" with regard to women's role.[66] In the Vichy state, as in Manchukuo, officials directed women first to abandon and then to pursue extra-familial work, as war conditions dictated.[67] Each state linked national and gendered identities and sought the restoration of conservative ideals of womanhood to reflect their national aspirations; "the order of bodies [was] a fundamental dimension of the political order."[68] In her examination of Vichy France, Miranda Pollard reveals how

> women's and men's bodies, identities, and sexual activities had to be defined and regulated according to the needs of a new France that would do away with feminine frivolity, promiscuity, and egoism. Feminized desire had to be erased. The sexual discourse of paternal men and maternal women was not, therefore, some self-evident, one-dimensionally moral aspect of Vichy. This discourse was intrinsic to Vichy's politics of antidemocracy and rénovation, constructing social utility and gendered citizenship in the new France.[69]

The *rénovation* sought by the Vichy regime explicitly cited maternal women as the embodiment of the nation's moral order. The hard-won rights, to choice in personal relationships, pursued by French women in the early twentieth century were decried by social conservatives as emblematic of the "liberty" that had cost France its national independence. Vichy's ascription of an exclusively maternal ideal for women attracted right-wing supporters while it alienated more socially progressive women and men. Remarkably similar narratives were advocated by cultural functionaries in Vichy France and in Manchukuo.

In Vichy France, officials dictated that "duty and sacrifice were the new virtues" for women, with motherhood as the cornerstone of their program for national revival.[70] The new woman was decried as the personification of French national weakness, for her lack of devotion to the domestic sphere, where her most pressing duty was to produce babies for the nation. Thus, women's extra-domestic freedoms were to be sacrificed for the Vichy cultural agenda, a step applauded by social conservatives. Vichy declared motherhood the ideal state for French women: "pure, clean, wholesome, blond (or not too dark), simply dressed – in conspicuous contrast to the 'fast,' seductive, dark New Woman. Vichy's ideal woman was portrayed not glamorously dressed but in a housecoat; not surrounded by men or in public space but, significantly, with children and with other mothers, in a world apart, of domestic order and innocence."[71] Vichy's idealization of the domesticated mother, "in a world apart," demonized new women, who were condemned for a pursuit of individualism associated with a weakened French state. France's future was declared dependent upon women pursuing national, not individual, aspirations. Lucien François, editor of the journal *Votre Beauté* (*Your Beauty*) succinctly argued: "The truth is that motherhood causes the physical qualities of a woman to blossom, develop, [and] be revealed, at the same time as it permits her mind to achieve its supreme harmony in keeping with her unique mission."[72] Motherhood thus enabled women, as mothers of France, to realize their biological, spiritual, and national destinies.

The destiny of France was thus premised upon women subordinating individual ambitions to the needs of the nation-state, which was deemed the province of men. Miranda Pollard stresses that "underlying many of these sermons on duty and virtue is indeed a determination to restate and re-inscribe patriarchal privileges."[73] Pollard's work reveals how the Vichy ambition of cultural *rénovation* is incomprehensible if its patriarchal foundations remain unexamined. Manchukuo officials also sought to legitimize their discourses of morality by weaving narratives of the ideal "good wife, wise mother" (*xianqi liangmu*) into nation-building strategies. Women-authored texts provide a powerful conduit into how colonial governance and patriarchal ideals structured the life choices available to women and, more particularly, women writers. Only by extricating the lived experience of individual women from colonial and nationalist ideals of womanhood can one understand the real impact of colonial society.

After the collapse of colonial regimes in China and France, little value was assigned to women's writings that were produced under foreign occupation and that appeared to prioritize criticism of the subjugation of women rather than of colonial subjugation per se. Jennifer Milligan argues that women writers in France during the 1920s and 1930s sustained "an overriding aim of reformulating or rejecting traditional, reactionary notions of female identity."[74] Later, in Vichy France, Edith Thomas and Elsa Triolet rejected in their writings the conservatism inherent to the Vichy program. Their efforts to reaffirm the individual emancipation of women appeared to transcend national priorities. These feminist writers were first condemned by the Vichy regime as "the most hideous monster[s] that the earth can bear"[75] and then were left to languish, as the title of Milligan's work suggests, as a "forgotten generation." Similarly, Mei Niang argues that Manchukuo's women writers were silenced in post-1949 China because of the Maoist regime's obsession with nationalist readings of works by writers such as Xiao Hong (1911-42).[76] In France and Manchuria, the forgotten feminist writings constitute a missing link, the absence of which distorts literary traditions and historical records. Feminist work has been consistently downplayed in popular culture as well as by the writers themselves. Lan Ling and Zhu Ti, two of the writers examined in this study, respectively describe their writings as "little reeds" and "little grass."[77] Their statements echo the claims of French *resistantes* that they were not resistance veterans, but rather that they did only "what had to be done."[78] Ironically, their self-dismissive modesty has contributed to the delegitimization of the feminist discourses that they sought to popularize.

Several recent works demonstrate the potential of Chinese women-centred analyses of literary production to contribute to studies of colonial life. Rey Chow's study of Zhang Ailing demonstrates how that author's "modes of narration sabotage the identity that Chinese modernism seeks between 'inner subjectivity' and 'new nation.'"[79] By analysing the significance that Zhang ascribed to portraying "the detailed and the sensuous," Chow uncovers new readings of literary subversion, the agency of women, and the Chinese quest for modernity that are obscured by the dismissal of Zhang's work as inconsequential.[80] Nicole Huang further enriches our understanding of the legacies of Shanghai's occupation-era women writers by highlighting "the formation of a new cultural arena that was established by a group of women who not only wrote, edited, and published, but also took part in defining and transforming the structure of modern knowledge."[81] Huang reveals how Zhang Ailing and her peers "manipulated textual strategies in order to compose wartime narratives in the guise of domestic and personal narratives."[82] As "authoritative cultural commentators," acutely aware of their historical position as witnesses to a fleeting moment in human history, they recorded their impressions of domestic life and daily survival.[83] Writing enabled them to support themselves while producing a permanent legacy of the colonial era. Huang's work challenges arguments that link these women's success to their production of nonpolitical, "domestic" literature. Huang argues that their rejection of the common "themes of death, hunger, scarcity, destruction, and social instability" makes their work more difficult to interpret accurately but does not invalidate their value to understanding colonial society.[84]

The development of accurate interpretive frameworks for women-authored texts is also essential for Manchukuo, where long-forgotten Chinese feminist writings coexisted with the Japanese colonial cultural agenda. In the early 1930s, Xiao Hong was the first major woman writer to challenge the patriarchal ideals that she linked with Manchukuo. Xiao Hong achieved a national profile for her writings, which were lauded by China's most prominent writer, Lu Xun. Xiao's public disavowal of Manchukuo during the war invested her writing with a patriotism that has since dominated interpretation of her work. But Lydia Liu has recently pointed out that nationalism was "not the only, or even the dominant," paradigm that lay at the heart of most popular modern Chinese fiction.[85] Liu dissects Xiao's oft-cited novel *Sheng si chang* (*Field of Life and Death*) to reveal that novel's use of the female body as a metaphor for "viewing the rise and fall of the nation."[86] Liu demonstrates that Xiao's work, which is often hailed as a "national allegory," should more properly be read as criticism of patriarchy and nationalism, and not of imperialism per se.[87] Research by Liu, Huang, and Chow destabilizes received interpretations of mid-twentieth-century Chinese literature, suggesting the need for greater attention to time- and space-specific, *women-centred* approaches that are attuned to the cacophony of voices that characterized contemporary Chinese literary worlds.

Xiao Hong abandoned Manchukuo, leaving an inspiring legacy for the young Chinese women who rose to take her place – Dan Di, Lan Ling, Mei Niang, Wu Ying, Yang Xu, Zhu Ti, and Zuo Di. These seven women together published hundreds of essays, novellas, poems, and other works critical of Manchukuo society and, especially, patriarchy. They shared complex relationships with the Manchukuo state: they were beneficiaries of the regime's cultural policies, which ultimately led to their persecution once that regime had collapsed. All of the women received part of their education and rose to intellectual maturity within Manchukuo. Their work was published in Japanese-owned institutions that blended Japanese and Chinese management, including the most prominent newspapers. Under Japanese rule, the women established formidable careers, as the nine volumes of their collected works that were published during the occupation attest. Each of the writers attained a high profile in Manchukuo, only to be condemned, ultimately, by colonial officials and their Chinese socialist successors.

In the early 1940s, colonial officials grew conscious of the transgressive nature of the writings of these women, but the writers faced far greater persecution after the occupation. Unlike Xiao Hong, who also shared an ambiguous relationship with Japan but who died during the war, these women paid dearly for their youthful careers. In 1943, Dan Di began the first of three terms of imprisonment. From 1943, work by Lan Ling, Wu Ying, Yang Xu, Zhu Ti, and Zuo Di was subjected to official investigation, censored, or banned. For nearly three decades following the establishment of the People's Republic of China in

1949, all of the women suffered for their colonial careers. Their legacy was all but erased from popular memory. The only Manchukuo women writers deemed worthy of notice or scholarly study in the Maoist era were those who had left Manchukuo and whose writings appeared to focus on anti-Japanese themes. Thus, Bai Lang (1911-80) won praise for lauding the Communist Party's leadership in the anti-Japanese struggle, while Xiao Hong's work was promoted for its patriotic stance.[88]

From the 1980s, a resurgence of interest in Manchukuo literature has led to an unprecedented range of interpretation of these women's work. Zhang Yumao lauds their empathy for the poor.[89] Shangguan Ying argues that Mei Niang's fiction is a vital record of regional history.[90] Xu Naixiang and Huang Wanhua favourably contrast Manchukuo's women writer's efforts to "expose reality" with the "graceful and restrained" (*wanyu*) style popularized by writers like Zhang Ailing.[91] The Northeast's frigid environment and its "pioneering" (*tuohuang*) lifestyle are credited with compelling local women to abandon such "graceful and restrained" writing styles to pursue "rough" (*cuye*) and "robust" (*xiongjian*) depictions of social reality.[92] Shen Dianhe and Huang Wanhua argue that the literature demonstrates the "passion and courage of Northeasteners" as well as the women's interest in the woman question and national liberation.[93] Liu Aihua argues that the writers' persistent deployment of words with negative connotations infects their work with a pessimism that reveals their antagonistic stances towards Manchukuo. Liu notes that in Dan Di's anti-imperialist novella *Andi he Mahua*, the author uses the word "sadness" (*bei'ai*) over twenty times and manipulates over two dozen different adjectives to voice emotions such as bitterness, disappointment, and pessimism to enhance the novella's negative narrative.[94] Feng Weiqun and Li Chunyan have lauded the "new discourses" that the post-Mao era has fostered.[95] This emerging body of Chinese scholarship underlines the need to re-evaluate not only the position of women in Manchukuo's literary world but the potential of women-centred approaches for the study of Japanese imperialism in Manchukuo.

The fourteen years of Japanese occupation in the Northeast permanently altered the lives of the local population. But despite the length of the occupation and its manifold ramifications for the people of the region, the Chinese cultural world of that era remains largely unexamined. Several factors have lessened the perceived value of these women's writings in particular. In China, popular fiction was long thought to have little value, historical or otherwise. Confucian maxims that directed women to "internal" household matters meant that their writings, regardless of artistic merit, were believed to have little historically relevant content. In the Maoist era, all literature from Manchukuo was tainted by its colonial genesis. Lan Ling, Mei Niang, Yang Xu, and Zhu Ti have reasoned that young people in China are currently more interested in business than culture and are repelled by the pessimistic nature of their work. The socially engaged nature of their work, which was designed to "expose the reality" of the Japanese occupation, militates against its current popularity, since it is so closely aligned with a historical context that is overwhelmingly associated with shame. This book resurrects the legacies of these women and their ability to shine light on Chinese lives under Japanese occupation in Manchukuo.

2

Foundations of Colonial Rule in Manchukuo and the "Woman Question"

THE HISTORIC MISSION SHOULDERED BY THE EMPIRE OF MANCHOUKUO IS GREAT. CONSEQUENTLY, THE RESPONSIBILITY OF THE PEOPLE OF MANCHOUKUO IS SIMILARLY HEAVY. TO LIVE IN THE ASPIRATION OF A NEW IDEOLOGY AND TO PURSUE A GRAND MISSION, IT IS NECESSARY TO BATTLE WITH OLD ABUSES AND TO FIGHT THE RECALCITRATION OF THE IGNORANT. THE PATH OF THE PIONEER IS ALWAYS A THORNY ONE.

– *Japan Today and Tomorrow, 1939*

The thorny path of the pioneer has rarely proved more trying than in Manchuria, which was the site of dramatic transformations during the first half of the twentieth century. Situated at the crossroads of northeast Asia, between China, Japan, Korea, and Russia, the region faltered from a vast preserve of Qing Manchu heritage to a strategic territory claimed by immigrants, militarists, and imperialist regimes. In the late 1800s, as Manchu rulers became conscious of their tenuous control over the region and the designs of neighbouring imperialist powers became increasingly evident, the Qing finally acceded to major Han migration to the region. By the late 1920s, Manchuria hosted a relatively sparse population of thirty million, spread over a land mass of more than 1.3 million square kilometres.[1] For decades, the Qing, Russian, and Japanese Empires had faced one another over the vast expanse, but Russia's defeat in the 1904-5 Russo-Japanese War and the collapse of the Qing dynasty in 1912 fuelled Japanese designs on the region. Just twenty years after the collapse of the Qing dynasty, sovereignty over the Manchu homelands was seized by the Japanese; in 1932 the establishment of Manchukuo formalized the long-standing Japanese presence in the region.

Manchuria's precarious international position in the early twentieth century is vividly represented in a Russian postcard dating from the eve of the Russo-Japanese War (Figure 2.1). Manchuria is represented as a woman. Firmly in the embrace of Russia, she has a line of suitors seeking her favour,

2.1 A postcard from the Russo-Japanese War era, depicts Manchuria as a woman in the arms of Russia. She appears oblivious to the dangers represented by the men of other nationalities, who also try to grab her.

including Japan, China, and Western powers. Oblivious to her plight, she dances with her eyes shut and a slight smile on her face. Her passivity is highlighted by her pink dress, which contrasts sharply with the men's attire. Manchuria appears distinctly Caucasian and vulnerable, a prize for which Russia and its rivals compete. The postcard depicts for public consumption Manchuria's contemporary vulnerability, its subject position within the international arena, and the multiple influences that acted upon the lives of women in the region.

A Civilizing Mission

Japan's invasion of Manchuria in 1931, and the establishment of Manchukuo the following year, was met with condemnation but no military resistance from the Chinese government. In the misguided hope that the League of Nations would uphold Chinese sovereignty, Chiang Kaishek, leader of the Republican government, refused to take up arms against the Japanese. Meanwhile, Japan sought international recognition for its fledgling client state with only limited success; diplomatic relations were established with El Salvador, Germany, Italy, Poland, Spain, and the Vatican. Most of the international community decried Manchukuo as a fraud. The Japanese attempted to legitimize their domination over the resource-rich region by arguing that the numerically superior Han had proved incapable of properly managing the volatile area since the Qing dynasty had collapsed, resulting in a dangerously unbalanced "melting pot of races."[2] Japanese apologists for Manchukuo claimed that ongoing friction in the region, along with unsettled international circumstances, dictated that the Japanese take their "rightful place" as the "heart" or "pivot of the five races,"[3] the Han, Hui, Japanese, Manchus, and Mongolians, a collection that notably excluded the region's considerable Korean and Russian communities. Only through the "scientific, conscientious, bold experiment" of Manchukuo, they argued, could the destructive militarists and communists be held at bay, enabling the stability requisite for the realization of East Asian modernity.[4] In 1940, Toshio Tamura, director of Manchukuo's Education Bureau, clearly articulated Japan's transformative mission in Manchuria: "Before the establishment of Manchoukuo, the country was a scene of strife, racially and individually, but with the birth of the new Empire this state of affairs was completely liquidated. Both the Government and the people are now united in building a better world, a world with an infinite capacity for development."[5] Despite claims of an idealistic modernization agenda to enrich life in Manchukuo, the state's genesis was far less altruistic and too distasteful for the Japanese to admit publicly: a small group of militarists, led by Ishiwara Kanji, had staged a successful, albeit unauthorized, coup in Manchuria that Japan's civil leaders in Tokyo dared not denounce, even if they were so inclined. Ishiwara heralded the birth of Manchukuo as a sacred opportunity, if not a responsibility, to restore East Asian sovereignty in the region and to expel the Western powers through a final battle between Eastern and Western civilizations.[6]

A member of Japan's royal family, Prince Konoe Fumimaro, waxed eloquent over the 1931 invasion that "afforded the inhabitants of Manchukuo an opportunity for their rejuvenation, with important ramifications for people living on both sides of the sea."[7] The "rejuvenation" Prince Konoe anticipated was not forthcoming, though he perceptively articulated the profound ramifications of the colonial state for both China and Japan. Louise Young has compellingly detailed the lures of empire that left contemporary Japanese in awe of their ever-expanding Asian presence: new lands were acquired for Japanese migration, easing population pressures and the anxieties of over-burdened farmers. Manchuria dazzled with seemingly limitless natural resources and a huge potential market. The region and its wealth fired the imagination of a population that had been mired in economic depression since the late 1920s. Yamamuro Shin'ichi has argued that in all of the Japanese Empire, Manchuria was "the only place that held a romance for Japanese."[8] The Japanese state compelled its men to pursue a myriad of farming, trade, and military opportunities for personal gain and national glory, to help build the "paradise land" (*letu*) that Manchukuo was contended to be. At the same time, the imperial state lauded Japanese women's strength and endurance, epitomized by "continental brides" and "continental mothers," as essential elements of Japan's grand mission abroad.[9]

2.2 *Five Races United,* a 1942 commemorative stamp, uses five women to represent the Han, Japanese, Korean, Manchu, and Mongol peoples. The image was widely used in Manchukuo propaganda to stress the ethnic harmony that officials argued lay at the heart of Manchukuo modernity.

Like their male counterparts, Japanese women were encouraged to take an active part in constructing the multiracial paradise in Manchukuo depicted in a stamp commemorating the tenth anniversary of Manchukuo, entitled *Five Races United* (Figure 2.2).[10] But despite the smiles adorning the faces of the five women of Han, Japanese, Korean, Manchu, and Mongol descent, the "ethnic harmony" (*minzoku kyōwa*) that officialdom advocated proved elusive. Manchukuo was stained not only by an overbearing military presence but also by an unseemly segregation that elevated the ruling Japanese above all others. Racism was a defining feature of Manchukuo society. Japanese enjoyed exclusive access to consumer goods such as white rice and required constant ceremonial submission from Manchukuo's non-Japanese subjects. Japanese workers earned higher salaries than their Chinese counterparts; Japanese factory workers commonly earned more than three times the wage of the Chinese.[11] Reference to the resident Chinese as Han was prohibited: the Chinese and the language that they used were labelled Manchuokuoan.[12] Manchukuo's racist underpinnings mitigated against popular acceptance of even the most positive ideological elements of the state's cultural agenda.

The establishment of Manchukuo formalized Japan's long-standing presence in the region, which bristled with Chinese and other migrants searching for a better life. Decades of Japanese investment, especially that associated with railway development, had cut a long, thin swathe across Manchuria, bringing settlers and disruption in its wake. The benefits of that development accrued primarily to the Japanese, whose rule extended only tentatively beyond the urban centres and territories bordering the railways.[13] Through the 1930s and early 1940s, opposition to Manchukuo became increasingly difficult to suppress, despite the tens of thousands of "bandits" – a term euphemistically applied to any who opposed the colonial regime – who were uprooted or killed by Manchukuo forces. As wartime depredations destabilized the rest of China, hundreds of thousands of workers crossed Manchukuo's borders, in both directions. War, economic necessity and opportunity, and family obligations weighed heavily on the population, which was caught in the crossfire of empires.[14] Remittances from workers in Manchukuo to their families in north China were as much an economic boon as they were a political irritant to those who decried Japanese rule.[15] To control the region's fluid population, a massive influx of Japanese resources and migrants would have been necessary. Japanese officials unveiled plans for a twenty-year migration of one million farmers and their families from Japan to Manchukuo.[16] Despite such grand imaginings, only some 300,000 Japanese farmers migrated to the colony and many of those, unable to cope with Manchukuo's bitter cold and "primitive conditions," quickly returned to Japan.[17] Dreams of empire may have captured the Japanese popular imagination, but they were destroyed by the realities of "pioneering life," divisive Manchukuo state policies, and the northern environment.

From its inception, the Manchukuo government pledged an international "open door" policy to fuel investment, economic growth, and stability.[18] But calls for foreign investment capital fell on deaf ears, and the Japanese were forced to rely on regional exploitation and investment from the home islands to fund their massive imperial project.[19] Further, prevailing prejudices against *zaibatsu* (massive conglomerates) in Japan necessitated colonial construction without their blatant domination. Louise Young cites an unofficial slogan of the Japanese Guandong army: "The *zaibatsu* must not come into Manchuria."[20] The Guandong army, the might behind the Manchukuo state, jealously guarded its interests, forcing economic development to shift from informal policies to state management. Eventually, formal five-year plans were adopted; the first was unveiled just weeks before the outbreak of war with China, on 10 June 1937. During the period of the First Five-Year Plan, the declining economic environment witnessed a doubling of living costs, which were not offset by wage increases. In 1941, as Manchukuo officials made final preparations for participation in a "Sacred War" against Great Britain and the United States, the Second Five-Year Plan was unveiled, creating expansive holding companies that supervised private, subsidiary firms to strengthen Japanese control over the economy.

War demands wracked the Manchukuo economy, forcing the rationing of diminishing supplies of basic necessities. Ann Kinney has shown that from the late 1930s, immisseration accelerated rapidly; from 1938 to 1940, inflation in the capital Xinjing has been calculated at 73 per cent.[21] Poverty became a defining feature of local Chinese life as the economic lure that had formerly compelled migrants to the region disappeared. Having survived a bitter, state-mandated unification of fifteen regional currencies in 1935, which effectively destroyed the native banking system, middle- and lower-class Chinese were pushed towards the breaking point by the strains of war mobilization just a few years later. Ramon Myer's study of Manchukuo's "modern enclave" economy reveals that by 1943 the colony had become one of the most important centres of industry and mining in Asia but "very little, if anything, produced in this modern enclave economy benefited ordinary consumers."[22] War demands prioritized heavy industry at the expense of Manchukuo's subjects. A majority of the population struggled to maintain mere subsistence while Manchukuo, advertised as the "Land of Soya Beans," led the world in soya bean production, growing in the range of four to five million metric tonnes annually, approximately 60 per cent of contemporary world production.[23] The strain of war, the misappropriation of resources, and excessive investment in heavy industry devastated all levels of society.

Sovereignty over Manchukuo was ostensibly vested in the local elites but was in fact dominated by the Japanese. Initial Japanese moves to co-opt the local population into their own rejuvenation, especially through county-level "Peace Maintenance Committees," were largely unsuccessful.[24] The 1934 enthronement of the last Qing emperor Aixin-Gioro Henry Puyi (1906-67) altered the era name from *Datong* (Great Unity) to *Kangde* (Tranquillity and Benevolent Virtue), but offered little of either. Puyi was a puppet manipulated to mask Japanese dominion. A subsequent "government reformation" on 1 July 1937, did not transform the essential nature of Manchukuo's "military fascist" regime, which remained firmly under Japanese control.[25] State-sponsored organizations, such as the Concordia Association (*Xiehehui*), "the spiritual womb of the Government," were established to promote the birth of a modern "ideal State" but eventually became little more than fronts for an onerous colonial presence that was ever more difficult to portray in a positive light. All officials, teachers, and prominent social figures were automatically enrolled in the Concordia Association; it was also a tool for mass mobilization – all youth from sixteen to nineteen were compulsorily enrolled in its youth league.[26] In October 1934, a subsidiary of the Concordia Association, the Manchukuo Women's Defence Association (*Manzhouguo fang furen hui*), was established to coordinate women's support for the state; by 1938, it had over 140,000 members.[27] On a daily basis, through such mass organizations, education, and the media, the population was exposed to Manchukuo ideology that had questionable applicability to their own lives and ambitions.

The socio-political aspirations of Manchukuo officials were enshrined in the Confucian concept of *Wangdao* (the Kingly Way).[28] A vague raison d'être for the colonial regime, *Wangdao* was promoted as an alternative to the "imported" ideals of nationalism and republicanism and was especially targeted against the Republic of China's "Three People's Principles" (*Sanmin zhuyi*), which were immediately banned.[29] (A political philosophy propounded by Sun Yatsen, the "father of the Republic," the three people's principles were nationalism, democracy, and people's livelihood.) A Confucian "return to tradition" was touted as a way to vanquish long-standing warlord rule, to create a "golden mean between the fascism and bolshevism" that, the Japanese argued, threatened Asia.[30] The anti-warlord, anti-communist alliance between Japan and Manchukuo is vividly illustrated in the 1938 cartoon *Oriental Lullaby*, by the artist Ichiro, published in the journal *Concordia and Culture in Manchoukuo* (Figure 2.3).[31] Japan is depicted as a man destroying Chinese warlords and the Comintern, while Manchukuo is portrayed as a woman dispelling communism while watching over "The Rising East," their baby. The hierarchy suggested in this cartoon is illustrative of the gendered nature of the *Wangdao* agenda. Although its adherents never clearly articulated a viable political ideology, they cited from the classic Confucian text *Li ji* (*The Book of Rites*) social and cultural ideals that bolstered the gendered aspirations of colonial officials. In unequivocal terms, state propaganda expounded a conservatism in which "men will have their rights and the women their home."[32] Liu Jinghui has demonstrated how the "New Wangdao Woman" (*Wangdao xia de xin funnü*), whose loyalty extended beyond the domestic sphere to the state, the nation, and society, was constructed as part of the process of building a "national spirit."[33] Prasenjit Duara cogently argues that this "tradition-within-modernity" model of womanhood was promoted in Manchukuo to legitimize

2.3 Ichiro's *Oriental Lullaby* illustrates the anti-communist mission that officials envisioned Manchukuo would fulfill. While Japan destroys Chinese warlords and the Comintern, Manchukuo makes its own unique contribution to "The Rising East."

"the regime's sovereignty claims."[34] Social conservatives were doubtless attracted by an agenda that contemporary observer Owen Lattimore judged "reactionary in the extreme."[35] But as the writings produced by young Chinese women in Manchukuo demonstrate,[36] such conservatism failed to garner much support from a population that accorded women and men more egalitarian roles: local Manchu women were famed for their assertive character, and Chinese migrants also tended to feel less compulsion to observe the conservative Confucianism that may have structured life back home.[37] Manchukuo officials failed to appreciate that gender identities are as difficult to dictate as nationalist loyalty. In spite of assertions in Japan that Manchukuo was "turning Japanese,"[38] local officials were vexed by the perpetuation of home-grown ideals that flew in the face of their *Wangdao* ideology. Japanese officials blamed Manchuria's remote "geographical situation" for ensuring that its populace was "little influenced by modern culture."[39] Yet, the modern culture that Manchukuo officials aspired to introduce was premised on the construction of a reactionary social order.

The Manchukuo cultural agenda was introduced with much fanfare. Cultural functionaries envisioned the emergence of a new citizenry and justified Japanese domination by claims to be "civilizing" the indigenous population. "Proper education" was thus accorded great significance.[40] In the early 1930s, the Manchukuo education system retained Republican structures and texts, although promotion of the Chinese Republic was banned in its entirety. Until 1941, a wide selection of Western books was allowed to circulate, but any literature advocating the Three People's Principles was immediately replaced with Confucian classics. Extensive alteration of the education system began in the mid-1930s, with the dismantling of liberal arts programs in conjunction with announced expansions of primary and vocational education. In June 1937, implementation of the New Education System formally divided liberal arts programs from vocational training, limiting access to the former. Most students were channelled into teacher-training or vocational schools. Colonial officials promoted New Education as the bedrock of successful career development while Chinese critics dismissed it as a guarantor of their continued subjugation. British missionaries, active until their incarceration following the outbreak of the Sacred War in 1941, also loudly condemned the disruptions to academic education, arguing that vocational studies left the Chinese little chance of prominent positions in the colonial order.[41] Fewer opportunities existed for advanced academic study, for female or male students. These were further restricted by onerous university-entrance exams. State funding for overseas study, which was seen to be essential for career advancement, caused intense competition among students, who desperately sought the means to improve their deteriorating lifestyles. In 1937, although Manchukuo's population exceeded thirty million, only 369 students studied abroad; of these, 226 students were in Japan. Less than 10 percent of these students were female, a reflection of biases against women pursuing higher education.[42]

Manchukuo promises of East Asian modernity were met with diffidence, indifference, and defiance. While significant sectors of the population may have been sympathetic to Japan's "civilizing mission" in 1932, by 1937 the sheen was gone. Manchukuo sovereignty was widely held in disrepute. Ishiwara Kanji, who conspired to establish Manchukuo, admitted in 1938 that "the sounds of military oppression fill the entire realm."[43] Officials managed control along rail lines and in major urban centres only through a major Japanese military presence. Their boasts of widespread indigenous support for an autonomous, Confucian-based Manchu monarchy were patently false. Any pretence at Manchukuo independence was shattered with the Japanese military's removal of Ishiwara Kanji from the colony to the home islands following his pleas for Manchukuo self-rule. By the early 1940s, "years of police persecution, ... of persistent hope and pervading fear" had taken its toll in Manchukuo, creating a demoralized, impoverished populace.[44] The state was weighed down by its own inability to realize the ideals of modernity that it so publicly advocated. Instead, Manchukuo grew ever more dependent upon a cumbersome military complex.

The "Woman Question" and Manchukuo Modernity

Debate over the woman question (*funü wenti*) predated by decades the Japanese invasion of Manchuria. Pre-eminent Chinese philosophers and social reformers from Kang Youwei to Liang Qichao and Lu Xun had long pondered the relationship of women to the state. From the late 1890s, analyses of Qing dynasty weakness often linked the perilous state of the empire with feudalism, the historical development of patriarchy, and a correspondingly low status of women: "women's emancipation came to symbolize a critical distinction between the 'feudal' Qing empire and China as a 'modern' nation-state."[45] Indeed, Liang Qichao argued that "the key to *all* reforms lay in women's education" to mobilize the 200 million "idle" women of China for duties as "good wives, wise mothers."[46] Liang's progressive views on women's education were therefore linked with conservative formulations of women's roles within the household. By the mid-1910s, public debate shifted to focus on women's equality in terms of love, sexuality, and individual emancipation, in contrast to the earlier emphasis upon effective liberation in the service of the nation and the national economy. New women who personified the abandonment of feudal traditions by aggressively pursuing careers outside their homes and choosing their own mates became powerful symbols of social change.

In *Women in the Chinese Enlightenment*, Wang Zheng underlines from women's perspectives how the May Fourth era (circa 1915-23) energized Chinese society. The May Fourth protest movement emerged from domestic dissatisfaction with China's weak international position, spawning calls to radically rejuvenate all aspects of society, from self-identities to literary styles.

May Fourth encompassed tangible political agitation (e.g., protest against the 1919 Versailles Treaty) as well as a more amorphous "thought revolution." Articulating ideals of emancipation and equality, especially that of women, enabled youth to reconcile inherited self-identities with an influx of foreign influences and pressures: "May Fourth cultural revolutionaries ... turned the *funü wenti* [woman question] into a cause célèbre" by injecting new words and concepts into the debate over the future of the nation and the people.[47] Wang compellingly argues that the "gender issue ... shape[d] Chinese society in the twentieth century."[48] Leo Oufan Lee has also noted that during the May Fourth period the concept of "modernity" came to be viewed as a new mode of historical consciousness, which was reflected in popular culture; Lee cites writer Hu Shi's argument that "each epoch has its own literature."[49] May Fourth compelled debate over the nature of modernity, producing distinct literary and gender ideals.

May Fourth vested literature with unprecedented political power, as debates over imperialism, cultural norms, and the status of women dominated Chinese writing in the "Renaissance" (1910s and 1920s) and in the "Enlightenment" (the mid-1930s). Yü Ying-shih distinguishes between the two movements: the "Renaissance was originally conceived as a cultural and intellectual project, whereas Enlightenment was essentially a political project in disguise."[50] During the Renaissance, social critics sought "to dig up the common tendencies toward self-submission and expose them."[51] Short stories were written to air "domestic shame" in the hope that "realistic literature" would transform the masses.[52] In 1919, writer Luo Jialun vowed, "Our thought revolution aims to change slavish mentality into independent thinking, to change autocratic mentality into egalitarian thinking, to change chaotic mentality into logical thinking."[53] Social activists, like Luo, enlivened Chinese society in a myriad of ways. By the 1930s, wide-ranging intellectual debates waged over a "multidimensionality and multidirectionality" of contemporary discourses that has since been downplayed.[54] Yü Ying-shih demonstrates how the Enlightenment of the mid-1930s "was carefully planned and implemented by underground cells of the Communist Party."[55] This movement constituted a "systematic attack on superstition and arbitrary authority," aimed at the Nationalist Party and the Japanese.[56] The Chinese Communist Party (CCP) promoted May Fourth rhetoric to counter Republican and Japanese promotion of Confucian ideals.[57] By the 1930s, as intellectual debate melded with political rhetoric, the divergent stances of the 1920s were simplified to the bywords of "May Fourth" emancipation – and women proved the perfect vehicle.

May Fourth discourses frequently linked national strength, cultural criticism, and the status of women. During the 1910s and 1920s, students waged war against "a pervasive, internalized passivity."[58] "Passive women" were cast as the ideal trope for a weakened China. "Independent personhood" (*duli renge*), for women and men, became a key slogan that signified a break with the

Confucian and authoritarian past.[59] Li Dazhao, a founder of the CCP, highlighted "the ideological connection between women's liberation and democracy."[60] In 1915, Chen Duxiu, another founder of the CCP and of the influential journal *Xin qingnian* (*New Youth*), wrote, "loyalty, filial piety, and chastity are not at all a master morality that extends standards to others from the self; rather, they are a slavery mentality that makes oneself subordinate to others."[61] Pre-eminent political activists denounced the "slavery mentality" that they associated with Confucian ideals and political autocracy. Vera Schwarcz has argued that Chiang Kaishek's adoption of conservative Confucian rhetoric in the New Life Movement, inaugurated 19 February 1934, paralleled the promotion of *Wangdao* in Manchukuo. The New Life Movement was a political campaign launched in the Republic by Chiang and his wife, Song Meiling, to promote traditional Confucian ideals with special focus on hygiene and manners. Schwarcz reasons that the rhetoric deployed by Republican and Manchukuo colonial officials alike, stressing obedience as a womanly virtue, "increased the likelihood that a patriotic outburst would turn anti-Confucian"[62] Later chapters demonstrate how May Fourth rhetoric was deployed by writers in Manchukuo to criticize what they believed were outdated ideals of womanhood.

The empowerment of women was a central concern of social activists in the May Fourth era, epitomized by the popularity of Henrik Ibsen's play *A Doll's House*, which was translated into Chinese and published in 1915 in the journal *Xin qingnian*. Nora, the protagonist, became an icon for "new youth." She rejected male chauvinist subordination of women, declaring "I have a more sacred duty, my duty to myself."[63] Nora's clarion call for women's individual emancipation resounded through urban China. Activists condemned Confucian ideals of the "good wife, wise mother" for "enchain[ing] women through the requirements of chastity."[64] All aspects of women's lives were debated, as "the description – or rather, the prescription – of the new woman was radically different from that of a filial daughter, good wife, and virtuous mother in the Confucian system."[65] New women rose to shatter female stereotypes by forging careers outside the home and choosing their own husbands. Japan, while marketing itself as a pre-eminent model for "modern education," was attacked as a "pernicious influence" for perpetuating outdated Confucian ideals as men were encouraged to study science and women housekeeping.[66] "May Fourth feminism ... held the incorporation of women into all social domains as the precondition for Chinese modernity."[67] May Fourth–inspired modernity was symbolized by new women who, like Nora, rejected ideals of womanly submission.

Feminist critiques emanating from within China were bolstered by literary and political currents in Japan. In Manchuria, as in much of China, Japan served as both a conduit and a constraint for cultural critique. Recent studies have underlined the vibrancy of the late Taishō (1912-25) and early Showa (1926-89) eras, even as Japanese society edged towards militarism. Intellectuals such as Fukuzawa Yukichi had argued that cultural criticism was a civic right and duty of intellectuals, requiring their independence from the state; he famously condemned Japan as "a hell for women."[68] Calls for reform gave rise to a diverse political and literary environment. While officially sanctioned discourses linked women's maternal duties and nationalism, activists also engaged in the "construction of new subjectivities" that rejected right-wing political ideology and conservative gender ideals.[69] Right-wing discourses linked nationalism with "traditional" social roles for women, but "new subjectivities" arose to reject such conservatism.[70] Japanese "new women" (*atarashii onna*) refuted the idealization of "women raised in boxes" (*hakoiri musume*) and asserted that the militarization of Japanese society required women to take more active roles in society.[71] Debate over, and among, "new women" became a defining feature of urban Japanese society. In 1926, the writer Takamure Itsue assailed "men, modern society, and the West [as] ... all equally hateful."[72] In 1932, political activist Yagi Akiko famously denounced the creation of the "slave" state of Manchukuo and called for Asian socialists to unite in opposition to Japanese imperialism.[73] Similarly, writer Ishikawa Fusae urged "mothers of humanity" to work towards social justice for all and to end the destructive wars that were ravaging Asia.[74] Such overt political discord was illegal in Manchukuo, but Manchukuo youth were enthralled by such dissonance while studying in Japan. Having been weaned upon May Fourth ideals of womanhood, they were inspired by cultural criticism in Japan, where new women challenged the patriarchal principles that they identified with oppressive institutions.

In Manchuria, from the late 1910s, women and men engaged in public debate over the woman question, as key aspects of the May Fourth agenda of women's emancipation took hold in the urban centres. James Carter has noted how, in Harbin, students actively debated "'the relationship between the liberation of women and the nation,' and 'the relationship between women's education and society,' themes that paralleled the debates surrounding the women's suffrage movements taking place simultaneously in England and the United States."[75] Debate continued throughout the 1920s. Once the dust of the 1931 Japanese invasion settled and domestic publication flourished again in the mid-1930s, debate over ideals of womanhood was reignited. Women's personal conduct and relationships with their families and the state were subjected to intense scrutiny as cultural functionaries sought to meld conservative Chinese Confucian ideals with their Japanese counterparts.[76] Good wives, wise mothers were idealized, as Prasenjit Duara has argued, as "a significant constituent of the symbolic regime of authenticity."[77] From the late 1930s, and especially after the launch of the Sacred War in December 1941, colonial officials aggressively directed women's energies towards bolstering their families, strengthening the economy, and contributing to the war effort. The officially sanctioned ideal of the self-sacrificing, obedient woman was promoted through positive reinforcement and negative critique. For the duration of the occupation, the emancipation that young, urban women in Manchuria had grown to expect and advocate since the May Fourth period was increasingly linked with Western individualism and was virulently attacked by conservatives.

Excellent sources exist for reconstructing officially sanctioned resolutions to the woman question in Manchukuo: including the *Funü* (*Woman*) page that featured throughout 1936 in Xinjing's *Datong bao* (*Great Unity Herald*), proceedings from conferences on ideals of womanhood, journal articles on "model housewives," and contemporary cartoons from *Xin Manzhou* (*New Manchukuo*). All these materials were produced in high-profile Japanese-owned, Chinese-language media. They articulate ideals of womanhood that reinforce the Manchukuo cultural agenda and are distinguished from popular Chinese

2.4 *Different Women* vividly represents the dichotomous construction of ideal womanhood in Manchukuo. Contrasts between the "new woman" in the right-hand column and the "good wife, wise mother" on the left informed much of contemporary popular culture.

literature by their overt idealization of conservative constructs of womanhood; representative titles include "Zai Man-Ri xi nüxing tan" (A Discussion of Women in the Manchukuo and Japanese Systems) and "Dadongya zhanzheng xia qingnian funü de juewu" (Young Women's Consciousness in the Greater East Asia War). Without exception, "model" women are portrayed in these works as submissive, meek, and, most of all, obedient to patriarchal and state instruction. Any perceived deviation is attacked ferociously; new women, in particular, are criticized for being lewd, selfish, and self-centred. The contrasting constructs of ideal behaviour are succinctly captured in the cartoon entitled *Different Women* (*Butong de nüxing*) (Figure 2.4).[78] The depiction of the new woman in the right-hand column is paralleled with the good wife, wise mother on the left. The new woman is shown applying makeup, playing mahjong, dancing, going to the theatre, and writing a letter, while the good wife, wise mother is cooking, doing laundry, cleaning, and helping her son and husband. Although the intention was to criticize the new woman, the cartoon suggests a more ambiguous interpretation. Cultural functionaries touted the good wife, wise mother as the ideal towards which all women should aspire, but the pained expression on her face suggests that the illustrator, Xiu Wen, was more favourably inclined towards the new woman.

In officially sanctioned media, new women were consistently urged to abandon their "drunken-life dream-death" existences to support Manchukuo's cultural agenda.[79] Two contemporary cartoons vividly lampoon new women. The self-absorbed, profligate *Twentieth-Century Girl* (*Ershi shiji de guniang*) is caricatured in *Xin Manzhou* (Figure 2.5).[80] In the drawing, a pregnant woman

2.5 *Twentieth-Century Girl* caricatures a new woman as fashionably attired, pregnant, and tearfully downing the contents of a bottle marked "sleeping pills."

③ 求婚

2.6 *Marriage Offer*, with a trendily attired woman leisurely smoking a cigarette, exemplifies conservative critiques of new women, who were criticized for being greedy, Westernized, and immoral. The caption reads: "Have character, have education, it is not as good as silver dollars. / Know life, know death, but [you] can't know women's hearts. / With self-pride, the clothes rack says to the people making the marriage offer, 'In the end, will she pick me?'"

with a short permanent wave wears a Western-style dress with high heels. Holding a bottle marked "sleeping pills," she tearfully consumes the contents to end her life and that of her unborn baby rather than realize her duty as a mother. Significantly, the title's reference to the twentieth century in general might encourage readers to interpret the caricature as a criticism either of new women or of the colonial constructs that dominated official rhetoric – that is, a pregnant woman in Manchukuo had nothing to live for. Despite such subtle ambiguity, the intended critique of the sexually unrestrained, individualistic Chinese new woman links her allegedly destructive character with Western influences. The self-centred, greedy behaviour of new women is also critiqued in *Marriage Offer* (*Qiuhun*) (Figure 2.6).[81] Money is portrayed as a more powerful lure than material goods and education to the woman who, also wearing a short skirt and high heels, leisurely smokes a cigarette. These depictions represent a host of criticisms of new women, who were portrayed as greedy, Westernized, immoral women. The Western-influenced appearances of these women contrast with the depiction of women with distinctively "Asian" features, clothes, and hairstyles in drawings accompanying articles that outlined officially sanctioned ideals of womanhood (Figure 2.7).[82] The "Asian" women are portrayed with upright posture and a seemingly greater dignity.

2.7 *Asian-Featured Women* shows distinctly "Asian" clothing and hairstyles alongside articles promoting conservative ideals of womanhood. The appearance of the women is notably different from depictions of new women.

An avowed goal of Japan's "civilizing" mission in Manchukuo was to bolster the participation of female students in the region's educational system. Even before the establishment of Manchukuo, most women rose no further than primary school, but after 1931 those who did were subject to curricula that increasingly concentrated on housekeeping and hygiene, the domestic sciences.[83] The gendered nature of Manchukuo education is marked by officialdom's aim to raise men to be "the national backbone" (*guomin gugan*). Male students were directed towards the sciences and physical training, while female students were encouraged to become good wives and wise mothers.[84] Boys and girls attended primary school together, but were separated in middle school, whereupon the numbers of girls in formal education plummeted. In 1939, roughly one-third of all primary school students were girls. However, they represented less than a quarter of middle school students. That same year, the capital Xinjing had one female high school with 303 students, but no girls' vocational schools; in the region's largest city, Fengtian, there were more substantial facilities, with 2,527 female students in ten high schools, and fourteen girls vocational schools (Figure 2.8).[85] Discrepancies between men's and women's education in Manchukuo were a source of constant criticism by women writers who longed for more substantial intellectual challenges and career opportunities.

Remarkable parallels existed between the policies of Manchukuo and Vichy France with respect to the proper education of women. In Vichy, the regime instigated classes that focused on girls' future domestic duties. It advocated that young women "must be well brought up ... They must be made into vigorous and healthy women, straightforward and modest, honest and unassuming, having an equable and cheerful nature of a very high moral standard ... They must also be made into good housewives, clean, organized, and thrifty."[86] In Manchukuo, the Welfare Department, for example, in conjunction with the Concordia Association, sponsored the Xinjing Domestics' Institute to train young Manchukuo women for work as maids and housekeepers in Japanese homes; students had to complete courses in etiquette, cooking,

2.8 *The Well-Equipped Mukden Girls High School.* The Manchukuo government advocated education for girls as part of its "civilizing" mission. The high school in this postcard was promoted as evidence of the official commitment to local education.

hygiene, laundering, and Japanese language. Although the Domestics' Institute may be an extreme example of Japanese efforts to domesticate Chinese women, the type of education it offered was the norm for women, who were expected upon graduation to "go back to the kitchen" (*zouhui chufang*). A prominent figure in the promotion of domesticated Japanese role models was Shimoda Utako, an educator who believed that Chinese and Japanese must work together in their educational institutions to foster a Pan-Asian modernity, based on "East Asian values," to educate all women on the importance of preserving Confucian concepts of female virtue.[87] In Japan, Vichy France, and Manchukuo social conservatives argued that families had failed to adequately socialize their daughters, and this necessitated that the state assume the task of educating the young women to become good wives, wise mothers.[88]

In Manchukuo, the adoption of Japanese ideals of womanhood was deemed by cultural functionaries to be an essential element of Japan's civilizing mission, to raise local women's consciousness, knowledge, and professionalism. Chinese housewives were exhorted to copy their Japanese counterparts, learning to "bear bitterness and endure labour" (*renku nailao*)[89] as they laboured in households consisting of "nine generations living together" (*jiushen tongdang*).[90] Educated women, especially those who had attended university, were encouraged to single-mindedly fulfil their study and work obligations and to avoid degenerating into "flower vases" (*huaping*) to decorate work places.[91] Thus, "new era" women were to fulfil more substantial, nation-oriented roles and not just "change from garbage into a toy" (*you feiwu gaicheng le wanwu*), a criticism of both "traditional" and "modern" women.[92] Japanese commentator Takebe Utako criticized Chinese women for becoming too "passive" (*yilai xing*) during the Yuan, Ming, and Qing dynasties, relying solely on giving birth, raising children, and protecting their individual bodies.[93] Thus, Manchukuo womanhood was distinguished from the roles of both "traditional" and "new" women.

From 1941 Sacred War demands dictated that women, just as men, had responsibilities for and vital contributions to make to the nation, as good wives and wise mothers, but also as workers, subjects, and citizens. Men's perceived innate ability to wage war was paralleled with women's abilities to raise children and work hard.[94] Increasingly, the latter was stressed. As noted by Prasenjit Duara, the "ideal was not to confine women to the home, but to contain and deploy them in the public in a way that would serve state and regime interests."[95] During the Sacred War, women's energies were to be mobilized and redirected from self- or family interests to those of the state. Relationships between women and men were cast in terms of duty: "Marriage for men and women is not at all for pleasure or sex, but for the development and extension of the race."[96] Men were chastized for abusing women. Writer Xi Yi blamed patriarchal violence for rising rates of lesbianism as women became increasingly disillusioned with male behaviour.[97] Women were urged to join hands and work together with other women and men to pursue newly defined prescriptions for the modern woman: "Just empty yelling will not get any response, we must make ourselves role models" to wake each other up.[98] Selfless, modest dedication to the state and family would fulfil women's responsibilities for actualizing paradise in Manchukuo.

Such ambitions remained elusive, however, and Japanese commentators, women and men, lamented the reluctance of Manchukuo women to embrace the "beautiful customs" that they associated with Japanese women. In *Qingnian wenhua*, Mochizuki Yuriko criticized the Japanese in Manchukuo, arguing that Japanese cultural ideals could be fully appreciated only when viewed and experienced in Japan. She stressed that Japanese colonists were neither representative nor inspirational in several important respects: they were young, most were single men who did not know how to live properly "without any gentle elders to guide them," and most remained segregated from their Manchukuo neighbours and exhibited little desire to associate with them.[99] Mochizuki blamed the failure of local Japanese to personify their own cultural ideals for hampering Manchukuo acceptance of official discourses on women's docility and chastity, which Mochizuki describes as Japanese women's "fate."[100] Japanese pronouncements on the virtues of docility, that "soft can conquer the hard" (*ruo neng ke gang*), fell on deaf ears in a colonial environment that relied on steady demonstrations of the state's military strength but far too few moral exemplars.[101]

Japanese criticism was especially directed towards urban Chinese women, whose lifestyle was contrasted with that of their rural counterparts, and condemned. In "Xin Zhongguo nüxing de dongjing" (Sounds of the New Chinese Women's Movement), Wei Zhonglan recounts the Japanese writer Hayashi Fusao's portrayal of Chinese women after a visit to north China in the mid-1930s: "China's urban women love to eat, they are too lazy to work, they talk trendily, and are not willing like Japanese women to eat bitterness. I also went to the Chinese countryside and saw the condition of women in the villages ... Chinese urban women cannot be called Han people. True Han women can only be found in villages."[102] Significantly, Hayashi's depiction of "true Han women" (*zhenzheng Han minzu zhi funü*) locates essential Chinese women's characteristics in rural women who lived outside the strong Japanese colonial presence of the cities. Hayashi further argued that for a woman, the "true Han people's spirit is to make fire, cook food, prepare noodles, collect manure, cut wood, wash clothes, go to the fields to harvest rice, watch the children, feed the animals[,] ... eat bitterness and bear it, obey her mother-in-law and husband, to go through peaceful days."[103] Hayashi lauded rural women's ability to obediently "eat bitterness and bear it," a notably conservative stance. But if his denunciation of urban women is considered in the context of Japan's imperial project, it becomes clear that his criticisms do more than describe the so-called decadence of the urban Chinese women he aimed to critique. The behaviour he cites manifests the resistance of those women to the colonial cultural agenda: Hayashi notes their overt refusal to mimic Japanese gender ideals, work diligently, or quietly accept economic deprivation. The dichotomy in depictions of rural women who "eat bitterness and bear it" and of the "lazy," "trendy" new women of the urban centres is emblematic of attempts to resolve the "woman question" in Manchukuo. This contrast illuminates the gulf that lay between state-sanctioned ideals and the women who were expected to embrace them.

In the early 1940s, conservative commentators consistently urged Manchukuo women to forsake individualistic lifestyles. In "Funü yu wenhua" (Women and Culture), Bai Wu argues that most women were consumed with individual needs: clothes, food, and providing pleasure for men, "a type of prostitute life" (*jinü shi de shenghuo*).[104] Blaming such behaviour on the lack of employment opportunities available for women, Bai urges urban women to reconsider their priorities and provide a role model to rural women of the "new reality" of self-sufficient, labouring housewives in the service of the state.[105] A similar critique informs "Xin Zhongguo nüxing de dongjing," as Wei Zhonglan condemns "women in the sewers," prostitutes, dance hostesses, and waitresses, as "pitiful maggots in a rouge hell."[106] Wei demands that these women "toss away high heels and wash away vanity" to focus on raising self-consciousness.[107] These critiques all link self-centred behaviour with Western influences and condemn new women as negative influences upon other women, their families, and the state. Women were encouraged to focus on roles that were "suited" to their "nurturing" nature (for example, nursing and teaching), echoing the type of emancipation advocated decades earlier by Liang Qichao.

Criticism of new women accelerated from December 1941 as the Sacred War transformed life in the colony. In 1943, Takebe Utako argued that few middle-class women in Manchukuo were capable of assuming their national responsibilities: "We Manchukuo women are only anxious for rations or to passively protect our lives."[108] Even though war had not yet touched the soil of the region, Takebe spurred women to "come together to devote heart and blood to eternal Manchukuo" through simple living, recycling, and physical fitness; women needed healthy bodies to support the national war effort.[109] Takebe expressly warns that "in the courthouses, in the streets, and in the alleys there are many loud-mouthed women broadcasting their husband's concerns."[110] The Sacred War demanded obedient, hard-working women who were single-mindedly devoted to the state, which was posited as the province of their husbands.

During wartime, resolutions to the woman question were often cast in light of international trends, but with specific reference to Asian conditions. While critics in prominent journals most often cited Japanese precedents, they also favourably described women's movements in France, Germany, Great Britain, the Soviet Union, and the United States.[111] From 1941, Manchukuo women were urged to emulate their counterparts in those other countries, to "survive with the nation, or die with the nation."[112] Cultural functionaries outlined gender-specific occupations: nurses and teachers were at the summit of "women-appropriate" jobs, which also included clerk, secretary, and waitress. At the height of the Sacred War, women who engaged in factory work were promoted as patriotic role models. American, British, and German success in motivating women to assume active roles on the factory floor to relieve the men who were needed on the frontlines was lauded.[113] Women who simultaneously embraced the roles of worker, wife, and mother were idealized: "In society, she is productive, in the home, she is a smart housewife."[114] The successful performance of these multiple roles was lauded as the best of "Asian traditions."

Japanese promotion of East Asian modernity in Manchukuo, which Prasenjit Duara has characterized as "modernity within tradition," was the central ambition of the Manchukuo Confucian revivalist Morality Society (Daodehui). Members envisioned the Morality Society "as a mediator between state and family" that would "cleanse the people's hearts" by realizing Confucian *Wangdao* ideals.[115] Supporters advocated a conservatism that they believed would liberate women by celebrating them as repositories of tradition in vital new roles, as "the new middle-class patriarchy made common cause with the Manchukuo state." [116] The Morality Society extolled an order in which "husbands were righteous and wives obedient."[117] Duara reveals strategies "whereby women were able to manoeuvre the goals of the Society to secure advantage for themselves and for other women. This was hardly easy, as many women must have experienced the pedagogy as a form of objectification. Counter-representations of the modern, Westernized woman were readily available to these women ... and until 1941 at least often carried positive images of liberated, Western, and Westernized women."[118] Duara's study of the Morality Society details how women members appropriated conservative Confucian ideals (cultivation of filial piety, obedience to patriarchs, and self-sacrifice) to carve out roles for independent social thought and action. Duara argues that the women "manoeuvred the language in the same moment in which they were constituted by it."[119] They articulated complex patterns of belief and behaviour that informed their relationships with family, the redemptive society, and the state. As these women forged their own self-identities within the public arena, they found meaning beyond "resignation, coping, and solace from grief and mistreatment."[120] Duara pinpoints strategies deployed by women within the Morality Society to manoeuvre state-sanctioned conservatism in their construction of negotiated ideals of womanhood. Different paths to similar goals were pursued by Manchukuo's young Chinese women writers, in close association with colonial institutions.

In Manchukuo, officially sanctioned resolutions to the woman question emphasized constructs of good wives, wise mothers that reconfigured fundamentally conservative Chinese and Japanese Confucian ideals. In the early 1930s, considerable resources were devoted to encourage the development of Japan-centric, patriarchal ideals of domesticated women. As the Sacred War necessitated the orderly mobilization of Manchukuo's subjects, submissive, labouring women in the service of men *and* the state were idealized. The individual emancipation advocated by new women was denounced as self-centred behaviour, which reflected a lack of enthusiasm for the Manchukuo state and its professed cultural agenda. Young Chinese women writers responded to officially sanctioned constructs by reconstituting ideals of womanhood to embody their own identities and aspirations. As will be shown in the next chapter, the gulf that persisted between their ideals and those advocated by officialdom and social conservatives is emblematic of the rifts that enlivened Manchukuo's literary world.

3

Manchukuo's Chinese-Language Literary World

If the historical record reaps anything but a harvest of bitterness from the years of the occupation, it will be this literary harvest of achievement.

– *Edward M. Gunn, Jr.*

During the first half of the twentieth century, dramatic shifts in the structure of Manchurian society gave rise to a vibrant Chinese-language literary world. Regional society was shaken by the May Fourth movement as it swept northward from Beijing in the late 1910s and early 1920s, bringing with it an unprecedented range of experimental literature.[1] Usage of the vernacular language, experimentation with subjectivity, and other diverse writing styles rapidly gained in popularity. By 1928, "new literature" flourished in the region.[2] Young writers raised their pens to condemn "traditional" customs, especially what they believed to be tragically outdated gender ideals. Among the most influential contemporary Chinese writers were Bing Xin, Ding Ling, Guo Moruo, and Lu Xun; their work was augmented by foreigners as diverse as Arthur Conan Doyle, Maxim Gorky, Rabindranath Tagore, and Émile Zola.[3] During the 1920s, local Chinese-language newspapers, blending Japanese ownership with Chinese management, emerged as the main venue for the publication of Chinese-language literature and as the central arena for debates on cultural change.[4] One of the most enduring of these institutions was the Japanese-owned *Shengjing shibao* (*Shengjing Daily*), which was established in 1906. Typical of other major regional newspapers, from 1916 its columns featured extensive debate of social issues, especially the woman question.[5] A remarkably active publishing sector, shifting public mores, and a heady mixture of domestic and international literary influences laid the foundations for a vital Chinese-language literary world that was forged within Manchukuo. In the process, unique literary styles were born, reflecting the harshness of the Manchurian environment and the hardiness of its people, and the cultural practices that attempted to reconcile one with the other.

The Early Occupation, 1931-1935

The Japanese invasion in September 1931 triggered a temporary collapse of Manchuria's burgeoning Chinese-language literary world. As the Japanese military moved to silence potential dissent, many newspapers – the most important venue for the publication of local literature – ceased publication, although prominent Japanese-owned newspapers such as the *Shengjing shibao* continued unabated. Writers' groups dispersed as investigations were launched against writers, publishers, and distributors. Fear extended to the reading public. Within weeks, restrictions were promulgated against public assembly, to forestall the expression of opposition to the new regime.[6] Symptomatic of the dramatic changes in public life is that within a year of the occupation almost one-third of the 24,000 teachers in the region were cashiered.[7] Access to "foreign" literature, specifically writings from other parts of China, was restricted.[8] Upon the founding of Manchukuo in March 1932, authorities further increased their vigilance over the sale of books. Within the following five months, over 650,000 copies of works were destroyed as book dealers were variously investigated, arrested, and thrown into jail, their operations forcibly closed.[9] The early occupation demonstrated to all those connected with Chinese literature – intellectuals, business owners, and the reading public alike – that colonial officials aimed for control over the production of local literature.

By the end of 1932, the atmosphere lightened and many papers and journals resumed publication, albeit reorganized in accordance with the "Publication Laws" (*Chuban fa*) of 24 October 1932. These laws, fifty-two in all, restricted production by requiring official registration for all publications. Their cumulative intent was to encourage the insulation of local society from the rest of China, to cultivate patriotism for the new state of Manchukuo, and to promote the concept of *Wangdao*. Any works deemed to endanger the "national foundation" by disclosing "military secrets" or by inducing "bad behaviour" were strictly forbidden.[10] Similar regulations, equally vague and, most importantly, haphazardly applied, were unveiled throughout the occupation. Their relentless reissuance over the course of the occupation attests to both their limited effect and to state intransigence in the realm of the written word. Rulers, writers, and readers all appeared to be keenly aware of the powers of the pen.

The early occupation triggered seismic shifts in Manchukuo's Chinese-language literary world in terms of locale, production, and prominent figures. In the early 1930s, a group of young writers, most notably Bai Lang, Duanmu Hongliang (1912-96), Liang Shanding (1914-95), Xiao Hong, and Xiao Jun (1908-88), with Lu Xun's active encouragement and support from Shanghai,[11] located the centre of the region's Chinese literary production firmly in the north in Harbin, relatively removed from the main centres of Japanese power in Dalian and Fengtian. Harbin played such a dominant role in this period that Liang

Shanding dubbed it the "hometown of literature."[12] These Harbin-based Chinese writers struggled to continue publication for several years after the occupation began, but by 1935 all of the major figures, except for Liang Shanding, had left Manchukuo to form the "exiled faction" (*liuwang pai*), which has since been the focus of Chinese and Western scholarship on writers from Manchuria. Following their departure, the centre of Manchukuo's literary world shifted southward to the capital Xinjing, and to Fengtian.

The work of the exiled faction has been acclaimed by Chinese nationalists for its vigorously anti-Japanese stance. In particular, Xiao Jun's *Ba yue de xiangcun* (*Village in August*) was celebrated for publicizing the heavy-handed nature of Japanese rule in Manchukuo and for arousing anti-Japanese war sentiment; his work was subsequently banned by colonial officials. Xiao Hong's departure in 1934, her public disavowal of Manchukuo, and her death during the war invested her work with a patriotic stance that cemented her position as a nationalist martyr, ignoring her feminist perspective, which had been lauded by her contemporaries. Based outside of Manchukuo for the last decade of the occupation, the exiled faction exerted a prolonged influence over their successors, most of whom idealized the social criticism that characterized their predecessors' work. Prasenjit Duara has noted that "writers such as the feminist Xiao Hong and her partner Xiao Jun, nourished on Gorky, Gogol, and other European writers, produced a radical literary culture that survived even after their departure from the region in 1934."[13] By the mid-1930s, Chinese literary production had resumed in Manchukuo. However, the only Chinese writer who had achieved a major profile in Manchukuo's first years and remained under Japanese rule was Liang Shanding, who later spearheaded efforts by young Chinese writers to rejuvenate the region's literary world. Liang's influence proved decisive in the revival of that world, both during Manchukuo and again in the 1980s.

A Literary Renaissance, 1936-1939

In the mid-1930s, small groups of young writers emerged in Manchukuo to revive the Harbin legacy of social criticism. Contrary to perceptions of Manchukuo as a cultural wasteland, during the final decade of Japanese rule over eighty literary factions formed, nearly twenty of which can be considered influential.[14] These groups ranged from those under official Japanese auspices, such as the Manchukuo-Japan Cultural Society (*Man-Ri wenhua xiehui*), to the Fengtian-based, independent, and aptly named Phoenix (*Fenghuang*), and the Harbin-based Marxist Gale (*Dafeng*). These literary groups formed within the parameters established by Manchukuo's "government control system" (*guanzhi tisi*).[15] Actual control, though, was difficult to administer because of the diversity of literary groups and the journals that they produced. Government officials, obsessed with securing control over the region, were too harried to assign the resources necessary to ensure the type of literary production they desired. Lively debates erupted between the various literary factions, towards, against, and irrespective of Manchukuo state policies. In the mid-thirties, within these debates, and between the cracks and crevices of haphazardly enforced Japanese colonial regulation, a vibrant Chinese-language literary renaissance developed.

In 1936 one of the most persistent and revealing debates erupted over the relationship of Manchukuo literature to China's literary world. Cultural functionaries vigorously promoted the "special, independent characteristics of Manchukuo literature" (*Manzhou wenxue de duli tese*) to segregate the cultural production of that state from the rest of China.[16] Writers enthusiastically extolled the region's unique environment and the pioneering nature of their literary work, but the May Fourth–inspired cultural criticism that dominated in China, and close ties to relatives and friends there, proved too resolute for colonial officials to stamp out. "Xinjing's ideological system" (*Xinjing sixiang tixi*), which officials envisioned would reflect the *Wangdao* authority that they sought, failed to rouse much interest or enthusiasm, as attested to by its absence from contemporary popular fiction. Even the June 1936 *People's Herald* Affair (*Minbao shijian*) in Harbin, in which more than ninety writers were jailed for alleged seditious connections to China, failed to sway writers to promote the independence of Manchukuo and *Wangdao* ideology.[17] In spite of increasing official surveillance, writers continued to pursue the type of critical literature advocated by Lu Xun, reinforcing cultural bonds with their contemporaries in the rest of China and undermining official demands to highlight a unique Manchukuo literature.

The recalcitrance of the writing community was met with an intensification of bureaucratic efforts at centralization and censorship. In September 1936, the Manchukuo Public Information Association was established "to maintain close contact among newspapers, new [*sic*] agencies and other public information enterprises, to control them and thereby to assure their sound development."[18] This initiative was bolstered on 1 July 1937 by the most extensive state-ordered restructuring of media to date, just days before the Sino-Japanese War broke out.[19] New bureaucratic departments and a publication office were established to monitor the following nine areas:

1 public opinion
2 literature and the arts
3 publication of important government policies
4 news coverage organizations
5 propaganda materials
6 publications, film, and "other propaganda materials"
7 broadcast and communications organs
8 intelligence
9 internal and external propaganda.[20]

Such micro-level control would have been possible only with a massive influx of personnel and resources, which were not forthcoming. Nonetheless, in conjunction with the eruption of war with the rest of China just six days later, promulgation of the new order spooked the struggling newspaper sector. Faced with the spectre of increasing bureaucratic intervention in an industry already burdened by supervision, seven major newspapers shut down.[21] But while newspapers were especially susceptible to state pressure, independent writers proved more elusive.

Writers in Manchukuo faced dual difficulties, which alternately enhanced and hindered their independence: financial compensation for their work was woefully inadequate and they risked losing even their pitiful incomes if they ran afoul of censors. All but the highest-profile journals and publishing companies had little, if any, money to offer writers for their work, so authors commonly received ten to twenty copies of a publication in lieu of payment.[22] Thus, most writers, women and men, were forced to undertake more than one career to make ends meet. For example, of the women discussed in this study Dan Di, Lan Ling, and Zhu Ti worked as teachers, and Mei Niang, Wu Ying, Yang Xu, and Zuo Di worked as editors, while their husbands were engaged in writing, editing, and other publication-related activities. In October 1939 a writer using the pen name M.G.M. argued in the journal *Nihon Hyōron* (Japan Debate) that a viable literary world had failed to materialize in Manchukuo because intellectuals could not rely solely on writing to earn an income.[23] Noting that official surveillance of Manchukuo's Chinese literary world was a negative, overly intrusive practice, M.G.M. stressed that local literature was doomed to inconsequence unless more freedom and money were provided to writers.[24] This dire evaluation, however, failed to account for the idealism of ambitious young writers who strove to carve out careers in the literary world regardless of the poor pay and risks.

From 1937 the expansion of Japanese aggression in southern China demanded the attention of Manchukuo officials, whose resources were increasingly commandeered by the war. Ambitious young writers were empowered by uneven enforcement of government regulations, as well as by the creation of new, vibrant publication sites that enlivened the local literary scene. Colonial officials were hampered in their efforts to mandate literary production by the dominant roles attained by local Chinese in the industry. Through the late 1930s, officials proved unable to extend the close scrutiny over Chinese popular literature with which they had earlier driven the exiled faction from the territory. Most of the Chinese writers who remained in Manchukuo were similarly alienated by the harsh nature of Japanese domination, but, either unwilling or unable to flee, they sought the means to articulate their dissatisfaction from within the colonial state. In 1939, the "year of factions" (*wenpai nian*), a flourishing literary production enlivened Manchukuo's cultural landscape.[25] Membership in these factions offered writers moral support, critical evaluation, and opportunities for publication. Membership in a clique proved essential to establishing a career in Manchukuo's Chinese-language literary world.

Yang Xu provides a particularly vivid contemporary description of a writers' faction in Xinjing in the late 1930s:

> They all call themselves the "capital city's literary youth," grasping the whole country's literary life. They, each of them, smoke cigarettes, drink wine, and sit in the teahouses leisurely talking about women, happily writing things, then play at being intimidating. As it turns out, who really understands literature? Write something, then there is a place for publication, after it's published, then they get together with each other to praise it. Later, people put titles on their heads, writer XX. Yes, it's just like this praising each other. Gradually they become a faction, then once a faction is created, everyone fights with each other, ugly faces all around. Sometimes, though, when two parties meet each other, their hands and mouths flap non-stop. Alas, that is literature! Actually, I find it very interesting.[26]

The informal, cutthroat nature of the business Yang Xu describes stands in stark contrast to the portrait fostered by colonial officials, of harmonious groups of writers striving to sanctify Manchukuo. In the colonial environment, personal relationships and personality loomed large in the formation of literary cliques and publication opportunities. In the late 1930s, Yang Xu won acceptance into just such a group of writers and forged a life-long friendship with Liang Shanding. In 1939, journals emerged as the dominant venue for publication, as "over a hundred writers, and a hundred different kinds of writing" emerged.[27] Of the many groups that formed in the year of factions, the three most prominent were the Chronicle of the Arts (*Yiwenzhi*), the Literary Selections (*Wenxuan*), and the Literary Collective (*Wencong*).

In the autumn of 1939, the Chronicle of the Arts faction organized in Xinjing. The most prominent members of this group included Gu Ding (1909-60), Jue Qing (1916-56), Xiao Song (b. 1912), and Yi Chi (1913-?). These writers, personally and professionally connected through participation in the short-lived but influential journal *Mingming* (*Clarity*), advocated an "art for art's sake" approach to writing.[28] The introduction to the first issue of the group's self-titled journal, *Yiwenzhi*, initiated debate over the function of literature. The Chronicle of the Arts urged writers "to carry on writing and printing. Whatever is written, whether it is as big as the sky, or as small as a sesame seed, if it is sincerely meant, then it will last forever."[29] This faction frowned on overtly political work and produced literature that refrained from explicitly violating Manchukuo's regulatory framework. To facilitate production they founded a well-funded bookstore and publishing company. For the most part, they limited publication in their journal to members of their clique. Manchukuo cultural functionaries lavished high praise on this "chosen" group of Chinese writers.[30] To date, these writers have attracted the most criticism from Chinese nationalists for their "complicated nature" (*fuza xing*): a seemingly close association with Manchukuo officialdom and the "non-political" nature of their writings.[31] The main members of this faction continued to publish throughout the occupation, although the group dissolved by 1941, leaving in its wake a considerably enlivened literary scene.

The members of the Chronicle of the Arts faction may have been united by common goals, but they were influenced by vastly different literary trends, which testify to the diversity of the early-twentieth-century Manchurian literary world. Gu Ding, without doubt the most excoriated Manchukuo writer, and the one who has since attracted the most critical attention (especially from Japanese scholars), pursued traditional Chinese and Japanese writing styles, devoid of an assertively political stance.[32] Rivals decried his work as an "official government brand" (*guan zhun li'an*).[33] Liang Shanding, in particular, criticized Gu for producing literature that did not reflect life in Manchukuo. Jue Qing, the "talented devil" (*guicai*), similarly opposed the popular yet politically risky style of "describing reality" and preferred to write of tacitly non-political "inner experiences" (*neixin tiyan*).[34] Xiao Song favoured English and American styles, while Yi Chi was influenced by Soviet "realism."[35] These writers' relatively non-confrontational stance towards the colonial state and their lack of overtly negative reflection on Manchukuo society have since dominated interpretations of their literary legacies. Most members of this faction neither actively championed nor condemned Manchukuo in their writings, reserving their ire instead for social realism, which was the bastion of their chief rivals, the Literary Selections and Literary Collective.

In December 1939, in Fengtian, Wang Qiuying founded the Literary Selections, with former contributors to the literary page of *Datong bao* (*Great Unity Herald*), Chen Yin (1914-?) and Yuan Xi (1920-79).[36] These men argued that Manchukuo's oppressive literary environment forced writers onto an "endless road, united in searching for a broad and smooth historical path" that would enable them to raise the consciousness of the masses.[37] Following Lu Xun's example, they urged writers to deploy literature as a weapon to expose the forces of darkness that plagued contemporary society. Wang Qiuying, in particular, was noted for the dark nature of his writings.[38] The Literary Selections attracted a wide audience for their work. The first issue of the group's self-titled publication, *Wenxuan*, published in the spring of 1940, was critically acclaimed and sold out rapidly. In response to this positive reception, the second volume, published in September 1940, doubled in size, with contributions from over thirty authors. The emergence of the Literary Selections confirmed the re-establishment of Fengtian as a hub of Chinese literary production.

Simultaneously in the capital, Xinjing, Liang Shanding organized the Literary Collective, with Mei Niang, Wu Lang (1912-57), Wu Ying, and others who had, like their colleagues in the Literary Selections faction, gained experience and exposure in the *Datong bao*. The Literary Collective, alone among its contemporaries, featured women among its most prominent members. This faction enjoyed support from Japanese intellectuals Kobayashi Hideo, Abe Tomoji, and Kishida Kunio. Liang Shanding, along with other members of the Literary Selections and the Literary Collective, encouraged writers to "describe reality" (*miaoxie zhenshi*) and even more explicitly to "expose reality" (*baolu zhenshi*), with particular emphasis on revealing the economic hardship, social disorder, and low status of women that they consistently associated with Manchukuo society. This faction's persistent engagement with negativity met with bureaucratic contempt but public acceptance. Their desire to expose reality vexed government officials, who noted that "there are obviously very many who agitate the people to contrary emotions, who write of the dark side, and who vigorously describe the red light districts."[39] By 1941, the Literary Collective had published four of the most influential books of the Manchukuo period: Liang Shanding's *Shan feng* (*Mountain Wind*), Mei Niang's *Di'er dai* (*The Second Generation*), Wang Qiuying's *Guiqu ji* (*Returning Home Collection*), and Wu Ying's *Liang ji* (*Two Extremes*).[40]

The writers of the Literary Collective were engaged in a quest for realism that was bolstered by Liang Shanding's promotion of "native place literature" (*xiangtu wenxue*), a literary form also advocated by Lu Xun as an effective tool for social criticism.[41] Hallmarks of Manchukuo's native place literature include use of the local dialect and specific reference to the local geographic and social environments. Representative works of this genre include Wang Qiuying's *Kuangkeng* (*Coalpit*), Yuan Xi's *Fengxue* (*Wind and Snow*), and Zhu Ti's "Da Heilongjiang de youyu" (The Melancholy of the Mighty Black Dragon River). These works all meld reverence for the land with the harsh realities of occupation life, in a language immediately familiar to the local reading public. Liang garnered support for native place literature from Wu Lang, editor of the popular journal *Simin* (*This People*), and Wang Qiuying, who beckoned writers to "construct local literature" (*jianshe difang wenxue*).[42] In the essay "Xiangtu he xiangtu wenxue" (Native Place and Native Place Literature), Liang praises the relative merits of Manchukuo's native place literature vis-à-vis the "transplanted literature" (*yizhi wenxue*) from Japan that was promoted by colonial bureaucrats who aimed to "Japanicize" Manchukuo's Chinese-language literary world.[43] Liang forcefully argues that, in order to attract a readership, literature must accurately reflect contemporary realities. Colonial officials adopted an ambiguous stance towards native place literature, as it could serve to distinguish Manchukuo from the rest of China, but it also proved a convenient tool for the expression of anti-Japanese sentiments through the celebration of local customs.

Despite the growth, for nearly a decade, of a regulatory framework designed to curtail criticism of colonial life, social realism prevailed in Manchukuo's Chinese-language literature. In 1938, Shinichi Yamaguchi noted that even among Japanese writers in Manchukuo, "realism seem[ed] to predominate among the main literary trends," linking these writers with their

Chinese counterparts.[44] In order to discipline writers whose work violated demands to promote positive depictions of Manchukuo, colonial officials expanded the activities of the Cultural Association (*Wenhuahui*), which had begun operations on 30 June 1937.[45] This state-sponsored group was dedicated to promotion of the conservatism that underlay Manchukuo's *Wangdao* ideal.[46] In August 1939 its central branch was transferred from the Japanese stronghold of Dalian to Manchukuo's capital, Xinjing, with branches established in Beijing, Fengtian, Harbin, and Tokyo.[47] The Cultural Association's authority was extended beyond the written word to encompass other cultural realms, including film, music, and painting. As Manchukuo's cultural world enlivened, officialdom sought ever more control over artistic production through regulation and the sponsorship of artistic organizations. Eight years after the occupation began, Manchukuo officials viewed their *actual* control over the arts as woefully inadequate yet essential to Manchukuo's success. In the late 1930s, a successful Chinese literary renaissance had been launched. Under the watchful eyes of bureaucrats, it was in danger of imminent collapse.

The Tightening of Colonial Censorship, 1940-1941

By 1940, the vibrancy of Manchukuo's literary scene, the rising stature of local Chinese writers, and the move towards the Sacred War led to heightened bureaucratic interest in establishing "appropriate parameters" for literature. Prasenjit Duara has noted that in Manchukuo until after September 1940, when Japan formed its alliance with Germany, "cultural control had been relatively lax and did not intrude into all dimensions of cultural production."[48] In the spring of 1940, firm steps towards dominion over Chinese literary production were being taken. On 30 March the Guandong Investigation Unit, responsible for probing allegations of sedition in Manchukuo, published "Outline of Countermeasures for Ideological Service" (*Sixiang duice fuwu yaogang*).[49] Three months later, in June, an Arts Reconnaissance Department (*Wenyi zhencha bu*) was established to control, direct, and investigate artistic production.[50] Fear spread through Manchukuo's literary world that, although informal meetings held to discuss literature might not be considered "political gatherings" per se, participation in them could have dire consequences. From the end of 1940 through 1941, the Manchukuo government issued an unprecedented volume of legislation designed to secure dominion over artistic creation. In December 1940, ministries responsible for the dissemination of news and the publication of literature were restructured. Jurisdiction over reading materials shifted between departments until January 1941, when journalism was formally distinguished from other forms of literary production and was subjected to stringent control.[51] These reforms in Manchukuo paralleled developments in Japan that aimed for rigorous state control over media.[52]

The ailing fortunes of journalism were a prelude to the torrent of rules and regulations governing other literary endeavours that issued forth in early 1941. In February and March, the most draconian measures to date were introduced to increase vigilance over writers who persisted in virulent social critiques. Colonial officials, through the State Propaganda Office, sought to streamline the "project of spiritual construction with the more advanced material construction of the state."[53] With explicit recognition that their cultural policies were failing, on 21 February the Eight Abstentions (*Ba bu*) were unveiled. Severe sanctions, ranging from censorship to imprisonment, were provided for those who engaged in the following:

- rebellious tendencies toward the current political situation
- criticism of the national policy without sincerity, or of a non-constructive nature
- agitation of citizens to antagonistic emotions
- exclusive use of darkness to depict life before and after the establishment of the nation
- use of decadent thought as the main point
- concerning love lust, to describe that moment with: recreational love that denigrates chastity, lust, abnormal sexual desire or acting wrongly out of personal considerations, incest, or adultery
- description of commission of a crime, written very cruelly or seriously
- use of matchmakers and domestics as the main topic, and especially exaggerated descriptions of the customs and human relationships of the entertainment districts.[54]

Cultural functionaries perceived all of the topics named in the Eight Abstentions, and which were prevalent in contemporary Chinese-language literature, to be criticisms of Manchukuo. In their minds, dark and pessimistic writing, portraying women's sexuality in ways that contradicted the ideal of chastity, or writing about any extramarital sexual activity denigrated the cultural ideals of Manchukuo and Japan. But despite ceaseless official interdictions, writers and readers revelled in the Eight Abstentions – not only did the forbidden topics make good reading, but treatment of them was enhanced by the aura of illegality.

The restrictions outlined in the Eight Abstentions reveal the nature of Chinese popular literature in Manchukuo ten years after the establishment of the state. Although these far-ranging directives were formally unveiled in February 1941, they were no surprise to writers. Since the inception of Manchukuo in 1932, officials had clearly enunciated appropriate parameters for literary production; these were constantly expanded through the decade. But the Eight Abstentions offered such wide-ranging guidelines that they allowed investigators tremendous leeway for censure and punishment. Had the Eight Abstentions been vigorously enforced, literary production would have been crippled. But they were not applied in a comprehensive manner. Officials soon viewed even the Eight Abstentions as inadequate and supplemented them with the "Summary of Guidelines to Art and Literature" (or Artistic Guidelines) (*Gangyao yiwen zhidao*), with the intention of "fundamentally transforming the role of arts and culture in the state."[55]

The promulgation of the Artistic Guidelines on 23 March 1941 caused Japanese writer Hasegawa Shun to observe darkly in the newspaper *Manri* (*Manchukuo Daily*) that Manchukuo's literary world had "crossed a Rubicon."[56] The Artistic Guidelines, comprising twenty-one regulations in five sections, dictated the adoption of Japanese literary traditions and professional organizations as models to facilitate realization of Manchukuo's "integrated, independent literature" (*hunran duli de wenyi*).[57] Henceforth, writers in the colony were automatically enrolled in state-sponsored organizations, which attempted to dictate the direction of their literary development. Manchukuo's writers responded, albeit briefly, in a suitably humbled manner. Gu Ding pronounced the Artistic Guidelines the "most significant matter" of the year.[58] Wang Qiuying mourned the "need to sweep away descriptions of the dark side."[59] These writers sensed impending restrictions on their intellectual activities, yet refrained from altering their established styles. As an ever-expanding regulatory framework was hoisted over Manchukuo's Chinese-language literary world, women writers, especially, continued to expose reality while their male colleagues more frequently paid for such activities with their freedom or their lives. Indeed, over the next few years, Tian Ben died in jail and Yuan Xi was imprisoned and later fled for Beijing, where Liang Shanding joined him shortly thereafter. Li Zhengzhong and Zhu Ti have since attributed official indifference to women's writings to a misogyny that dismissed their work as inconsequential.[60] Until 1943 most women writers were spared the intense investigation of their lives and work that dogged their male counterparts.

From 1941 in Manchukuo, as in Beijing and Shanghai, the Japanese aggressively fostered state-sponsored organizations through which they sought to structure artistic production.[61] Manchukuo media chief Muto Tomio stressed that in order for the "arts to fulfil the national system's needs, we still need to focus on the organization of professionals."[62] Muto's call did not go unheeded. By 1941 the Cultural Association had expanded to nine departments with over one thousand members, including most prominently Gu Ding and Xiao Song.[63] On 27 July 1941, the Manchukuo Writers and Artists Association (*Manzhou wenyijia xiehui*) was established.[64] Directed by Yamada Kiyosaburo, its branch members in Xinjing included Gu Ding, Jue Qing, Liang Shanding, Wu Lang, Wu Ying, Xiao Song, and Yi Chi, and, in Fengtian, Wang Qiuying and Yuan Xi.[65] High-profile writers in Manchukuo were officially, and *compulsorily*, mobilized to "assist in the promotion of the Greater East Asia Sacred War."[66] Despite such mobilization, the Cultural Association and the Writers and Artists Association achieved minimal success in promoting positive Chinese-language literature production.

In Manchukuo, Chinese-language journals typically blended pro-

Manchukuo, pro–Sacred War news with dark and pessimistic literature. Most journals were structured with officially sanctioned news and editorials in the front sections, followed by literature in the back. To encourage adherence to state regulations, editors were randomly imprisoned for several days and released without charges.[67] Despite such intimidation, editors continued to publish dark and pessimistic literature. Editors published the negative literature that was submitted to them in the belief that censors would be sidetracked by the positive nature of the front portions of the publication. Many editors were sympathetic to writers' efforts to expose the shortcomings of Manchukuo society; it could be argued that such literature was produced with the intent of assisting officialdom to realize the changes necessary for establishing Manchukuo's "paradise land." Others anticipated that in due time local Chinese would grow sympathetic to the state, and that the Chinese literature would grow more positive of its own accord.[68] Two of the highest-profile journals in Manchukuo, *Xin Manzhou* (*New Manchukuo*) and *Qilin* (*Unicorn*) exemplify this approach to publication. Both were Japanese-owned yet managed under the joint guidance of Chinese and Japanese editors. At *Xin Manzhou*, Wu Ying and her husband Wu Lang (Figure 3.1) worked within the editing pool and oversaw production of several of the most controversial works of the era, including Lan Ling's explicitly anti-patriarchal short story "Richu" (Sunrise). On 1 June 1941, the journal *Qilin* was launched in Xinjing as the successor to the defunct *Simin*.[69] Edited first by Xiao Song and later by Yi Chi, the journal aimed "to raise readers' spiritual development" through highlighting the strengths

3.1 Wu Ying (centre) and her husband Wu Lang (right) in the early 1940s.

necessary to overcome adversity.[70] *Qilin* published a great quantity of dark literature, including Wu Ying's short story "Ming" (Howl), the anti-patriarchal, anti-colonial tone of which spawned an official investigation of a writer who officials had previously perceived to be beyond reproach.

One of the most prominent journals in the Japanese Empire, the *Daban Huawen meiri* (*Chinese Osaka Daily / Osaka mainichi shimbun*) began publication on 3 November 1938. Produced by the *Osaka Daily* and the *Tokyo Daily News*, it was published in Japan, with draft offices in Osaka, Beijing, and Shanghai, for distribution across East Asia. During its long, successful run, this bimonthly (until 1944, then monthly) journal published thirteen volumes. The *Daban Huawen meiri* was an organ in which Manchukuo writers could publish work, while at home or in Japan, that exposed readers to subjects officially prohibited in Manchukuo. In the preface to the edition marking the publication's first anniversary in 1939, the editors stress that their policies were not dictated by the Japanese state or by the army, but rather by the editors' "stand on a position of freedom" (*zhan zai ziyou de lichang shang*).[71] This respect for freedom of expression enabled them to publish several works that were highly critical of life in Manchukuo, including Dan Di's *Andi he Mahua* (*Andi and Mahua*) (1940), which she wrote in Manchukuo while on summer vacation from school in Japan. *Andi he Mahua* is explicitly critical of the foreign invasion of Manchuria, yet the editors named it the journal's best mid-length novella for 1940.

The increasingly virulent material produced in violation of the Eight Abstentions and the Artistic Guidelines did not go unnoticed by colonial officials. By September 1941 Muto Tomio had published several missives condemning "the very troublesome matter" of dark literature published in violation of government regulations.[72] He demanded that special attention be devoted to this urgent issue, and investigations were launched against several high-profile Manchukuo writers. On 29 November 1941 the state's chief investigation unit circulated Internal Bulletin Number 3650, which provided detailed, critical analyses of works by eight writers, including Dan Di, Liang Shanding, and Wu Ying.[73] Their works were collected, examined for anti-Japanese content, and criticized for their anti-Manchukuo stances. Such intensive surveillance became commonplace after the commencement of the Sacred War.

The Japanese attack on Pearl Harbor on 8 December 1941 exacerbated the already tense environment in Manchukuo. Aggressive action was taken to integrate local literary production with the empire's security concerns. A state-issued *Manzhou lishi* (*History of Manchukuo*) glowingly, albeit inaccurately, portrayed the contemporary Japanese and Manchukuo literary worlds as "government-controlled cultures" that worked jointly towards the "rejuvenation of east Asia and a return to tradition."[74] Heavy-handed campaigns of coercion were intended to inspire Chinese obedience but furthered local alienation. In late December 1941 widespread arrests of students, intellectuals, and workers suspected of anti-Japanese activities were conducted; the most infamous, the Harbin Leftist Literature Incident of 31 December saw Chen Ti, Guan Monan, Wang Guangdi, and others imprisoned for allegedly seditious writings and suspect political activities.[75] The following month, in January 1942, further centralization of media was undertaken with the formation of the Tranquillity and Benevolent Virtue (*Kangde*) News Society. Newspapers in the capital were amalgamated into the *Manwen* (*Manchukuo News*) and in Fengtian, the *Manri* (*Manchukuo Daily*).[76] As the state prepared to celebrate its ten-year anniversary on 1 March 1942, arrangements were underway to establish a Literature and Arts Reconnaissance Unit (*Wenyi zhencha bu*) to manage writers' "inner" thoughts; it began operations in June 1942.[77]

The Sacred War, increasing bureaucratic surveillance of Manchukuo's literary world, and the wave of arrests at the end of 1941 triggered another exodus of Manchukuo writers. In 1942, Liu Longguang, Mei Niang, and Yuan Xi, among others, established homes in Beijing, which was also under Japanese occupation but where writers were not subject to such close surveillance. In June 1942 these expatriates participated in the formation of the North China–Manchukuo Writers Association (*Huabei Manzhou xiehui*).[78] As refugees living in another Japanese-occupied space, they were later credited with the creation of a literary style that was distinct from that of Manchukuo and other Chinese territories.[79] From outside Manchukuo, most maintained relationships with their compatriots back home.

A Proliferation of Organizations, 1942-1945

Beginning in the spring of 1942, leading figures in Japan's literary world, with state support, embarked on a conciliatory initiative towards their counterparts in other parts of the Japanese Empire. Tentative steps towards the creation of a trans-Asian literary world were taken with the convocation in Tokyo of the first Greater East Asia Writers' Congress, from 3 to 10 November 1942.[80] The impetus for the congress came from former Japanese army employees, Chinese academics, and writers throughout the Japanese Empire. Since August 1940, Japanese intellectuals Kikuchi Kan and Kume Masao (who in 1942 became executive director of the Japanese Literary Patriotic Association) had pushed for measures to integrate the Sino-Japanese literary worlds; the Sacred War expanded their vision to include Japanese-held territories across Asia.[81] Congress supporters expected that it would "discuss ways and means of how literary circles ... can offer cooperation toward the prosecution of the Greater East Asian War and the creation of literature and art characteristic of East Asia."[82] In Beijing, Liu Longguang, Mei Niang's husband and head of the North China Writers' Association, joined a chorus of local writers who argued that colonial authorities could assuage concerns over a lack of "spirit" in contemporary literature through the provision of awards to promote writers and to raise their low status.[83] The Greater East Asia Writers' Congress, which was organized under Japanese auspices, stressed Japanese culture as the basis for Asian cultural development, but vital contributions were also made by delegates from occupied China; the literature department of Beijing University was responsible for judging Chinese-language works.[84] Gu Ding and Wu Ying were among seven representatives from Manchukuo to attend the first congress in Tokyo. The official goal of the first congress was to foster a "spirit of Greater East Asia" (*dadongya jingshen*) but in a subsequent article in *Qilin* outlining the proceedings of the congress, Wu Ying glowingly describes the artistic camaraderie she encountered, without a single reference to the spirit of Greater East Asia.[85]

The official aims of the Greater East Asia Writers' Congress paralleled colonial directives in Manchukuo and inspired similar levels of local support. Promotion of the "spirit of Greater East Asia" in Manchukuo necessitated enhancement of the Artistic Guidelines, which resulted in the publication, on 8 December 1942, of the Outline of the Fundamental National Policy (*Jiben guoce dagang*).[86] It demanded that writers in Manchukuo re-evaluate their priorities and that they "construct the national spirit, praise war objectives, and allow for a fundamental comprehension of contemporary conditions."[87] Literature was to faithfully advance the objectives of the Sacred War and to laud the modernization of Manchukuo under Japanese leadership. The outline also ordered the restructuring of administration of media on a provincial basis, with top officials responsible for the content, control, and distribution of news and literature. These measures reinforced existing regulations by explicitly linking the production of Manchukuo literature with the regimentation required by Sacred War demands.

Throughout 1943 Japanese-sponsored literary organizations in Manchukuo proliferated, though their influence on local Chinese literary production was minimal. The Manchukuo Literary Association expanded membership and on 26 May 1943 opened a subsidiary, Manchukuo Literature (*Manzhouguo wenxue*), with members Gu Ding, Jue Qing, Liang Shanding, and Wu Lang.[88] A Greater East Asia Association (*Dadongya xiehui*) was also formed, with Gu Ding, Wang Qiuying, Wu Lang, and Xiao Song among its members. The creation of a Publication Association (*Chuban xiehui*) was a further bid for bureaucratic dominion – a so-called New System (*xin tizhi*) – over the literary world through the investigation, approval, and distribution of Chinese literature that promoted Asian traditions and the Sacred War.[89] The formation of these groups, and the parallel growth of a bureaucracy to monitor them, achieved limited success in altering the content of Manchukuo literature. Their growth does, though, attest to a continued vibrancy of the Chinese-language literary world during the final years of Japanese colonial rule and the significance attached to it by Manchukuo officials.

From 25 to 28 August 1943 the second Greater East Asia Writers' Congress was held in Tokyo. Six delegates from Manchukuo, including Gu Ding and Wu Lang, joined representatives from Japan and the other occupied areas in

China to call for a "New East Asia Literature Concept." Three departments were established within the congress to discuss literary objectives and the creation of a unified publication system, to promote translation work, and to develop a system of awards for literary excellence. For the first time, the congress issued awards based on literary merit, explicitly stating that they were not distributed on the basis of affinity with Japanese directives. The first Greater East Asia Literature Award was presented to Yuan Xi (formerly of Manchukuo) for his novel *Beike* (*Seashells*), while works by fellow Manchukuo writers Jue Qing, Mei Niang, and Shi Jun were also honoured. The congress recognized these writers for work with an explicitly negative outlook. Yuan Xi, fearing official retribution in Manchukuo for the popularity of his dark writings, had in October 1941 moved to Beijing. After the 1943 congress, he was imprisoned but later released through the personal guarantees of Liu Longguang and Takeuchi Yoshiro, a sympathetic Japanese judge stationed in China.[90] The bond between these three men illustrates the complex social ties that existed in Japanese-occupied northern China.

From the latter half of 1943 through 1944, Manchukuo writers, having attained popular and critical recognition, threw caution to the winds with the publication of some of their most subversive works to date. The October issue of *Qingnian wenhua*, a special women's edition, contains work that openly violated Manchukuo's literary regulations: Dan Di's "Jie" (Warning) recounts the experiences of an unwed mother who abandons her newborn baby; Lan Ling's "Richu" (Sunrise) denounces parental authority; Wu Ying's "Yu" (Lust) exposes sexual tensions in a widow's remarriage; and Zuo Di's "Nü nan" (Women's Difficulty) portrays childbirth as a form of torture. Together, these works contravene almost all of the Eight Abstentions. During this period, as well, dark native place novels, such as Liang Shanding's *Lüse de gu* (*The Green Valley*), Yuan Xi's *Ouyangjia de ren* (*The Ouyangs*), and Wang Qiuying's *He liu diceng* (*The Bottom of the River*), were published. Each of these works has been noted for being "impregnated with the valiant life force of Manchuria's wilderness and mountain forests" while openly "criticizing the old race system."[91] Collectively, they conjure some of the darkest portraits of life in Manchukuo.

In the fall of 1943, following publication of *Lüse de gu*, Liang Shanding – Zuo Di's husband and the writer with the highest profile in Manchukuo – found himself at the top of the state inspection bureau's black list, and the couple's home was searched. Liang had remained in Manchukuo since the start of the occupation, but by 1943 intrusive official surveillance lay too heavily upon him. He fled to Beijing, where, with Yuan Xi's help, he found work at the New People's (*Xinmin*) publishing company and edited the journal *Zhongguo wenxue* (*Chinese Literature*).[92] As he settled in Beijing, Liang pessimistically observed: "China's writers are now like beggars ... Their left hand is tightly grabbed by officials, and the right hand must beg publishers for money. That beggar can never back away."[93] Liang vividly describes the pressures facing

Chinese writers during the Japanese occupation, but he fails to account for the idealism that drove him and his colleagues to pursue their careers in the first place. In Liang's absence, his novel *Lüse de gu*, which had forced him to abandon Manchukuo and his family, was successfully received by literary critics in Manchukuo. Prasenjit Duara has recently argued that the post-Mao rehabilitation of this novel as anti-Japanese or anti-imperialist is a misreading of its "critique of whatever power structure existed."[94] Whatever the novel's intended target, it was published within a state that increasingly prosecuted such transgressions. Liang left Manchukuo to resume his career in the less restrictive environment of Beijing, where, You Bingche argued, "narcotics cases, kidnapping, theft and robbery, family problems, corruption in the various echelons of the government, and other social problems occupied most of the space of the newspaper. Even the literary section reflected the predominance of the negative element in society at that time."[95] As Liang discovered, Beijing's less-regulated literary world shared with its Manchukuo counterpart a proclivity for negative writing and thus could serve as a refuge for writers who were able or willing to leave Manchukuo.

The negativity that dominated literature in Beijing and Manchukuo attracted the attention not only of cultural functionaries but also of Japanese writers and social activists who disapproved of Japanese military aggression on the mainland. In both Japan and China, sympathetic Japanese encouraged Chinese writers to produce realistic, emotionally charged works that accurately reflected life in the colony. In April 1943 Kitamura Kenjiro argued that if Manchukuo writers followed the dictates of colonial officials and "depart from emotion and bury their heads in constructive [pro-state commentary], what kind of condition is that? Isn't this tragic? Writers should have the intention to write on the constructive side, but they must be allowed mainly to write on the side of emotions. Only with this kind of rich foundation can Manchukuo literature finally have a hundred flowers bloom."[96] Kitamura promoted exposing reality, urging Chinese writers to depict life in Manchukuo accurately, warts and all. Thus, even though Chinese-language literature in Manchukuo was subject to surveillance, it managed to retain a critical tone that was appreciated by sympathetic Japanese. The considerable popularity in Japan of Manchukuo writers is reflected by the numbers of works that were translated into Japanese, including work by Liang Shanding, Mei Niang, and Zuo Di. A prominent example is *Manshū sakka shōsetsu shū: Tanpopo* (*Dandelion: A Collection of Short Stories by Manchukuo Writers*), a 1940 volume that contains the writings of seven authors, including Wu Ying.

In 1944, colonial officials in Manchukuo, faced with uncooperative Chinese writers and the sympathetic Japanese who spurred them on, adopted a decidedly martial tone. On 4 January the Manchukuo Literary Association initiated use of the slogan "wielding pens as swords" (*yi bi dai jian*) to steel the hearts and minds of Manchukuo subjects for the Sacred War.[97] Those pens proved to be double-edged swords, as Chinese writers continued to produce literature that violated the Manchukuo regulatory framework. Official anxieties over artistic production, in conjunction with paper shortages, led to a state-ordered amalgamation of the largest journals, *Minsheng* (*People's Life*), *Pengyou* (*Friend*), *Qilin*, *Qingnian wenhua*, *Xin chao* (*New Tide*), and *Xingya* (*Rising Asia*), into *Xin Manzhou*. Shortly thereafter, in September, a writing contest, called the Greater East Asia Sacred War and Our Consciousness (Dadongya shengzhan yu women de juewu), dominated the pages of *Xin Manzhou*.[98] Contest organizers hoped for an outpouring of patriotic fervour for Manchukuo, but their efforts issued forth only more in-depth depictions of economic deprivation and adversity. Thus, the closely monitored *Xin Manzhou*, a high-profile, Japanese-owned venue for the publication of pro-Manchukuo news, also functioned as an important arena in which Chinese articulated their disenchantment with contemporary society.

The third and final Greater East Asia Writers' Congress was held in Nanjing on 12-14 November 1944. Manchukuo sent eight representatives, including Gu Ding, Jue Qing, Xiao Song, and the congress chair Wu Lang. The foci of this congress were "helping each other in the Greater East Asia war struggle," "reviving the culture of East Asia," and creating a "new East Asia cultural spirit." While the agenda had not substantially altered in the two years since the first congress, the atmosphere certainly had. Edward Gunn has noted the "desperate drive" to mobilize writers that characterized the final year of the war, as well as the lack of progress made on this front by the congresses.[99] Liu Longguang, who was by then the most powerful editor in north China, wearied of continued participation, leaving his wife, Mei Niang, whose poignantly anti-colonial and anti-patriarchal *Xie* (*Crabs*) was acclaimed novel of the year, to attend alone.[100]

As the final months of the Japanese occupation passed, heavy restrictions made publication increasingly difficult. Continued bureaucratic efforts to boost public morale were exemplified by a Rally of the Arts for a Decisive Battle (*Juezhan yiwen dahui*), which was held in Xinjing on 1-3 December 1944. The anticipated rally did not materialize. Manchukuo's literary world was plagued by a ponderous bureaucratic apparatus, critical reversals in the prosecution of the Sacred War, and severe paper shortages, which first forced the publication of journals and books on substandard paper and then, in 1945, the withdrawal of most printed material from circulation.[101] In February 1945 Zuo Di's short story "Meiyou guang de xing" (A Lustreless Star), which recounts "women's tragedy" in Manchukuo, was published in Beijing in a collection of women's fiction; its title captures the negativity of Chinese literature published in the final days of Japanese occupation. The last volume of collected works published in Manchukuo was Zhu Ti's *Ying* (*Cherry*). Appropriately, it was released in the late spring as the cherry blossoms, symbol of imperial Japan, fell to the ground and were blown away by the wind, followed shortly thereafter by the colonial state of Manchukuo.

Throughout their occupation of Manchuria, the Japanese proved unable or unwilling to provide the resources necessary to effectively structure literary production in accordance with the rigorous regulatory framework that they promulgated with great fanfare. Bureaucratic control over literature was frustrated by the difficulty of recruiting personnel who possessed sufficient ability to read and to accurately interpret literature and who had access to materials that often sold out quickly.[102] Publishers negotiated between censors and writers by combining within the same publication pro-Manchukuo and negative material. To make matters worse for Manchukuo officials, publishers, and even censors could be sympathetic to efforts to expose the government's shortcomings, and many of those who were not could be placated or paid by zealous editors. Finally, validation from Japanese supporters and official organizations such as the Greater East Asia Writers' Congress militated against harsh treatment of prominent Chinese who, in spite of ceaseless restrictions to the contrary, depicted Manchukuo life in bleak terms. Few moral or financial incentives existed to entice writers to abandon the idealism that initially drove them to establish their careers. The militaristic, racist nature of Manchukuo society and the penurious conditions that Chinese writers endured did little to contribute to the production of pro-Manchukuo literature. Women writers tended to be particularly critical of Manchukuo society, yet because they were women, and consequently held in little esteem by the authorities, they were subject to less intrusive scrutiny than were their male counterparts. In spite of the negativity of women's writings, until 1944 only Dan Di and Wu Ying were subject to official investigation; in Manchukuo's final year, they were joined by Lan Ling, Yang Xu, Zhu Ti, and Zuo Di. Men were subject to more constant surveillance and persecution throughout the occupation. Nonetheless, despite widely publicized systemic attempts to control literary production, Manchukuo officials were incapable of fully bringing Chinese writers to heel.

The incessant propagation of restrictions on literary production became an essential element of anti-Manchukuo narratives in the post-liberation period. All writers who had enjoyed any success in such an apparently oppressive environment were denounced as "traitors to China." Many Manchukuo censors and Maoist radicals were blinded to the critical nature of the Chinese-language literature produced under Japanese rule. The bureaucratic regulatory framework established in Manchukuo did loom large over the literary world but not in the intended manner. Chinese writers worked around state regulations to expose reality and to raise the consciousness of their readers. Indeed, as will be shown in subsequent chapters, it was precisely while they lived their lives under Japanese rule that many Chinese writers were exposed to literary styles and to radical ideologies that inspired them to critique Manchukuo life. While in Japan, Dan Di, Mei Niang, and Wu Ying all enjoyed access to progressive and revolutionary literature, including the work of Chinese communist writers such as Guo Moruo that was banned in the colony.

In Japan, they also forged relationships with sympathetic Japanese, who encouraged, if not financed, their activities. As well, Chinese could purchase subversive materials in the imperial metropole and have them shipped home, bypassing censors that operated between China and Manchukuo. Complex disjunctures in official bureaucratic regulations and the realities of colonial life enabled the creation of a Chinese-language literature in Manchukuo that highlights the strengths of those whom the Japanese sought to subjugate and provided the means for them to dream of a free, post-colonial, *Chinese* world. In a tragic irony, the highly politicized Chinese movements that swept the region from the 1950s to the 1970s silenced all Manchukuo writers as "traitors to China," finally achieving the submission that colonial officials had so long sought.

Perhaps nowhere is the chasm between the Manchukuo cultural agenda and the ways that Chinese in Manchukuo lived their lives more evident than in the gulf that existed between the ideals promoted by colonial officials and those pursued by Manchukuo's most prolific women writers. Despite propaganda that dictated ideals of submissive, obedient good wives and wise mothers, the most prolific Chinese women writers in Manchukuo raised their pens to denounce the state's patriarchal foundations.

4

Forging Careers in Manchukuo

By the ruins of terror's triumph, children build their dust castle.

– *Rabindranath Tagore*

Within three years of the establishment of Manchukuo, the prominent writers Bai Lang, Duanmu Hongliang, Xiao Hong, and Xiao Jun had fled the region. Their departure temporarily quieted the colony's burgeoning Chinese-language literary world. But almost immediately, young Chinese writers rose to emulate their famed predecessors. By 1939, local Chinese-language literature flourished again. In Manchukuo's reinvigorated literary scene, women played integral roles, both as objects of analysis and as advocates of social change. This chapter contextualizes the lives and careers of Manchukuo's most prolific Chinese women writers: Dan Di, Lan Ling, Mei Niang, Wu Ying, Yang Xu, Zhu Ti, and Zuo Di. The writers who abandoned Manchukuo by 1935, to date the most acclaimed of the region's twentieth-century Chinese writers, and those who remained within the Japanese colony were divided by geography but united by a shared cultural heritage. Far removed from Manchukuo, the former group constructed harshly critical portraits of life in the colony. The latter, within Manchukuo, produced anti-patriarchal literature critical of Manchukuo society. Children when the Japanese occupation began, they later sought to realize the ideals of individual emancipation that had inspired Chinese youth in Manchuria during the Republican period. This chapters reveals how, as young adults, they used Manchukuo education and career opportunities to their advantage, to satisfy their personal and professional ambitions.

Family Backgrounds

The waves of migration that flooded Manchuria after the late Qing period brought Han Chinese, Hui (Chinese Muslim), Japanese, Korean, Manchu, Mongolian, Russian, and other peoples to the region. Many were attracted by the sparsely populated land and the economic opportunities radiating from massive Japanese investment; most, including the Japanese, settled into the lower or middle classes. In the pioneering region, many prided themselves on their ability to "endure hardship" (*chiku nailiao*).[1] Recent migration and poverty were features common to much of Manchuria's population in the first half of the twentieth century. These same features characterize the family backgrounds of the women who are the subjects of this study. Most of their families were attracted to Manchuria by economic opportunity. Several came from southern China and locations in the north, including Beijing, Hebei, and Shandong. Dan Di's father migrated from further afield, from Hunan, to work as a soldier during the 1904-5 Russo-Japanese War.[2] After the war, he settled in the region and married a Korean orphan. Other families did not come from so far away. In 1925, Zhu Ti's father, a merchant, migrated with his wife and three children from Beijing to Jilin city in search of a more lucrative market.[3] Another economic migrant, destined to become the most financially successful of the group, was Mei Niang's father, Sun Zhiyuan. As a teenager, he migrated from Shandong to Changchun, to work as a messenger, ultimately becoming a major industrialist in the region.[4]

These migrants sought economic opportunity in Manchuria during a period of informal Japanese dominance. Japanese investment overshadowed domestic Chinese and Russian endeavours, stimulating growth in all sectors of the regional economy and enticing migrants to the rapidly developing region. Following the establishment of Manchukuo in 1932, however, the families did not continue to prosper, and several declined precipitously. Their impoverishment reflects the shift in regional development from a relatively free-wheeling environment to formal, Japanese-dominated, state-dictated economic policies that focused on resource extraction, heavy industry, and, eventually, Sacred War demands. For all but a select group of Japanese, economic opportunities dwindled. Mei Niang's father, for example, lost the Russian connections that had contributed to his rapid rise and he refused the opportunity of collaboration with the colonial administration.[5] Lan Ling's father and Zhu Ti's parents eventually abandoned Manchukuo for their hometowns, which were also under Japanese occupation.[6] Lan Ling's father left in 1936 and briefly returned in 1941; he then permanently relocated with his second wife and their youngest son to his home village in Hebei. Zhu Ti's parents left Manchukuo for Beijing in 1943. The experiences of these families suggest that the economic opportunities that had lured Chinese migrants to Manchuria in the first place disappeared as Japanese dominance intensified.

All seven of the women writers were born or raised in Manchuria. Wu Ying was born in Jilin city in 1915; Dan Di in Tangyuan county, Heilongjiang, on 15 August 1916; Yang Xu in Fengtian on 8 June 1918; Zuo Di in Yanji, Jilin province, on 13 August 1920. Three of the writers moved to Manchuria with their families as babies: Lan Ling was born in Pingjing, Hebei, on February 3, 1918; Mei Niang in Vladivostok on 24 December 1920; Zhu Ti in Beijing on 16 March 1923. All spent their formative years in Manchuria before the Japanese occupation began. Mei Niang was raised in Changchun, Yang Xu and Zuo Di in Fengtian, Zhu Ti and Wu Ying in Jilin, and Dan Di and Lan Ling in Qiqihaer. In these cities, they grew up alongside Japanese, Korean, Russian, and other peoples, relatively free from the racism that later characterized Manchukuo society. When the Japanese occupation began in 1931, the eldest of the writers was sixteen years old and the youngest, eight. Their youth precluded their deciding on their own whether to stay or to leave. All remained with their families.

The writers' ethnicity reflects Manchuria's reputation as a melting pot. Lan Ling, Mei Niang, Zhu Ti, and Zuo Di were all born to Han parents. But Dan Di was Han and Korean, Wu Ying was Han and Manchu, and Yang Xu was Hui. Their backgrounds are suggestive of Manchuria's rich ethnic fabric. As discussed in Chapter 2, colonial officials promoted Manchukuo as a kingdom of multi-ethnic cooperation. But few of the women wrote of ethnicity, and none echoed the official rhetoric. Instead, in their writings, they cite ethnicity as difference. For example, Yang Xu celebrated the Hui dietary restrictions that enabled her to escape what she perceived to be the restrictive environment of boarding school.[7] Hui avoidance of pork made life at a Han Christian boarding school impossible for her. Likewise, Wu Ying noted that the infant son of a Japanese socialite she interviewed instantly recognized that she was not Japanese; in her interview, she contrasts Chinese and Japanese ideals of raising children, reflecting favourably on the former.[8] In the hundreds of fictional works by these women, the Japanese are rarely discussed, and then only negatively. For example, in Mei Niang's *Xie* (*Crabs*), the Japanese work ethic is shown to be disruptive to Chinese social practices. In Dan Di's *Andi he Mahua* (*Andi and Mahua*) foreign invasion destroys family stability. Despite the women's diverse backgrounds, the ethnic harmony idealized by colonial officials is not reflected in this literature. Prasenjit Duara, too, has noted the "stunning silence" regarding ethnicity in Manchukuo literature.[9] The absence of any positive correlation between the writers' ethnicities and state rhetoric is symbolic of the resistance to the Manchukuo cultural agenda that united these disparate writers. Self-identities were expressed in opposition to, rather than in support of, Manchukuo rhetoric; regardless of their ethnic backgrounds, these women all self-identified as Chinese.

The women were raised in a variety of family forms, from nuclear to extended. Dan Di, Wu Ying, Yang Xu, and Zhu Ti were raised in relatively stable, middle- to lower-class households with two parents and several siblings.[10] Lan Ling, Mei Niang, and Zuo Di came from more tumultuous family backgrounds. Lan Ling's family consisted of her mother, her father, his second wife, and several younger children.[11] In 1936, when she was eighteen years old, her father left Manchukuo. As the eldest sibling, she was forced to shoulder additional responsibilities for supporting the family. Mei Niang was born in Vladivostok but raised in Changchun in an extended, wealthy household. Yet life was far from idyllic: her mother was a concubine who was hounded to suicide soon after Mei Niang's birth.[12] In Mei Niang's teenage years, family life dramatically altered as her stepmother died and her father remarried again, before his own death in 1936. Zuo Di's family was also transformed by the death of her mother when Zuo was eleven.[13] A semblance of normalcy was restored to her life when her father remarried, two more children were born, and the new family bonded. Although the writers' families assumed various forms, their parents all struggled with adversity.

Most of the women were raised in relative poverty. Dan Di later recounted how her life was shaped by her early education and poverty. Her father's employment as a middle school teacher in Qiqihaer ensured that the family was poor, despite his scholarly standing.[14] Their dire straits dictated that Dan Di help supplement the family's income. She collected wood, leaves, and mushrooms in the forest, sold pig's blood in the market, and worked in the fields during harvest. Like Lan Ling, she accompanied her mother to pawn shops and learned first-hand the odious cost of credit, different strategies to overcome poverty, and the untenable position of Manchuria's lower classes.[15] The instability of the writers' youth is also reflected in the tumultuous career of Zuo Di's father, Zuo Junming, who was the principal of Fengtian's Teacher Training Institute when his daughter was born in 1920; he changed positions half a dozen times between then, the loss of his final job in 1936, and his death in 1938.[16] Although these families lived in poverty in Manchukuo, most were likely better off than they would have been in their hometowns, which suffered the instability that plagued Republican China after 1931.

Mei Niang is the only member of this group who was born into wealth. In the 1920s, her father, Sun Zhiyuan, worked his way up from a position as a messenger in a British firm, becoming a major regional industrialist.[17] His success was achieved through hard work, mastery of English, Japanese, and Russian, and a timely marriage into the family of a prominent militarist. In the spring of 1932, when Mei Niang was twelve, Sun rejected a vice-presidency of the Manchukuo Central Bank and the family left the colony for a year, travelling between Dalian, Jinan, Qingdao, and Tianjin. But prohibitions against the conversion and export of currencies from Manchukuo caused a precipitous decline in family finances. Held hostage to their property, the Sun family returned to Manchukuo. Sun Zhiyuan's death shortly thereafter resulted in the breakup of the family, as Mei Niang and her siblings were sent to boarding school in Japan. In Mei Niang's youth, the comforts that she had become accustomed to began to disappear. The experience of her family is an important reminder that those who chose to leave Manchukuo forfeited their personal property. They had to choose between remaining with their established lives under Japanese colonial rule in a region that had never known more than tentative Chinese rule, or leaving with nothing for an uncertain future in the splintering Republic of China. These families chose to remain.

The family backgrounds of the writers had a critical influence on their lives. Their families were attracted to Manchuria by economic opportunity, and most remained throughout the occupation, despite a lack of enthusiasm for Japanese dominion. They did not prosper, but they did gain a degree of stability unattainable elsewhere in China. As will be shown below, the women seem to have inherited the same ambition and tenacity that had both fired their parents' trek to Manchuria and kept them there.

Childhood to School

One of the most formative experiences shared by the women was their early home education, which blended Confucian classics and May Fourth literature. In their natal homes, they learned to read Confucian texts and later embraced the May Fourth literature that was introduced into Manchuria in the early Republican period and later inspired much Manchukuo cultural production. All of the women began their formal education in the Republican period and completed it under Japanese rule. As detailed in Chapter 2, Japanese ambitions for Chinese women in Manchukuo were most evident in the colonial education system. But the contrast between the conservatism advocated by officialdom and the ideals cultivated within the writers' families and local popular culture proved deeply unsettling for the young women. Within that gulf was cast the seeds of their rejection of the Manchukuo cultural agenda.

According to their own recollections, as young girls Mei Niang, Yang Xu, and Zhu Ti all exhibited traits suggestive of their future characters. All were noted for unorthodox behaviour. Mei Niang's father played a decisive role in moulding her character; he encouraged her to be independent, "like a man" (*xiang nanren yiyang*).[18] To the shock of local residents, Mei Niang drove a horse and carriage through the streets of Changchun. Yang Xu was a similarly rambunctious girl who was constantly in trouble for playing with her friends rather than following her parents' admonitions to focus on her studies.[19] At school, Yang was a popular and fashionable student, noted for her flashy style, her skills on the harmonica, and an outspoken nature. As a young girl, Zhu Ti demonstrated a "formidable" (*lihai*) character, as she refused to be bullied by either of her siblings; she later noted that writing was therapeutic in her struggles at the onset of adolescence.[20] From a young age, these women did not subscribe to the conservative ideals of modest obedience that Manchukuo officials advocated. They were outspoken and assertive, reflecting the character traits that had enabled their parents to survive as pioneers in Manchuria.

Literature played fundamental roles in the writers' childhoods, during which they were exposed to both traditional and contemporary Chinese literature. Home education may have varied from private tutorials or parental mentoring to casual reading but was seen by their parents to be an essential component of their young lives. At the age of three, Mei Niang embarked on an eclectic classical Chinese and Western education at home, with tutorials in English.[21] She spent several years studying under a classically trained Confucian scholar and the Russian wife of a local bank manager. Dan Di dated her writing ambitions to her study of Tang poetry, which she also began at three, under her father's guidance.[22] Lan Ling and Wu Ying later cited the benefits of access to reading materials at home, ranging from the classic Qing novel *Hongloumeng* (*Dream of the Red Chamber*) to the latest May Fourth work.[23] Each of the women cited regional, national, and foreign literary influences: Xiao Jun and Xiao Hong; Ba Jin, Bing Xin, Ding Ling, Guo Moruo, and Lu Xun; Lord Byron, Maxim Gorky, Rabindranath Tagore, and Émile Zola were early influences on them, a range that reflected the disparate writing styles appreciated within contemporary Chinese culture. Classical and vernacular Chinese, social realism, and romanticism melded to create a rich Republican literary landscape. The young women aspired to leave their own marks on this diverse cultural world.

Formal education began between the ages of five and seven. Like many urban girls in Manchuria, the future writers attended primary school but, unlike most, they all went on to complete middle school. In 1931, their education was briefly interrupted by the Japanese invasion, although they all eventually completed their studies in the colonial system. Although all the girls attended school, they did not all do so without controversy. Lan Ling and Yang Xu both noted their parents' misgivings concerning the education of girls. These misgivings had little to do with Manchukuo education per se. Lan Ling's mother believed that girls must have basic reading and writing skills but worried that "excessive" education would distract them from a more proper focus on household responsibilities.[24] Her mother, who had been raised in a rural household, spent her days as she believed every woman should: consumed with household affairs, including cooking, sewing, and raising children. Thus, in 1928, when Lan Ling completed four years of primary education, her mother believed further study was unnecessary and potentially harmful. But her father, employed as a minor clerk in the local government, was swayed by May Fourth ideals. He insisted that all their children, irrespective of sex, continue with their schooling to the utmost of their ability.[25] Lan Ling's completion of a four-year degree at a teacher-training school, in 1935, reveals much about her ambitions as well as her parents' relationship. Her father overruled her mother's objections, allowing Lan Ling to receive an education that eventually enabled her to support the family after her father left Manchukuo. Yang Xu's parents feared that their daughter would not be suitably married if she continued past middle school; her education ended in 1938, when she ran away to escape a marriage that they had arranged for her.[26] The conservatism of Lan Ling's mother and Yang Xu's parents would have attracted them to the Confucian curriculum mandated by Manchukuo officials: their propagation of Confucian ideals for women dovetailed with an equally conservative Republican education, and thus would have appealed to parents who wanted assurance that their daughters would be vested with conservative values and kept safe from interaction with boys. These girls, however, were inspired by May Fourth ideals that challenged the conservatism that informed women's education in both the Republic of China and in Manchukuo.

Before and during the Japanese occupation, dormitory life was standard for middle school students. Mei Niang and Yang Xu wrote of their experiences. Mei Niang began to board at Jilin Municipal Middle School for Girls in 1931, when she was ten years old, and she credited dormitory life with introducing her to the "rich emotions" (*nonghou de ganqing*) of a collective womanhood.[27] Her childhood had been shaped by the suicide of her mother, a prickly relationship with her stepmother, and a father who doted on her. Living with other girls whose backgrounds varied yet who shared similar interactions with patriarchy awakened Mei Niang to a common subjugation that she believed lay at the heart of women's lives. In the mid-1930s, Yang Xu attended a British-run predominantly Han Chinese school in Fengtian that operated until 1941 by adhering to Manchukuo's educational guidelines. Yet while she attended the middle school, she did not board there. Yang was grateful for the relative freedom this accorded her, since she viewed boarding school "as restrictive as [life in] Yama's court" (*Yan wang si de guanchu*); she condemned it for segregating girls and boys, thereby retarding her female classmates' natural emotional and sexual development.[28] Yang also noted that live-in students found themselves under intense pressure to respect the Christian teachers' condemnation of the motion picture industry. In *Wo de riji* (*My Diary*) she mocks their moral posturing, noting that strict censorship meant that the mostly lacklustre films rarely changed and that she often saw those same Christian teachers at the theatre whenever she went.[29] In their writings, both Mei Niang and Yang Xu reveal how Manchukuo education made them more conscious of institutionalized discrimination against women.

In the early 1940s, Mei Niang and Yang Xu explicitly condemned the restrictive nature of girls' education in Manchukuo. They blamed it for perpetuating outdated gender ideals at women's expense. Mei Niang cited specific changes to the education system following the establishment of Manchukuo: forbidden topics included modern and contemporary Chinese history and former Republican president Yuan Shikai.[30] To the mid-1930s, the curriculum remained focused on Chinese and Western texts, but newly employed Japanese staff undertook to inculcate conservative ideals of womanhood, which stressed docility, obedience, and composure.[31] By middle school, girls were separated from boys and immersed in courses that did not prepare them for the meaningful careers outside the home that many envisioned. In Mei Niang's novella *Xie* (1941), the sympathetically portrayed female protagonist Sun Ling pronounces herself "especially put out" (*tebie meiqu*) by Japanese-style home economics courses.[32] Mei Niang was similarly uninspired by officially sanctioned gender ideals and refused to "go back to the kitchen" upon graduation.[33] Yang Xu also clearly articulated her refusal to silently accede to such an education: "School, family, society ... seem to be combining to take advantage of me, this pitiful girl. As soon as I think about hope, reality immediately makes me run into a stone wall. Am I not to moan while being attacked from all sides?"[34] Manchukuo education made these women more cognizant of the contrasts between the modernity that they envisioned and the conservatism of *Wangdao* ideals, convincing them of the latter's inferiority.

Two of the writers, Mei Niang and Dan Di, pursued advanced education in Japan. After the death of her father in 1936, Mei Niang was sent by her guardians (her stepmother and uncle) to study in Japan, coincidentally at the same time that Xiao Hong, a leading figure of Manchukuo's exiled faction, also resided there. Although Mei Niang's dream was to study medicine, she soon discovered that the only avenue available to her in a Japanese college in the mid-1930s was to become a good wife, wise mother.[35] Such a lack of opportunity alienated the young woman, who dreamed of "modern" opportunities premised on the ideals of independence with which she had been raised. Indeed, a frequent theme in her work is the inadequacy of Japanese-style education for women. Mei Niang was more drawn to Tokyo's Chinese-language bookstore (Neixin shudian) and her future husband, Liu Longguang, who worked there. Her education was cut short in 1938 by her guardians' refusal to allow her to choose her own partner, Liu. Mei returned to the capital, where she began to work at *Datongbao*. In 1939, Liu followed her to Manchukuo, where they married against her guardians' wishes. Over the next few years, Mei and Liu lived in Manchukuo as well as various Japanese cities. She abhorred the growing presence of Japanese imperialism, fascism, and patriarchy in Chinese society but believed that these constituted political, not racial, problems.[36] She was moved by the wartime hardships under which the common people of Japan strained, and she refused to condemn all Japanese for their nation's aggression against China. While in Japan, she was also repulsed by rampant discrimination against Korean workers, which inspired her short story "Qiaomin" (Expatriates).[37] Mei Niang took advantage of the education and employment opportunities available to establish a platform from which to critique contemporary society. While in Japan, she wrote three of her most famous works, "Bang" (Clam), "Yu" (Fish), and the novella *Xie*. She polished her Japanese-language skills and began to translate progressive Japanese literature, notably that of Kume Masao, into Chinese. She permanently returned to China in 1941. From her new home in Beijing, she continued to write of Chinese colonial life in Manchukuo and corresponded with fellow women writers, such as Wu Ying, who resided in that territory.

Alone among the women of this study, Dan Di (Figure 4.1) won a highly competitive scholarship for advanced education in Japan. In 1935, after completing middle school, she began teaching but within two years successfully passed the qualifying exams for study in Japan. In 1938, she started classes at the Women's Senior Middle Teacher Training Institute in Nara. For Dan Di, life in Japan was disheartening: "Left to myself, all is desolate" (*liugei wo de, jin shi qiliang*).[38] In the essay "Gan" (Feelings), she notes that "When I start to think about myself, there is nothing that I can say. I am like other girls. After graduating from middle school, I suffer from my roused yearnings. The disasters of life and emotions make the days pass with such melancholy and depression."[39]

4.1 Dan Di, circa 1940.

In her writings, she contrasts Japan's coldness, the autumn leaves falling, and the lament of a flute, with her warm hometown memories among the "people on the banks of the Nen River. They all dress warmly and have full bellies."[40] She grew disconcerted by her Japanese classmates who "rarely sing, rarely smile, [and are] corroded by a silent melancholy."[41] She noted fundamental differences between Chinese and Japanese women. In 1942, she attended a women's history class, which underlined, for her, those differences. She noted that contemporary Japanese gender analysis theorized that women had been subjugated by men since the "primitive era" (*yuanshi shidai*) because of their inferior physiology and economic structures that discriminated against them.[42] To her chagrin, the class portrayed the history of women as solely "forgotten women, toyed-with women whose fate is already as if they are dead."[43] She rejected the idealization of women's passive subjugation. Dan Di's experiences in Japan confirmed for her the inferiority of Japanese ideals of womanhood.

Dan Di's forthright character is illuminated in Mei Niang's essay "Jinian Tian Lin" (Remembering Tian Lin). Mei Niang recounts the violent outburst that ended the relationship between Dan Di and her boyfriend, Tian Lang (1912-45), a Chinese student from Manchukuo attending university in Kyoto, on Dan Di's discovery that Tian had entered into an arranged marriage; his request that she remain his mistress infuriated her.[44] She turned to Mei Niang for support, and the two shared their conviction that "men running around with wild feudalistic standards are already a spent force."[45] To the surprise of everyone and at the risk of expulsion for having had a boyfriend (a strictly prohibited practice), Dan Di informed school authorities of the altercation. Dan Di's involvement with a Chinese partner (whom she felt had betrayed her) and

Japanese authorities (to whom she turned for security, comfort, or revenge) illustrates the conflicting and competing ties of contemporary life. Dan Di was deeply shaken by the end of this long-term relationship, which no doubt influenced the tone of her writings. She also credited her meagre Manchukuo scholarship with forcing her to write to pay for living expenses.[46] By the time Dan Di returned to Manchukuo in 1942, the negativity of her writings had already alarmed colonial officials and she was assigned to teach in Kaiyuan, Liaoning, at the local Women's Middle School, a relatively insignificant posting for a student who had received five years of rare state funding for advanced education in Japan.[47]

Living in Japan affected Mei Niang and Dan Di in ways that Manchukuo officials could not have predicted. In the early 1940s, Japan's literary world was not as restrictive as its Manchukuo counterpart. Greater access was available, in bookstores and libraries, to literature from China and the West. Tokyo's Chinese-language bookstore was stocked with the works of writers such as Marx, Lenin, and Xiao Hong; in Tokyo, Mei Niang was able to purchase Xiao Jun's virulently anti-Japanese novel *Ba yue de xiangcun* (*Village in August*).[48] Dan Di and Mei Niang were inspired by these works, which officials at home condemned as treasonous. Ironically, young Chinese were encouraged to travel to the heart of the Japanese Empire, where they were exposed to the literature deemed most offensive by the Manchukuo government. Both women returned to Manchukuo with an intensified belief in the superiority of modern Chinese cultural ideals and with more powerful means to articulate that conviction.

Manchukuo's women writers were thus raised within a complex weave of conservative and progressive, Chinese, Japanese, and Western ideals. Inspired by the spirit of independence that life in the pioneering region of Manchuria necessitated and by May Fourth ideals of women's emancipation, they criticized the subjugation of women that they believed was endemic to the Manchukuo cultural agenda. Manchukuo education touted a conservatism that repulsed them, and it gave them common ground. In Japan, Mei Niang and Dan Di became friends. At home, in school, and abroad, these women pursued a vision of modernity that was seemingly incongruous with the professed ambitions of Manchukuo officials. As the following sections attest, their adult lives and careers were contoured by their youthful ideals.

Becoming Wives and Mothers

As discussed in Chapter 2, a defining characteristic of new women in Republican China was their advocacy of free choice in marriage. Women who chose their own partners emerged in the May Fourth era as dramatic symbols of modernity and sexual equality. In Manchukuo, new women also attached great importance to personal control over their romantic pursuits. Manchukuo officials may have condemned new women for a presumed lax morality, but these women deemed individual control over their bodies integral to their identities as modern Chinese women. Aiming to personify the ideals of emancipation that informed their writing, the seven women writers all refused to accept arranged marriage. The subjects of this book rebuffed parents who contrived to arrange marriages for them. In time, all of the women became wives and mothers but on their own terms and after roundly critiquing officially sanctioned ideals of good wives, wise mothers.

Mei Niang and Yang Xu rejected arranged marriages at great personal cost. While studying in Japan, Mei Niang fell in love with a Chinese economics student from Manchukuo, Liu Longguang. In 1938, her guardians refused to recognize their relationship, severed her financial support, and forced her to return prematurely to Manchukuo. In 1939, Liu followed her to Xinjing, whereupon she infuriated her family by breaking off an engagement that they had arranged for her.[49] Liu and Mei began to live together, and the home they shared became a salon for young writers in the capital. Despite a tumultuous beginning, their marriage produced three children and lasted until Liu's untimely death in 1949. Yang Xu similarly rejected an arranged marriage, a practice that she condemned at the time as "ignorant."[50] She blamed her father, but both parents hoped that she would not emulate her elder sister, who had balked at the suggestion of an arranged marriage and chose her own husband. In 1938, at the age of nineteen, Yang Xu was in love with a writer named Xiadi, and "declared war on [her] father" (*dui fuqin xuan zhan le*).[51] She packed her bags and fled for Xinjing and Xiadi, who waited for her there.[52] Their relationship ended a few years later in 1940; he was considerably older than her and, initially unbeknown to her, had a wife and child. Yang Xu would not enter into a marriage that was anything less than an equal partnership. In 1942, while working as an editor at the *Guomin huabao* (*Citizen's Herald*), she met the man she would marry, Zhang Hong'en. He was employed as supervisor of printing at *Xin Manzhou* (*New Manchukuo*). Yang noted that he was stable and forthright, not at all like the type of men she had previously dated: "In the morning the Qin dynasty, in the evening the Chu dynasty" (*chao Qin mu Chu*).[53] They married in 1943, bringing to an end Yang's single life, which she dubbed "woman's dangerous road" (*nüren de weixian zhi lu*).[54] Yang Xu's parents, however, were unmoved by Zhang's personality and their mutual dedication. Her father never accepted their marriage and her mother did so only grudgingly, travelling from Fengtian to Xinjing to attend their wedding celebrations for a brief two days. Yang Xu's friends were surprised that the outspoken young woman would marry such an unprepossessing man. Despite the disapproval of family and friends, however, this union lasted for sixty-one years, producing three sons and a daughter.

Zhu Ti also alienated her parents with her choice of a husband. She met her future husband, Li Zhengzhong, when she was fourteen.[55] Their relationship developed from Li's frequent visits to an aunt who lived next door to Zhu's family in Xinjing. Zhu Ti's parents disapproved of Li's impoverished background. Though a promising writer pursuing postsecondary education in law,

4.2 Zhu Ti and Li Zhengzhong, circa 1942.

Li did not appear capable of providing the level of financial support for Zhu Ti that her parents envisioned. As her parents prepared to leave Manchukuo in search of more lucrative business opportunities back in Beijing in 1942, the young couple married (Figure 4.2), so that she could remain with Li and his family in Manchukuo. Their marriage has lasted for over sixty years and produced three children.

Just as Mei Niang, Yang Xu, and Zhu Ti chose their husbands, so did the other women, though in less acrimonious ways. Wu Ying and Zuo Di met their partners at work. Wu Ying (Figure 4.3) met her husband, editor and writer Wu Lang, in the editing pool at *Simin* (*This People*). They married in 1935 and had one son. In her marriage, Wu Ying violated officially sanctioned ideals of good wives, wise mothers in two important respects: she remanded her son to her parents to raise, and the couple lived at a hotel to spare Wu Ying from housework. In an interview in 1943, she laughingly observed that despite her modern marriage, she alone was responsible for the housekeeping, which she avoided so that she could devote more time to her professional pursuits.[56] In her personal life, she refuted the conservatism through which Manchukuo officials sought to structure Chinese women's lives. In 1941, she introduced her protégé, Zuo Di (Figure 4.4), to her colleague Liang Shanding. Zuo and Liang married in May 1942; this marriage was her first, his second, and the last for both of them. They had four children in a relationship that was wracked for two decades by official persecution, from both the Manchukuo regime and its Maoist successor. Like the rest of the writers, Wu Ying and Zuo Di married men with

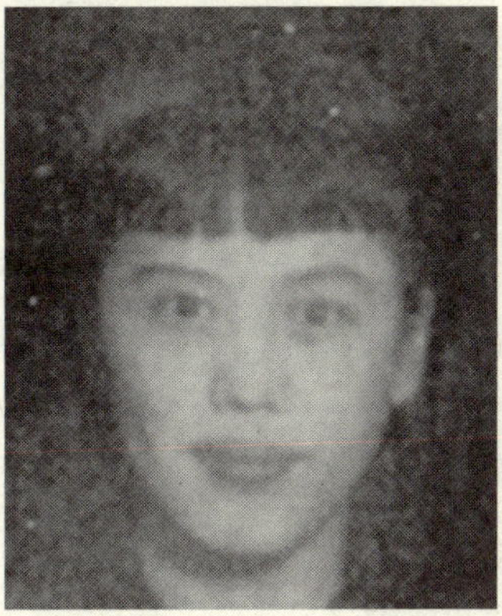

4.3 Wu Ying, circa 1940.

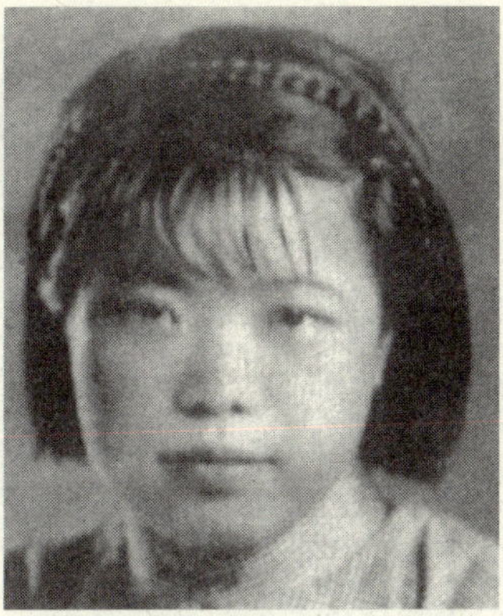

4.4 Zuo Di, circa 1940.

similar professional ambitions. They also married two of Manchukuo's most renowned writers. Liang Shanding and Wu Lang played decisive roles in Manchukuo's literary world, as writers, editors, and mentors for younger writers.

Five of the women writers – Mei Niang, Yang Xu, Zhu Ti, Wu Ying, and Zuo Di – married only once. Even when their husbands died young, they did not remarry. In contrast, Dan Di's personal life was shaped by an almost unfathomable level of persecution. Her first husband, whom she met at work in 1946, divorced her when she was imprisoned (for the second time) by the Chinese Communist Party (CCP) in 1947. She married her second husband in 1960, and they had one child. In 1966, she was imprisoned for a third time, and her second husband died shortly after she was released. Her third marriage, while she was in her seventies, lasted only a few years before her own death in 1992. Lan Ling's personal life was also deeply affected by the turmoil that accompanied the Japanese invasion. With her parents' approval, she had married a neighbour after her first engagement was broken. Her first fiancé, Cao Mengbu, was an underground CCP member and a science teacher at Qiqihaer's Mongolian Banner Teacher Training School.[57] He mentored the young poet, introducing her to Soviet literature and to what became her favourite novel, Maxim Gorky's *Mother*. In 1937, when Cao left Manchukuo to join the anti-Japanese resistance, Lan stayed behind to support her family. In 1941, after no contact for several years, her father broke their engagement, whereupon she was affianced to a young writer, Hu Dounan. Hu was a graduate of Beijing's prestigious Qinghua University and worked in Qiqihaer as a middle school teacher.[58] They married at the end of 1942 and had one child. Upon the liberation of Qiqihaer, Cao returned with the CCP army, acknowledged their broken engagement, vouched for her character with the local communist authorities, and left.[59] Following Hu's death in 1949, Lan married Qiu Jingshan, a returned Chinese student from the Soviet Union who subsequently held high positions

4.5 This composite photograph features Lan Ling in her early twenties with a later picture of her husband, Qiu Jingshan.

in China's prestigious Foreign Languages Press. They remained married until his death in 1997 (Figure 4.5).

For most of the couples, married life did not last long. In 1949, Mei Niang's husband Liu Longguang died as the ship in which he was returning to China sank in the Taiwan Straits. Lan Ling's first husband, Hu Dounan, died of natural causes after only seven years of marriage. In 1957, at the height of the Anti-Rightist campaign, Wu Ying's husband, Wu Lang, who could no longer face prolonged political persecution for his Manchukuo career, committed suicide. Dan Di's marriages were tragically short, interrupted twice by her incarceration. Zuo Di's marriage to Liang Shanding lasted seventeen years, but political persecution separated them for eleven of those years.[60] The marriages of Yang Xu and Zhu Ti each lasted for over sixty years but were also marked by terms of imprisonment or hard labour. The women's marriages brought happiness that was all too brief and children who had to bear for decades the burden of their parents' youthful careers. It is striking how much misery the women endured in their personal lives for their literary lives in Manchukuo.

The writers consistently critiqued the contemporary construct of good wives, wise mothers yet, ironically, came to personify many of its essential elements. None of the women chose to remain single. Mei Niang was widowed for over fifty years; in imperial China, she would have been lauded as a chaste widow. Zuo Di did not remarry after her politically motivated divorce. Wu Ying died shortly after her husband's suicide. Lan Ling was married to Qiu Jingshan for over forty years, and Yang Xu and Zhu Ti were married to their husbands for over six decades. All became mothers. Although Wu Ying relinquished control over her child to her own parents, the rest struggled to simultaneously fulfil career and household responsibilities. As they matured, they came to embody many of the traits of the good wives, wise mothers ideal that they had so roundly criticized. Their critiques of officially sanctioned ideals of womanhood are outlined in the following chapter. In light of their personal lives, those critiques might more properly be interpreted as condemnation of the conservatism of the Manchukuo cultural agenda, rather than of marriage and motherhood per se.

Forging Careers

Two main factors drove the women to establish careers in Manchukuo: money and idealism. In Manchukuo, as in the rest of China, few writers could survive solely by their pens. All of the women worked to earn a living as they fulfilled their personal ambitions to write; poverty ensured that most combined writing with other pursuits. They used the opportunities available to them in Manchukuo to make money in a manner that was meaningful to them. The career paths that they chose reflected contemporary opportunities pursued by new women elsewhere, in the Republic of China and in Japan. Their careers highlight the potential that existed for Chinese women to pursue their own ambitions while living under Japanese colonial rule in Manchukuo.

Dan Di, Lan Ling, and Zhu Ti were employed as teachers, one of several careers that educated women in Manchukuo were encouraged to pursue. Dan and Lan trained at the Heilongjiang Provincial First Women's Teacher Training Institute; they both graduated in July 1935.[61] On graduation, Dan Di began teaching at the primary school she had attended as a child. After one year, she returned home to prepare for the highly competitive state scholarship exams for advanced studies in Japan. In 1937, she won a scholarship and left for Japan. In 1942, upon completion of her studies, she was assigned to Kaiyuan Women's Middle School in Liaoning province. In 1936, Lan Ling began her first teaching assignment at Qiqihaer's Tongxin Primary School. In April 1941, she resigned to focus on writing, but returned to teaching again in June 1944, when censorship made publishing overly difficult for her. Zhu Ti graduated from Jilin Provincial Women's Middle Subsidiary Teacher Training School in 1942.[62] She immediately began teaching at Jilin Beishan primary school in Xinjing. Reflecting official gender ideals and the career paths of most female teachers, all three of these women were assigned to teach in primary or women's schools. Although women in Manchukuo were encouraged to pursue careers as teachers (a profession advocated by officials to especially suit women's "nurturing" nature), they were paid little for their efforts. All three of the women supplemented their teaching incomes by writing, and Dan Di and Lan Ling also sewed and made frequent trips to pawn shops.[63]

Manchukuo propaganda promoted education as an essential element of regional modernization – a literate population was meant to symbolize the progressive and enlightened nature of *Wangdao* rule, bolstering the image of the state by empowering its youth. But in their writings, these women argue that the Manchukuo education system was incapable of empowering women. Lan Ling and Zhu Ti both wrote of their experiences as teachers. In 1944, Zhu Ti criticized Manchukuo education in her short story "Wo he wo de haizimen" (Me and My Children). The female protagonist, a teacher, argues that her duty is to save students "from the contagious poisons in the common world."[64] The teacher cuts short her honeymoon to shield her students from contemporary social ills, encouraging them to single-mindedly pursue their youthful ideals despite her privately held fears that their efforts will be to no avail. Lan Ling later acknowledged education's potential for personal growth, but she had reservations regarding the Manchukuo emphasis on Confucianism and filial piety, especially as they pertained to women.[65] Even more vexing for her was the required Japanese-style housework studies class (*jiashi ke*) for girls. As a teacher, she was disappointed with the content and direction of girls' education. Both Lan Ling and Zhu Ti had been drawn to education by idealism, but were dismayed by the Manchukuo cultural agenda that they were hired to promote. Although during the first year of the occupation approximately one-third of the region's teachers left their positions, many teachers who were resistant to Manchukuo propaganda remained. The sample of this study suggests the cooperative as well as subversive roles of teachers within the education system. Of these three women, all were the subjects of official investigation. In 1943, while teaching, Dan Di wrote "Jie" (Warning) and was arrested and imprisoned shortly thereafter on charges of intending to flee Manchukuo. In 1944, two of Zhu Ti's short stories, "Xiao Yinzi he ta de jiazu" (Little Yinzi and Her Relations) and "Ying" (Cherry) were banned, and Lan Ling's home was searched, twice. While it is impossible to reconstruct their in-class activities, the critiques of contemporary society that dominated their writings, and eventually outraged Manchukuo officials, must also have influenced their work as professional educators.

Teaching was not the only profession available to educated women. In 1938 Zuo Di completed a two-year course at Fengtian's South Manchuria Pharmaceutical College. She briefly worked as a pharmaceutical clerk in Fengtian, but low wages and the death of her father prompted a move to Xinjing in search of more lucrative work. Connections with an uncle who worked at the law courts, a middle school education, and Japanese language skills landed her a job as a clerk at the National Propaganda Department (Hongbao). In the capital, she acquired her dreamt-of independence. At the same time, her wages helped to support her family after the loss of its primary wage-earner, and she sent money home for her younger siblings. Forging careers in Manchukuo necessitated various degrees of contact with state institutions. Zuo Di was driven by financial necessity and ambition, and empowered by her Manchukuo education, to work in the National Propaganda Department. She then used the income she earned to help support her impoverished family and to further her own career ambitions.

Of all the writers of this study, Yang Xu pursued the least orthodox career path. In 1938, she fled to Xinjing to escape an arranged marriage and found work as a clerk in the Manchukuo Central Bank. She described her search for employment in the Xinjing job market "as difficult as finding a pearl. [I] spent the energy of nine cows and two tigers signing up."[66] Despite long hours at the bank, she earned only a subsistence-level wage; her salary proved inadequate to support her even when sharing rent with two co-workers.[67] In 1939, she began to supplement her income by coaching evening singing classes at the state's official movie production company, Manchukuo Movies (*Manying*).[68] The double workload proved unbearable, and she had to resign from Manchukuo Film. Buoyed by her experiences, however, she soon left the bank to join the Japanese-sponsored Arts Drama Troupe (*Wenyi huajutuan*).[69] Yang's decision to abandon her steady bank job and become a performer scandalized family and friends. Her friends denounced her actions as "treason and heresy" (*da ni bu dao*).[70] Whether their disgust was a result to her career choice or the closer proximity it brought her to the Japanese was not clearly articulated, but they erected "a battle line" (*yi tiao zhanxian*) against her for abandoning a life of relative security to enter a profession that was considered dubious at best, immoral at worst, and far too close for comfort to the Japanese.[71] Undaunted, Yang spent the next two years pursuing a singing career. She joined the Manchukuo Entertainment Recording Company (*Manzhou xuyin zhushi huishe*) to become a staple on the Manchukuo music scene. She graced the cover of *Qilin* (*Unicorn*) (June 1942; see Figure 4.6), performed frequently on radio, and made records on the Shanghai-based Victory (*Shengli*) label.[72] She also starred in a dramatic production of Cao Yu's critically acclaimed play *Sunrise* (*Richu*) and performed at Manchukuo's exhibition at the Pan-Asian Exposition in Seoul, Korea, in 1941.[73] Yang was perhaps best known to contemporaries for singing the Manchukuo national anthem on record. According to her own recollections, she was summoned by Japanese cultural functionaries and ordered to perform the anthem.[74] Significantly, in the early 1940s, she wrote several lengthy essays about her experiences in Manchukuo's singing industry but does not once refer to her most high-profile performance, suggesting an at least ambiguous relationship with it.[75] Contemporary writer Li Zhengzhong has argued that her performance of Manchukuo's national anthem was comparable to writers' membership in Manchukuo's cultural associations – high-profile Chinese were forced into compromising public positions regardless of personal preferences.[76] Yang Xu's career estranged family and friends who believed her best option was to settle down and marry, out of the limelight. Instead, she pursued a reasonably well-paid profession that thrust her onto the national stage. From there, she overtly challenged conservative ideals of womanhood. By the end of 1942, however, she abandoned her performing career to focus on writing, editing, and married life.

Once Yang Xu, Mei Niang, Wu Ying, and Zuo Di began to publish their writings, they relied exclusively on income from their literary pursuits, which

4.6 Yang Xu was a popular singer and writer whose image graced the cover of one of Manchukuo's most popular magazines, *Qilin* (*Unicorn*), June 1942.

came to dominate their lives. All of the women married men who were involved in the production of literature. Mei Niang, Wu Ying, Zhu Ti, and Zuo Di married prominent authors or editors and their personal and professional lives intertwined, as would be expected in the relatively small pool of educated local Chinese. In Manchukuo's highly suspect literary world, only the most committed endured – and they found support in each other. Wu Ying and Zuo Di, and their high-profile husbands, Wu Lang and Liang Shanding, edited newspapers and journals, published their writings, and were members of government-affiliated organizations, yet they lived in penury. Their sparse incomes testify to the low pay for Chinese intellectuals in Manchukuo. Even the most high-profile writers who were publicly affiliated with Japanese colonial institutions could barely manage to support themselves. Sympathetic Japanese intellectuals had criticized this failing as early as 1939, to no avail.[77] But the writers were not deterred by low incomes, as they were also driven by idealism and ambition. Ironically, the low levels of remuneration that they received forced them to produce even more writing critical of contemporary society to make ends meet. Only Mei Niang inherited wealth that could have allowed her a degree of independence, yet she was ideologically committed to earning her own income. Wu Ying, Yang Xu, and Zuo Di, and their husbands, were entirely dependent upon income from literary work. When their writings violated Manchukuo law, they risked their livelihoods, if not their freedom or their lives.

Most of the writers began to publish while in their teens. Lan Ling's first poem was inspired by an underground CCP member in Qiqihaer, Ba Lai (the pen name of Jin Jianxiao), and was published when she was fourteen.[78] Ba Lai edited a literary supplement, *Wutian* (*Grasslands*) for the *Heilongjiang ribao* (*Heilongjiang Daily*) from 1934 to 1935, when he was arrested and later executed by the Japanese for links with the CCP.[79] Lan Ling's first published poem, "Pa ta jin na yinyu de jia men" (Afraid He Will Enter That Dark House's Door), was printed with Ba's help. An enthusiastic teacher assembled Mei Niang's writings from middle school to publish a collected volume of her writings when Mei was sixteen.[80] Yang Xu and Zhu Ti first published their writings when they were eighteen.[81] Dan Di and Wu Ying began to publish at nineteen. Their young age is significant. By 1935, most of Manchukuo's prominent writers had fled. These women established their careers at young ages in a relatively barren literary world. While their predecessors balked at working in close proximity to the colonial state, these women knew nothing else. Manchukuo appeared to be a permanent entity, which institutionalized a decades-long informal Japanese presence in the region. If they were to survive, they had to work, and they found literary work appealing. Writing earned them money, however meagre, and allowed them to experiment with self-expression. Thus, it was rewarding to them on several levels: they could achieve their independence, help their families, and articulate their discomfort with contemporary society. The critical nature of their work must also have assuaged any conscientious objections to working closely with the occupying forces. For their part, Manchukuo officials appear initially to have viewed their work as harmless – the writers were young, had been partly educated in Manchukuo, and were *only* women after all. Their writings might criticize Manchukuo society, but these critiques were not unlike those produced by progressive writers in Japan. Perhaps most importantly, the women did not express any support for the Republic of China. In fact, many of their critiques would have been equally applicable to contemporary Republican society.

In Manchukuo, colonial officials discounted Chinese women's literature at their peril. As discussed in Chapter 3, these women sought to "describe" and "expose reality" by detailing the "dark side" (*yin'an mian*) of society.[82] Two of the women, Mei Niang and Wu Ying, were founding members of the Literary Collective, the Xinjing faction that most forcefully advocated "exposing reality." In 1939, the Literary Collective published Mei Niang's *Di'er dai* (*The Second Generation*) and Wu Ying's *Liang ji* (*Two Extremes*). Mei Niang, throughout *Di'er dai*, implicitly argues that the social turmoil that epitomized Chinese life in Manchukuo was induced by Japanese colonialism and patriarchy. Wu Ying's *Liang ji* critiques conservative patriarchal mores for oppressing and alienating women; representative titles of short stories include: "Nü pantu" (Woman Rebel) and "Xin kundao" (New Female Path). Following Lu Xun's example, they aspired to expose the darkest elements of society in a bid to raise the social conscience of the masses. In a direct affront to official demands that writers exclusively adopt Japanese role models, Dan Di even cited Francis Bacon as an inspiration for her writing, quoting his saying, "Truth is the principle of the era."[83] These women believed that as educated new women they enjoyed special insight into the nature of Manchukuo's shortcomings and that they were obliged to use their positions of privilege to articulate their well-informed contempt.

Against a backdrop of colonial regulations proscribing negativity, pessimism, and discussion of sexuality, the women wrote candidly of their despair and desires. Their writings appeared in high-profile, Japanese-owned Chinese-language newspapers and journals, including *Daban Huawen meiri* (*Chinese Osaka Daily*), *Datong bao* (*Great Unity Herald*), *Jiankang Manzhou* (*Healthy Manchukuo*), *Qilin* (*Unicorn*), *Qingnian wenhua* (*Youth Culture*), *Shengjing shibao* (*Shengjing Daily*), *Simin*, and *Xin Manzhou*. In addition, Dan Di, Wu Ying, and Zhu Ti each published one volume of collected works during the occupation period, Yang Xu published two, and Mei Niang four.[84] These were typically produced in quantities of two to four thousand – for example, two thousand copies of Wu Ying's *Liang ji (Two Extremes*) (1939), three thousand copies each of Yang Xu's *Wo de riji* (1944) and the first edition of Mei Niang's *Yu* (1943), and four thousand copies of Mei's *Xie* (1944).[85] These statistics do not accurately reflect the number of readers who had access to their work. Books, journals, and newspapers commonly enjoyed a shared readership, especially after paper restrictions were implemented in the early 1940s. While it is difficult to assess the influence of their work, their writings were published in, and the women participated in editing, the most prominent publications in Manchukuo. Contemporary reviews of their work and the public debate over ideals of womanhood caused by Yang Xu's essay "Gongkai de zuizhuang" (Open Indictment) in the pages of *Xin Manzhou* evince the seriousness with which Chinese critics and other readers viewed their work.[86]

At various stages, and in different capacities, three of the writers worked at Xinjing's official, Japanese-owned Chinese-language daily newspaper, *Datong bao*: Mei Niang (contributor and proofreader, 1936 and 1938),[87] Wu Ying (reporter, 1940), and Zuo Di (editor, 1942-3). *Datong bao* was a vital state organ devoted to the promotion of pro-government news and commentary, but it also published fiction and op-ed material. Within its pages, Mei Niang criticized contemporary gender ideals, and Zuo Di edited her husband's controversial novel *Lüse de gu*, which was first heavily censored, then banned, and led to the couple's eventual abandonment of Manchukuo. Thus, within the pages of the pre-eminent Chinese-language newspaper in the capital of Manchukuo, the women engaged in cooperative and subversive intellectual activities. They worked for a newspaper in which they published material that violated Manchukuo's literary guidelines, and they were paid for it. Far more commonly, though, they worked at journals, which tended to be less subject to official scrutiny than was *Datong bao*.

During the Japanese occupation, most of the women were employed as editors at journals. Wu Ying attained the highest profile as an editor for her work at *Simin* (1939-40), *Manzhou wenyi* (*Manchukuo Arts*) (1942), and *Xin Manzhou* (1942-4).[88] She was also a member of the Japanese-sponsored Manchukuo Arts Association (1942-3) and the Manchukuo Library Auxiliary Association (1942-3).[89] As her editorial responsibilities increased, Wu Ying continued to author essays under several pen names, but she wrote her last work of fiction in 1943. She mentored Zuo Di, who was briefly employed by the Manchukuo Library Auxiliary Association (1940), where she participated in the preparation of the Japanese-language journal *Manshū fujin* (*Manchukuo Women*).[90] When this magazine folded, Zuo Di was transferred to the editing pool at *Xin Manzhou* (1940-3). In 1942, she was appointed an editor at the Culture Society (*Wenhua shi*) (1942-3). She eventually left that position to follow her husband into exile in Beijing. After abandoning her career as an entertainer in 1942, Yang Xu worked as an editor for *Guomin huabao* (1942).[91] While on probation for attempting to flee Manchukuo in 1944-5, Dan Di joined the editorial staff at *Manzhou yinghua* (*Manchukuo Movies*). In Beijing, Mei Niang edited *Funü zazhi* (*Ladies' Journal*) (1942-3). As editors, they selected, proofread, and approved material for publication. While the particular details of their duties may never be known, their ambition to expose reality, and the persecution that eventually besieged them, suggests their editorial proclivities. Their transition from writing to editing also evidences the closely knit nature of the contemporary literary world.

Three books highlight the editorial achievements of Wu Ying and Zuo Di. In 1941, they edited the critically acclaimed *Shijie ming xiaoshuo xuan* (*Selection of World Famous Novels*) and *Xuesheng xiao zidian* (*Primer Dictionary for Students*). *Shijie ming xiaoshuo xuan* was highly regarded by contemporaries for introducing readers to Western writers.[92] It should be noted that the volume's Western content conflicted with the early 1940s official promotion of Japanese literature as the sole legitimate basis for cultural development in Manchukuo. Two years later, in February 1943, Zuo Di edited *Nüzuojia chuangzuo xuan* (*Selected Writings of Women Writers*). This volume features the work of five of the most prominent women writers of Manchukuo: Bai

Lang, Dan Di, Mei Niang, Wu Ying, and Xiao Hong. In the introduction, Zuo praises their use of "women's exceptional wisdom and delicate writing style to analyse the lifestyle of the masses of women living in society."[93] Significantly, *Nüzuojia chuangzuo xuan* includes work by the self-exiled Bai Lang and Xiao Hong, stressing their contributions to the development of feminist discourses in Manchukuo, not the Chinese patriotism for which they were lauded by Chinese nationalists and banned by Manchukuo officials. It is a testament to colonial officialdom's lax attitude and low regard for women's writing that work by these exiled writers was published in Manchukuo a decade after they had fled, during which time their notoriety had only increased. Their inclusion in this compilation explicitly links the most prolific women writers in latter Manchukuo with their literary predecessors, to stress a common feminist legacy.

One further example provides insight into the simultaneous cooperation and subversion possible in prominent Manchukuo institutions. In 1942, Wu Ying was chosen to represent Manchukuo as a delegate to the first Greater East Asia Writers' Congress in Tokyo. Her participation in the congress legitimized the Manchukuo literary scene, which Japanese critics singled out for its critical reflection on colonial life. In a subsequent article published in *Qilin*, "Chuxi Dadongya wenxuezhe da hui suo gan" (Feelings about Attending the Greater East Asia Writers' Congress), Wu details the high level of respect Japanese participants accorded to her and her fellow Manchukuo delegates. She notes that many Japanese were ardent supporters of Manchukuo's Chinese-language literary endeavours. Wu tacitly redefines the purpose of the congress by stressing a resurrection of the culture of "each country in the Eastern ocean ... connecting nations with their national spirits."[94] But the official aims of this congress explicitly stressed the transplantation of *Japanese* literature throughout Asia, not the revitalization of distinct Asian "national spirits." Wu briefly notes that the Sacred War was being fought to liberate all Asians, offering no substantial evaluation of the congress proceedings, yet writes extensively of the friendships she cultivated in Japan. Wu stresses the support of Japanese intellectuals that could legitimate, in the eyes of colonial officials, the work of Chinese writers, thereby problematizing the enforcement of literary regulations in Manchukuo. High-level cooperation between Chinese and Japanese writers lent a legitimacy to Manchukuo literature that could be manipulated by the Chinese to further their own ambitions. The subversive potential of that cooperation contradicts the charges of treasonous behaviour for which these authors were later excoriated in the Maoist era.

In Manchukuo, Beijing, and Japan, contemporaries lauded the impact of these seven women on the Chinese-language literary world. In 1936, upon the publication of her first work, Wu Ying was hailed by literary critics as "a symbol of vitality and hope" for Manchukuo literature.[95] In 1939, to recognize the popularity of her collected works, *Liang ji*, and to enhance the fame of the Selected Works faction (of which she was a founding member), Wu Ying was awarded that faction's highest distinction, the Number One People's Artist Award.[96] In 1941, her short story "Xuyuan" (Dilapidation) captured the top prize in a writing contest organized by the Japanese-sponsored Manchukuo-China Arts Exchange (*Man-Zhong wenyi jiaohuan*).[97] Dan Di's first novella, *Andi he Mahua*, was heralded by Chinese writers in Japan (where it was published) for her unflinching portrait of colonial hardship in Manchukuo; *Andi he Mahua* won the *Daban Huawen meiri*'s first prize for best mid-length novel in 1942. When Dan Di's collected works were published, in December 1943, Wu Ying and other Chinese critics pronounced her Manchukuo's "most advanced woman writer."[98] But while she was hailed by Chinese critics as "ahead of her times" (*hou lai zhe ju*), she sat in a Manchukuo prison.[99] The irony could not have been lost on her supporters. The critical and popular reception of these writers was a double-edged sword: by 1943, the women had attained a profile that officials could no longer ignore.

In the early 1940s, Mei Niang received the most critical and popular attention of the writers. Of the four collected volumes she published during the occupation, her second, *Di'er dai*, was credited by critic Han Hu with introducing "liberalism" (*zizhu zhuyi*) to Manchukuo.[100] In 1943, her short story "Yu" won the Greater East Asia Writers' Congress Second Prize for Literature, but it was also condemned by the ranking contemporary Japanese scholar of Chinese literature, Yoshikawa Kojiro, as "among the most degenerate pieces" he had ever encountered.[101] Mei Niang's positive portrayal of Fen, the love-starved adulterous heroine of the story, was the antithesis of officially sanctioned constructs of good wives, wise mothers. Despite Yoshikawa's discomfort, the collection *Yu* proved extremely popular; it was republished six times within half a year.[102] Finally, in 1944 the title work from her fourth volume of collected works, *Xie*, which recounts the decline of a wealthy family in Changchun during the Japanese occupation, was acclaimed Novel of the Year by the Greater East Asia Writers' Congress.[103] Mei Niang, as the rest of the writers under discussion, won acclaim for work that was overtly critical of patriarchy and Manchukuo society.

All seven women were praised for their critical reflection on the nature of Manchukuo society – by Chinese, Japanese, and joint Sino-Japanese organizations. All of the works cited above reflect negatively on contemporary society and the subjugation of women. The women did not laud *Wangdao* ideals, Manchukuo, or the Japanese. As will be seen in the following chapters, proselytizing for the colonial state was not a condition of their critical or popular success. Each of the women worked within Manchukuo institutions for their own personal and professional gain, only to attract the attention of officialdom in the final years of the occupation. They achieved popular appeal and critical acclaim, wrote hundreds of articles, stories, and poems, edited journals, and earned money that enabled them to live independently and help support their families. In the process, they left a trail of achievements that eventually led to their downfall in the People's Republic of China. It is worth bearing in mind that the bulk of their legacy was completed by 1945, a creative period that ranged from three to ten years for each author and that ended before any of them turned thirty years old. Their youthful careers sealed their collective personal and professional fates.

5

Disrupting the Patriarchal Foundations of Manchukuo

"In a word, the life that women lead, it really is a tragedy; never-ending hardships combine to create a tragedy."

– *Zuo Di, "Nü nan" (Women's Difficulty)*

In Manchukuo, a weighty combination of state institutions, education, and popular culture were marshalled by officialdom in the attempt to inculcate Japan-centric, conservative ideals of womanhood. The women studied here met those ideals with their refusal to renounce the Chinese constructs of modernity that had inspired them as young girls. In their work, Manchukuo's most prolific Chinese women writers confronted two adversaries that they believed worked in tandem to deny their individual emancipation: Manchukuo society and its patriarchal foundations. The subjugation that they experienced or observed as women living in Manchukuo compelled them to careers as cultural critics. This chapter highlights the critiques of patriarchy that inform their legacies, underlining their opposition to the ideals of womanhood promoted by the administration in Manchukuo.

Progressive women's movements in Japan, Europe, North America, and elsewhere in China encouraged Manchukuo's young Chinese women writers to reject not only conservative Chinese ideals of womanhood but also imported Japanese ideals, which they viewed as the proverbial "icing on the cake."[1] In their writings, Zuo Di, Yang Xu, and Mei Niang all specifically cite the negative impact of patriarchal ideals on Manchukuo society. The title character in Zuo Di's story "Liu Qi" laments the lack of opportunity for women in Manchukuo's "men-centred society" (*nanren wei zhongxin de shehui*).[2] Yang Xu consistently criticized "male chauvinist society" (*nanxing wei zhongxin de shehui*).[3] In the preface to *Wo de riji* (*My Diary*) she explicitly states her intention to expose as "naked" (*chiluo*) her inner self through dissection of ideals of womanhood as they manifested in her own life.[4] Yang Xu's assertion that "I am an ordinary woman" (*Wo shi ge pingfan de nüren*) could not have endeared her to censors, who immediately banned her second volume of collected writings.[5]

Mei Niang similarly asserted that an essential element of exposing reality was "talking about women's suffering" (*shuoshuo funü de kunan ba*).[6] In her highly popular, explicitly anti-patriarchal short story "Yu" (Fish), the female protagonist Fen condemns "male-centred society ... which recognizes that men should have all the rights and interests, to oppress me and tyrannize me."[7] In 1943, in an open letter to Wu Ying published in Beijing's *Qingnian wenhua* (*Youth Culture*), Mei Niang declared that the subjugation endured by women in "male chauvinist society" (*nanxing zhong shehui*) made women more conscious (*juewu*) and progressive (*qianjin*) than men, requiring them to shoulder special responsibilities: "Women in this society experience a great deal of suffering and pain that men can't imagine ... Only women can change this world into heaven."[8] Manchukuo's sexist society, these authors argued, required rehabilitation by those who had been tempered by its worst excesses, women.

Yang Xu's forthright rejection of conservative ideals of womanhood is clearly articulated in her essay "Gongkai de zuizhuang" (Open Indictment): "Because I have such straightforward speech and attitude, I often forget that I am a woman. I don't use lady-like serenity and tenderness, and lady-like smiles and charm. What I have to do, I just do. What I have to say, I just say. I am content to laugh out loud – content to let my character be bold and unconstrained."[9] Such "bold and unconstrained" behaviour (especially her compulsion to do and say what she must) flew in the face of the Manchukuo ideal of modest and submissive women. Yang asserted that she preferred her male friends "not to look at me as a woman" (*bu ba wo kancheng nüren*) so that they could talk openly and honestly as equals, which she felt was impossible with "lady-like behaviour."[10] Throughout her writings, Yang insists that such a forthright attitude is a strength, common to educated, modern women like herself. But she also notes that behind her back snide remarks were made about women engaged in cultural production in general, and about her in particular.[11] As a celebrity of considerable renown, Yang felt entitled to conduct her personal life in a manner that she associated with the much-vaunted ideal of modernity. Her essay "Gongkai de zuizhuang" prompted a rebuttal in *Xin Manzhou* (*New Manchukuo*) by her former co-worker, Jia Ren, entitled "Zhi Yang Xu nüshi" (To Madame Yang Xu). Jia refutes Yang's portrayal of female office workers as "vases," protesting that Yang's modern ideals were shared by them all.[12] Yang Xu and Jia Ren both publicly rejected conservative ideals of womanhood as antithetical to Manchukuo's ambitions for the region; such ideals were not "modern."[13] Indeed, Jin praises Yang for her "determination to not fear social rejection and to not tolerate Confucianism ... [She is] absolutely fighting against [her] evil environment [*e huangjing*]"[14] Jia heralds Yang as a "contemporary new woman" (*shidai de xin nüxing*), the antithesis of a good wife, wise mother.[15] In "Ji Yang Xu xiaojie" (Notes on Miss Yang Xu), Shang Qiuhe argues that Yang was not the same as "ordinary women" (*yiban nüren*) but rather was "too progressive" (*tai qianjin*). Shang claims that "in this too progressive era, too progressive people can't help sinking into contradictions."[16]

The debate inspired by Yang Xu's work points to a deep well of dissatisfaction articulated by educated Chinese women.

The women under discussion often expressed their dissatisfaction with contemporary Manchukuo gender ideals with reference to Western precedents. In Zhu Ti's "Xiao Yinzi he ta de jiazu" (Little Yinzi and Her Relations), the narrator recounts how a foreign film awakened her to the violence inherent to patriarchal society: "Men's brutality is limitless."[17] The middle-class narrator is moved by the suffering of her next-door neighbour, a young girl who is raped by her adoptive father, yet she is apparently blind to her own subjugation by an overbearing husband, who demands that she not interfere in the private life of other families. The narrator's inability to stand up to her spouse in order to save the powerless young girl suggests the complicity of women in their subjugation in Manchukuo. In Zuo Di's "Liu Qi," the title character is inspired by Madame Curie, whom she pronounces "the greatest female in the world" (*shijie weida de nüxing*) for her selfless devotion to the betterment of society.[18] The nurturing persona of Madame Curie would have appealed to conservatives, who advocated health services, and especially nursing, as an ideal profession for ambitious young women (Figure 5.1). But Liu Qi is outraged to read German philosopher Arthur Schopenhauer's misogynistic assertion that a woman "certainly needs a man to lead her, to manage her" (*yiding xuyao yi ge nanren lingdao ta, guanli ta*).[19] Liu Qi's visceral (and positively portrayed) reaction to Schopenhauer underlines the author's own opposition to the patriarchal subjugation of women and implicitly supports the independence that

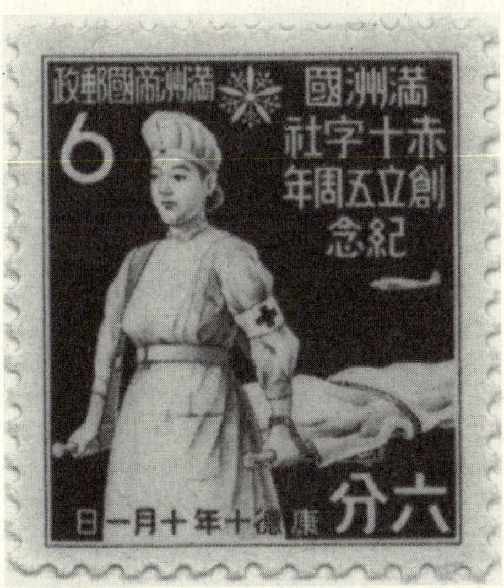

5.1 A stamp commemorating the fifth anniversary of the founding of the Manchukuo Red Cross Society. The image of a nurse celebrates officially sanctioned career opportunities for young professional women in Manchukuo.

she associated with Madame Curie. In a similar vein, Mei Niang praises the spirit of Nora, the heroine from Henrik Ibsen's *A Doll's House*, for inspiring her respect for Western writers, including Lord Byron, Mary Shelley, and Émile Zola.[20] Further positive reflections on Western role models include Yang Xu's citation of Alexandre Dumas' novel *Camille* as an inspiration for her romantic pursuits and Dan Di's reference to Francis Bacon in her search for truth.[21]

An overt paean to Western culture is provided by Henri Matisse's drawings, which accompany the original 1943 publications of Dan Di's "Jie" (Warning), Wu Ying's "Ming" (Howl), and Zuo Di's "Nü nan" (Women's Difficulty) in the journal *Qingnian wenhua* (*Youth Culture*). This special issue, published during the Sacred War, reveals a disregard for official demands that only positive, uplifting Japanese role models be deployed. Matisse's portraits are distinctly European in facial features and clothing, and they differ dramatically from those of the Asian women in illustrations accompanying articles praising good wives, wise mothers, as shown in Chapter 2. The prominence accorded drawings by a Western artist, when officialdom dictated the essential superiority of Japanese culture, underscores the subversive intent of this literature: "Jie," "Ming," and "Nü nan" all critique Manchukuo society by describing the patriarchal subjugation of local women. "Jie" and "Ming" were both specifically cited by censors for their anti-Japanese tone. These three literary works thus link explicit cultural criticism with a seeming appreciation of Western culture as late as the final years of Manchukuo.

Three topics are particularly useful in demonstrating women writers' critical approach to the patriarchal society of Manchukuo: "patience and endurance" (*rennai*); love, marriage, and childbirth; and sex. By problematizing the ideals of patience and endurance that officials identified as essential to construct of the good wife, wise mother, by stressing the importance of personal choice in relationships rather than submission to the state, men, or familial commands, and through questioning the value attached to women's chastity, these writers directly challenged the patriarchal foundations of Manchukuo.

Patience and Endurance

> "Why can't I bear suffering? Why can't I bear suffering?"
>
> *Mala in Zhu Ti, "Shengming zhi xiyue" (The Joy of Life)*

Mala, the female protagonist in Zhu Ti's short story "Shengming zhi xiyue," underlines the significance that both Chinese and Japanese in Manchukuo attributed to women's cultivation of patience and endurance in the face of hardship. Contemporary literature directed towards or written by women abounds with the nouns patience (*ren*), endurance (*nai*), and their compound form, *rennai.* Two distinct patterns of representing patience and endurance emerge. Officially sanctioned ideals tend to promote the long-term, passive acceptance of hardship, which is defined primarily in terms of economic deprivation. Especially during the Sacred War, women who heroically and uncomplainingly coped with shortages of consumer goods were idealized. Women who cultivated patience and endurance were praised by officialdom as positive role models. But the seven writers under discussion here most often linked women's patience and endurance with the patriarchal oppression of women, to counsel rejection of it.

A revealing depiction of patience and endurance is found in Wu Ying's story "Ming" (Howl). Pregnant and no longer able to endure her husband's abuse, the female protagonist refuses to continue "living like a pig in this great world."[22] She yells at her drunken husband:

> I dare say, in this world there isn't a woman whose patience and endurance can compare to my senseless and blind patience and endurance. This patience and endurance, I have not bragged about it in front of people. I often conceal it in front of people because I know this is my natural-born weakness. This weakness is passed on from the hands of my grandmother and mother. They pass it on to me, according to the rules, like leaving their daughter a kind of wealth. Continuously, one generation after another generation, to me. Naturally, according to the rules, I will give it to my descendants. Listen, ah! This is such a pitiful tradition![23]

In "Ming," patience and endurance are condemned as "a pitiful tradition" bequeathed to the young woman "according to the rules" by her female forebears until it is perceived to be a "natural-born weakness." The protagonist's growing awareness of this weakness is the catalyst for her transformation into a "rebel woman" (*fanfan de nüren*).[24] She refuses to perpetuate the "senseless and blind" ideal that she blames for enslaving generations of women. Eventually, her anger overwhelms her, causing her to miscarry. At the end of the story she abandons her husband to embark on a new life, alone. Wu Ying empowers the woman through a sympathetic depiction and by providing her the only voice in the novella; her husband does not respond to her provocation. The female character dominates the narrative with an assertiveness that effectively inverts officially sanctioned gender roles and the virtue of patience and endurance in particular. Wu's portrait of this woman's rejection of her husband and of impending motherhood violates literary regulations such as the Eight Abstentions through unambiguous rejection of the construct of the good wife, wise mother ideal. Contemporary censors, evaluating her work from a nationalist rather than feminist stance, considered the husband's characterization to be a thinly veiled condemnation of Japan: they alleged that the female protagonist was the personification of Manchukuo, rather than an angry woman.[25]

The most egregious manifestation of patience and endurance is passive victimhood. In Zhu Ti's story "Du Bohai" (Crossing the Bohai Sea), which was banned for its portrayal of Manchukuo society, the protagonist avers that she "has no more patience and endurance because she has had no news of her travelling man."[26] After waiting five years for him to return to Shandong, she refuses to continue passively biding time. As the woman searches for her husband in Manchukuo, she is raped, convicted for murder, and exiled. In exile, she learns that she does not need her husband to survive: "To lose a man's cooperation is no reason to be disheartened about one's own life."[27] Her refusal to passively accept her fate sets her on a course of action that excoriates Manchukuo while teaching her the value of self-reliance. In Lan Ling's short story "Richu" (Sunrise), Lian castigates her mother's belief that prayer will deliver her from a miserable life. Lian "is unwilling to patiently endure for a long time the darkness and damp" that she believes has consumed her mother.[28] Her mother's acceptance of a miserable fate compels Lian to forsake a similar life and actively pursue her own happiness. She rejects a marriage arranged on her behalf and elopes with her lover to Manchukuo; doubtless, contemporary readers would have read their flight to freedom in the colony as ironic. In Mei Niang's "Yu" (Fish), the female protagonist determines to leave her common-law husband, the father of their child: "When he was fooling around before, I used women's greatest patience and endurance to forgive him."[29] He repaid her by secretly marrying another woman. Throughout this literature, patience and endurance is cultivated to women's detriment. In Zuo Di's "Nü nan" (Women's Difficulty), a new mother expresses her disgust at a religious pamphlet that suggests, "If one wants to go to heaven, there is only one condition, and that is to continue to bear and endure [life] like a rock."[30] The woman rejects religion as deceitful, mocks the concept of heaven, and identifies patience and endurance as a key component of women's suffering.

Explicit rejection of patience and endurance manifests in the use of vulgarities peppering the language of female characters. At times, Wu Ying's fiction is overwhelmed by local slang and curse words.[31] But the deployment of these words does not diminish the characters' integrity nor does it detract from readers' empathy for them. In "Cui Hong" (Cui Hong), for example, the former prostitute Cui Hong's use of vulgarities is coupled with her honest, no-nonsense nature. Her condemnation of the "motherfucking bastards" who "looked at me like a piece of meat ... like monsters gnawing on human flesh!" is designed to elicit sympathy from readers, not to appall them.[32] In the novella, Cui's former profession and her coarse language are sympathetically depicted while the pretentious middle-class characters who surround her are plagued by their own pettiness. Their unwarranted arrogance is contrasted with Cui's honest, albeit coarse, character to reflect negatively on conservative ideals of women's propriety.

Patience and endurance do appear to have value, however, for both women and men in times of trouble. In the 1943 essay "Yidian chunzhen ji guren" (A Little Sincerity Mailed to an Old Friend), Yang Xu suggests that life is so miserable in Manchukuo that there is no choice but to bear the suffering: "Life really is a mystery, a very sad story. We are all very unfortunate. In these sunny spring-like days, we find attacks of wind and rain storms. We have no power to conquer this attack aimed to destroy us, we just have to bear it. To bear it with tears pouring inside, pouring into the depths of our memory."[33] This pessimistic tone typifies Yang Xu's entire body of work, which consistently recounts the "attacks" of everyday life. Lan Ling echoes this sentiment in her short story "Yehang" (Night Navigators) as the female protagonist, Jun, receives a note reading: "In this fluctuating war, it's a time when all people are suffering, but bear it with patience and endurance! Without war, peace can not come."[34] Jun is inspired to believe that the postwar order will recompense her current suffering. Neither of these works, it should be noted, despite condoning patience and endurance, link these characteristics with constructs of ideal womanhood or shed any positive light on Manchukuo society.

In this literature, patience and endurance are most often condemned as integral elements of women's subjugation. These writers blame a tradition passed down from mother to daughter for blinding successive generations to complicity in their own subjugation. They advocate resistance against patriarchal privilege by rejecting women's "virtuous" passivity. Although patience and endurance might have value, these writers place far more emphasis on women's cultivation of personal relationships to emancipate them from the "pitiful traditions" of the past.

Love, Marriage, and Childbirth

> Love has no rules, no standards. As long as we love each other, the dark can be bright, hell can be heaven. Ah! How magnificent love is, how intoxicating love is, ah!
>
> – *Yang Xu, "Fangfu shi yi chang wennuan de meng" (As If a Warm Dream)*

The literature under discussion problematizes the good wife, wise mother ideal through depiction of women's romances, marriage practices, and childbirth. The authors idealize love affairs with partners of their choice, relationships that might properly (but not necessarily) be consummated by marriage and childbirth. Cultural functionaries lauded women's obedience to the state and to men, positions that these writers challenged throughout their work. Even as they entered the workplace, matrimony, and motherhood, the women did not praise the Manchukuo cultural agenda, or even describe it in much detail. This literature did not legitimate the colonial state or its "modern" ambitions for women. Rather, as Yang Xu asserts above, the writers proposed that only through the intoxication of love, not by submission to *Wangdao* or good wives, wise mothers ideals, could the darkness of life in Manchukuo be dissipated.

Yang Xu's writings are pertinent to any consideration of romance in Manchukuo, since her second volume of collected works, *Wo de riji*, was banned for explicit depiction of women's romances. In that volume, Yang Xu argues that "falling in love is a kind of instinct" that is all-consuming for young men and women: "When youth get together, falling in love is like a kind of contagious disease."[35] Conservatives would doubtless have agreed with her assessment of the potency of adolescent love, for they argued the necessity of sequestering women and arranging marriages precisely in order to avoid the dangers that they linked with romance and women's "excessive" individual freedom. But Yang Xu *celebrated* love as she warned women of the pitfalls of marriage, both arranged and chosen. She condemned the patriarchal cloistering of women for preventing the development of healthy, equal relationships between women and men. She argued that women were subjugated in loveless marriages at the mercy of their husbands: "A woman is his bird in a cage. He can do whatever he wants to, toying with the bird."[36] Yang candidly rejected women's passivity. In 1941, in her essay "Ji" (Mail), she denounced a woman's position in marriage as a slave to her husband, a fate she compared to imprisonment: "No matter what, do not get married; it's simply no different from a [criminal] conviction. The so-called household brings a woman only handcuffs and a cangue to tie you up, you won't have any freedom whatsoever. What is love? It is what will make women jump into a cage, and after jumping into the cage, everything is finished."[37] Yang condemned women's lack of freedom in marriage, in the "so-called household," which she characterized as a cage. In the early 1940s, she rejected arranged and free-choice marriages. This stance was no doubt influenced by her doomed relationship with the writer Xiadi, but Yang also questioned the nature of her own character. In *Wo de riji*, she rhetorically asks, "Could I be that kind of a 'good wife, wise mother'? Not a chance, not with my type of 'wild horse character'" (*yema xing*).[38]

Yang Xu's definition of marriage as a form of imprisonment altered following her own nuptials in 1942. In 1943, in "Fangfu shi yi chang wennuan de meng" (As If a Warm Dream), she pronounced marriage to be love's proper "solution" (*guishu*), "otherwise how could that fire-like love be handled?"[39] Marriage, she argued, constituted a woman's "best escape" from a dating scene unfairly biased against women, since "time hurries people to become as old as a devil, and women's years are basically few!"[40] Yang reversed her earlier stance on marriage to propose that women trade their youth for security – but with men of their own choosing, all the while remaining wary of men who, as relationships get serious, "grab their heads and scurry like rats."[41] She asserted that men were encouraged to view love as "merely life's decoration," and she ascribed their cavalier position to gender ideals that granted men unrestricted career opportunities and uninhibited access to the opposite sex.[42] She argued that women were forced to place greater value on their relationships than men because of regressive gender ideals that restricted women's economic opportunities and denied them access to a range of men. Yang maintained that men, despite their interest in women, can not and need not attribute the same significance to marriage as women must because patriarchal society denied women the ability to sustain themselves, forcing a wife's reliance on her husband for financial security.[43] Further, the sheltering of women from men reduced not only a woman's potential choice of partner but also the possibility of a happy or even suitable match. Yang reasoned that marriage existed for the mutual benefit of individual women and men – not for the strength of the nation – and therefore it had to be made more accommodating to women.

Yang Xu's combative stance is also reflected in other women's writing. The title character in Zuo Di's "Liu Qi" dismisses married life for women as "a meaningless existence": "I once thought of marriage, but that is always a dead end for women. I must struggle on with fate."[44] The fictional Liu Qi renounced the dead end for women in marriage, as Yang Xu had, and dreamed of a public career, serving the people. At the climax of Wu Ying's short story "Ming," the protagonist abandons her abusive husband in search of a new life. In "Xin youling" (New Ghost), Wu Ying describes the destruction of a young woman's life as she slowly comprehends that an arranged marriage "will not bring any benefit."[45] The woman is taken for granted by her husband, a university student whose studies and fellow students inspire revulsion for his illiterate, bound-foot wife. Her unrequited devotion to him only reinforces her husband's acceptance of his male friends' self-assured belief that "women are easy to handle."[46] His extramarital affairs with women his wife decries as "female goblins" tear their marriage apart. Wu Ying paints a damning portrait of an abused woman and her intellectual husband who, despite her despair, nonchalantly pursues other women.[47] The young woman's arranged marriage is depicted as ruinous: she is deprived of the means to sustain herself and must deal with a husband who treats her with contempt, a condition apparently exacerbated by his education.

Yang Xu, Wu Ying, and Zuo Di were not the only writers to call for more equitable marriage practices; Mei Niang and Zhu Ti also stressed the importance of love, mutual commitment, and monogamy. In Mei Niang's *Ye he hua kai* (*Flowers That Blossom in the Night*), the female protagonist Daidai avers "life without love has lost all meaning."[48] The type of relationship that Daidai idealizes also inspires the female protagonist, Fen, in Mei Niang's "Yu": "The two of us would go to work together, come home, read, eat, entertain guests, and use our youthful spirits to serve society."[49] Fen's ambition to share a meaningful life with her partner is shattered upon discovery that, unbeknownst to her, he had submitted to his father's pressure to enter an arranged marriage. Rather than submit to her husband's demand that she accept a subsidiary position as a concubine in his new household, Fen leaves to seek "spiritual liberation" (*jingshen de jiefang*) elsewhere.[50] In Mei Niang's "Bang" (Clam), the protagonist Meili is distraught over her impending arranged marriage. In Manchukuo, she argues, all women were expected to marry and were pressured to do so before the age of forty, when they were believed to have exhausted their marital options.[51] Meili states that she is not averse to marriage but wants to choose her own partner, Qi. In fact, she envies the "qualifications of contemporary wives" (*shidai de qizi de tiaojian*): excellence in housekeeping, cultivation of a "pure and fresh mind," and strong child-rearing skills, but swears that she would rather become a prostitute than enter into an arranged marriage in which she expected to be "bullied" (*qifu*) from morning till night by her husband's family.[52] Thus, Meili anticipates realizing the attributes of a good wife, wise mother but chafes at the restrictive path accorded her. She recognizes that she has few alternatives to escaping her parents' machinations and rhetorically asks Qi: "Where [can we] go? Tianjin, Beijing, or even a little further to Shanghai or Nanjing? Where is it not the same?"[53] In 1939, when "Bang" was written, each of these cities was occupied by the Japanese, who promoted a conservative cultural agenda that stressed women's obedience, filial piety, and respect for marriage.

Zhu Ti also critiqued the untenable position of women in traditional relationships. In the preface to her collected writings, *Ying*, she notes that several influences affected her writing aspirations:

> Truthfully, when I wrote these things, besides applying a strong native place flavour, I also had another little thought. No doubt, readers of this volume will immediately see this kind of thought in the short story "Ying," where it is more clearly carved on the surface. From start to finish, I feel that it is a huge insult if women must rely on men to provide for them. Naturally, I don't oppose man and woman living together, but I am deliberating on how that lifestyle can finally be made more equitable, and how to improve its structure. Man and woman living together is the singular ever-evolving artery of humankind. However, to be a woman, from start to finish one must have the self-awareness and ambition to be able to live independently; only in this way can one accomplish a woman's essential character.[54]

Zhu Ti privileges 'woman' as the focus of her analysis to promote attributes essential to her definition of ideal womanhood: self-awareness, ambition, and independence. Her work critiques inequitable gender constructs that subjugate women, undermining their ability to achieve "a woman's essential character" (*nüren de benshen*). Zhu Ti states that she "naturally" does not oppose men and women living together but rather aims to enhance their relationships, to make them more "suited" to women; literary regulations from 1941, at the latest, pressured writers to idealize married life.[55] Zhu Ti thus reiterates essential elements of May Fourth discourses of women's emancipation in terms that do not violate a sacred tenet of Manchukuo's cultural agenda – that young single women strive to become good wives, wise mothers.

In "Du Bohai," Zhu Ti questions women's "natural" drive to sustain their marriages despite all odds. The female protagonist, Mother, leaves Shandong in a desperate search for her missing husband, who had left for Manchukuo five years before: "Naturally Mother wants to be beside [her husband]. That is a desire every woman has."[56] The woman's obsession with finding her husband results in tortuous hardship, convincing her that she does not need a man in order to survive. In "Da Heilongjiang de youyu" (The Melancholy of the Mighty Black Dragon River) as well, Zhu Ti describes the refusal of her protagonist, Yana, to resume living with her former husband, the father of her daughter, because she no longer loves him: "She didn't have the heart to continue with the faded love. Mother believed that was a kind of crime, the greatest insult a woman could give a man."[57] Zhu argues that marriage must be founded on mutual love and respect, or be ended – whether there were children or not.

The destructive potential of traditional ideals dominates Wu Ying's short story "Liang ji" (Two Extremes), which critiques the life-long widowhood of Zhang Granny Six, whose husband died when she was seventeen after only one year of marriage. Personifying the conservative ideal of widowed chastity, Zhang lived into old age as a model widow, wearing no makeup, flowers, or bright clothes, and rarely leaving her house.[58] Seething with bitterness, she resents all the children in the neighbourhood. Zhang may have fulfilled the widow ideal, but her behaviour turns her into a social pariah. She swears at all within earshot that she is grateful that she bore no sons so that she doesn't have to watch them grow up to become one of the wastrels that surround her. A particular target of her scorn is unmarried women. She asserts that all women must "have a master, have a family."[59] Zhang laments young women's lost virtue, oblivious to what is vividly clear to the reader: the "virtues" that she mourns are the genesis of her misery, which makes her a tragic figure in the community. "Liang ji" illuminates the divisive social gulf that resulted in Manchukuo from disparate ideals of womanhood. Wu Ying mocks the model widowhood that squandered the life of a young woman who had no option but to aspire to mores that contributed neither to her own happiness nor to the well-being of the community. Her "virtue" is depicted as pathetic, wasteful, and harmful to all around her.

Zuo Di's "Meiyou guang de xing" (A Lustreless Star) also details patriarchy's destructive nature through the tragic life of a fictional actress, Luoli, and her friendship with the narrator, a female intellectual who lives next door to her. The narrator, who has moved beside a film studio, finds herself surrounded by women she perceives to be "very bad": they "wear makeup and [trendy] clothes, sing lurid songs like fairy maidens, shrilly laughing, shaking their hips and limbs as they saunter along in front of so many people."[60] She contrasts their "frivolous and dissipated" behaviour with that of the exemplary "simple unadorned" (*zhipu*) Luoli, who, she is surprised to discover, is also an actress.[61] Luoli's life story, told through flashback, challenges the narrator's preconceived ideas about "dissipated" women. Luoli informs the narrator that her father, a "moral" (*beide*) merchant-official with three wives, was "an animal without feelings" for having driven her mother out of the house after she gave birth to her, her second daughter.[62] When Luoli was a young girl, her father intercepted a letter to her from a boy and then demanded that she kill herself for violating the family's honour. Instead, Luoli ran away, barely escaped being sold into prostitution by an uncle, and eventually fell in love and married, only to later be abandoned by her husband. All of the men in her life – her father, her uncle, and eventually her husband – betrayed her, leaving her no option but to pursue an acting career to support herself and her baby. Ironically, the narrator notes, she was cast only in comedic roles, underlining the blindness of her male directors to the toll that patriarchal abuse had taken on her life; the narrator muses that, in light of Luoli's personal life, her forte should be tragedy. In "Meiyou guang de xing," patriarchal ideals trebly ruin women's lives: first, by destroying their mother's lives; second, by casting daughters into untenable situations; and third, by condemning them as "bad women." Each man in Luoli's life contributed towards her plight as she became a "lustreless star," steadfastly maintaining herself and her daughter, and awakening the narrator to her own prejudices.

The only author among this group to praise traditional marriage practices was Wu Ying, in several essays in the early 1940s. One example suffices to shed light on their significance.[63] In 1940, Wu Ying, under her real name, Wu Yuying, published the essay "Zhangfu fushi" (Serving Husbands) in *Xin Manzhou*. She argues that tradition-based gender divisions in marriage should be encouraged to guarantee that "men rule outside, women manage inside" (*nan zhi wai, nü zhu nei*).[64] She stresses that a family's primary objective should be the economic stability guaranteed by a hard-working man responsible for supplying his wife and children with "clothes, food, and housing" (*yi, chi, zhu*).[65] Women, she argues, have their own responsibilities within the household, and they must recognize the value of those gender-based roles to the stability of the family, society, and nation. In this essay, Wu Ying exactly articulates the essence of the *Wangdao* good wife, wise mother ideal. It is significant, though, that Wu Ying published the work under her real name rather than the pen name for which she was most widely known. The absence of any positive reflection on conservative ideals in work published under her pen name evidences at least an ambiguous stance towards such conservatism. The use of her own name in this particular instance suggests the necessity for prominent Chinese to demonstrate occasional deference to officially sanctioned ideals.

The good wife, wise mother ideal incorporated childbirth as *the* consummation of marriage and every woman's civic duty. The literature written by these seven women, too, portrays birth as an essential element of women's lives but commonly describes it as "a kind of natural punishment" (*yi zhong ziran de xingfa*).[66] Women's lives revolve around a duty that is both a blessing and a curse. In Wu Ying's "Qian sipo" (Fourth Sister-in-law Qian), the title character is a successful professional who obsesses over her need to produce a son. She cries, "In the end hard work doesn't count, only giving birth to a son will be considered a success."[67] Qian argues that regardless of a woman's career accomplishments, "having a son is having protection. If not, it is just like sitting in a bottomless boat."[68] Her perception that she needs to produce a son for her husband compels Qian to sacrifice her happy marriage, her career, and, ultimately, her sanity to a motherhood that she fears her barren body can never achieve. Qian's desperation points to a dominant message in this literature: childbirth is "women's greatest distress" (*nüren zuida de kunan*).[69] In Zuo Di's "Nü nan," the narrator's aunt pronounces childbirth "every woman's hardship," an ordeal that women fear will kill them.[70] Fear and pain are cited as constituent elements of a pregnant woman's life even though, in "Nü nan," the narrator's suffering is recompensed, as the newborn baby "filled my void, she made me feel unlimited gratitude."[71] Childbirth is problematized as the narrator celebrates the birth of her child, but only in retrospect and after severe suffering. In Wu Ying's work "Ming," the protagonist is incapacitated by her fear of giving birth to a girl. But her distress is not linked to the physical pain of giving birth or to a presumed need to produce a son. Rather, she is terrified that a girl will suffer the same horrible fate that she was forced to endure. Feverishly, she prays for a miscarriage. After she loses the baby she rages at her husband and the doctor, whom she believes conspired together against her, for their "fear that women have too many kids, and occupy more of your property" (*pa nüren shengyu de duo zi, duo zhanju nimen fencun de*).[72] Childbirth, the achievement ascribed by conservatives to women in Manchukuo, is often associated in these women's literature with pain, torment, and the uncertainty of women's lives.

In the writings of these women, the greatest horror is reserved for the trauma attending the birth of children to young, unmarried mothers. In Lan Ling's poem "Zai jingjing de yulinli" (In a Quiet Forest), a young Buddhist novice learns that her pregnant, unwed mother had been driven out of her home by her father and had died after she gave birth to her, alone in the forest.[73] The genesis of the novice's lonely existence was her mother's maltreatment by all the men in her life: her lover refused to take any responsibility for their unborn child and her father threw her out of her home, directly leading to her death. While this poem could be interpreted as a morality tale warning of the pitfalls attending pregnant single women, the sympathy with which Lan Ling describes the young novice and her mother implies strong criticism of the men and their behaviour. Similarly, in Dan Di's short story "Jie" (Warning), Qin's mother worries about her unwed, pregnant daughter's future, but both mother and daughter live in fear of Qin's father. After discovering Qin's pregnancy, her father condemns her for "carrying the disaster of life, [and she feels] unlimited humiliation, fear, nervousness" as he drives her from their home.[74] He blames her for having fallen victim to her lover's "totally base, animalistic seduction."[75] Qin barely survives giving birth alone, drenched in blood, in the forest. Both "Zai jingjing de yulinli" and "Jie" depict young, pregnant single women whose lives are ruined by men who alternately love and reject them. In these tales, men abandon their pregnant lovers, and fathers renounce their daughters, with impunity. The women are left on their own to deal with the ramifications of a moral order that favours the men who abandoned them and condemns only women for engaging in premarital sex. In the face of expulsion from their homes, the girls and their mothers are powerless as they, alone, bear the blame for children born out of wedlock.

In this literature, love, marriage, and childbirth are all problematized by the authors' explicit rejection of what Yang Xu vividly described as Manchukuo's "hot as a furnace" (*honglu*) patriarchal structures, which sought to meld women into obedient good wives, wise mothers.[76] These writers instead advocated women's equal access to relationships through which they could establish families with men of their choice. The ideals articulated in their writings reflect the personal ambitions that guided the writers into their young adulthood and into marriages of their own. Despite the critiques outlined above, each of the women eventually became a wife and mother.

Sex

> Women's road is narrow, especially in this society, which uses virginity (zhencao) to judge women.
>
> – *Mei Niang, "Bang"*

In Manchukuo, sexuality was a defining element of ideals of womanhood held by cultural functionaries and popular Chinese writers alike. No other aspect of women's lives was more subject to attempted state control. A key component of Manchukuo's modernity project was the restriction of Chinese women's "sexual freedom" through the introduction of a network of regulations designed to promote the conservative cultural agenda. From the establishment of Manchukuo, ceaseless restrictions against writing about sexuality were promulgated. Writing about "recreational love that denigrates chastity, lust, abnormal sexual desire or acting wrongly out of personal considerations, incest, or adultery" was explicitly banned from the early 1940s but nonetheless remained a prominent feature in popular literature.[77] In the final years of Manchukuo, these prohibited topics became even more pronounced, as writing about sex proved popular with readers while also being an effective vehicle to articulate self-identities that signalled dissatisfaction with the Manchukuo state and its patriarchal foundations. Frank discussion, or depiction, of women's sexual lives directly challenged the legitimacy of Japanese claims that chastity was the "cornerstone" of female virtue.[78]

Yang Xu's *Wo de riji* was banned for its interrogation of women's pursuit of romance and the sexual freedoms associated with it. Yang rejected the ideal of chastity propagated by Manchukuo officialdom in the belief that it militated against women's fundamental equality with men. She asserted that both sexes should regard love and sex as "instincts" (*benneng*), which women must actively cultivate in order to foster healthier relationships, for both women and men.[79] Yang even provocatively defined ideal men in terms of their character traits and physical attributes, commodifying them as if they were "not worth a penny."[80] In *Wo de riji*, Yang Xu outlines her ideal man: "On the surface, he should have a strong healthy body, he should be quiet and full of sensibility. [He should] handle matters with experience, make people feel that their person will not be violated, have fire-hot emotions, rich sympathy ... furthermore, [he] cannot be a miser."[81] With the exception of "fire-hot" emotions, these qualities are remarkably similar to constructs of good wives, wise mothers. Yang also eroticized the pristine environment of her girls' school by recounting her passionate though unrequited crush on her Han Chinese Japanese-language teacher, Mr. Liu. His "virgin-shy" (*chunü xiu de*) response to her teasing made her desire him even more; she credited him with putting her on the road to becoming a "rebel woman" (*fanpan de nüxing*).[82] In each of these examples, Yang Xu subverted officially sanctioned constructs of women's chastity and modesty by arguing her right to realize her desires.

Mei Niang also consistently challenged sexual double standards in her writing: sex, or discussion of it, can punctuate the narrative as female characters take pleasure in "losing their bodies."[83] In 1943, the leading Japanese scholar of Chinese literature, Yoshikawa Kojiro, denounced Mei Niang's best-selling "Yu" (Fish) as "among the most degenerate pieces" he had ever read.[84] Yoshikawa was repulsed by the pregnant protagonist, Fen, who boldly rejects her partner to have an affair with his cousin, whom she also later determines to leave.[85] Fen defends her quest for love as natural, refusing to accept any relationship in which she was less than an equal partner.[86] The story's popularity is attested to by its re-publication six times within a year and the awarding to it of the second prize at the Greater East Asia Writers' Congress in 1943. In Mei Niang's story "Bang," the protagonist, Meili, laments the sexual double standards that prevail in Manchukuo, asking why she is expected to be a virgin when her fiancé, Qi, is no longer one himself. Meili "loses" her virginity with Qi:

> Qi's scorching hot breath went from Meili's ear into her heart.
>
> Slowly, the hand rubbing her back moved around to her chest.
>
> Meili's heart was ferociously pounding, following Qi's warm hand. Meili felt a kind of wondrous feeling, a kind of slight numbing, an uncontrollable impulse.
>
> Meili felt her cheeks burning.
>
> "Li, you really are beautiful, your face is like a flower."
>
> Suddenly, Qi, heavily panting, used a kind of irresistible hot strength to move onto Meili, two legs were pressing down on Meili's body.
>
> "Dear, you, you ... "[87]

Meili passively encourages and then fully enjoys her boyfriend Qi's advances. She responds with an "uncontrollable impulse," as both are consumed by passion, yet afterwards it is only Meili who is punished for their activities. But she refused to be cowed, arguing that sexuality is a natural part of women's life that should not rightfully be denied: "No, I must not blame myself. That is a natural instinct [*benxing*]. Everyone must have it, to refuse it would be immoral. I mustn't feel sorry for losing my virginity."[88] Thus, Meili's engagement in premarital sex, an activity explicitly condemned by Manchukuo authorities, is sympathetically portrayed by Mei Niang as an instinctual act that young, unmarried women should engage in without remorse.

In Zhu Ti's "Yuantian de liuxing" (A Shooting Star in a Faraway Sky), the protagonist, Madan, celebrates recovery from an illness by drinking whiskey and dancing in the lounge of a ship, which becomes her "kingdom" (*wangguo*); drunk, she believes that her male companions (the captain and a doctor) are her "subjects and prisoners of war" (*chenxia he fulu*), utterly beholden to her.[89] With her inhibitions lowered by the alcohol, she is seduced by the captain and abandons herself to the "limitless pleasure" of sex with him.[90] "As if in a dream, Madan's veins were pulsating. Madan's breath lost its regular pattern. Finally, Madan let herself completely go to the limitless pleasure, Madan felt everything pressing down on her body, Madan thought what she could use to resist, Madan did not move."[91] Madan engages in this pleasure at her peril. She awakes in the morning to be tortured by her conscience and then humiliated by the doctor's lack of interest in her. Madan reels from one man to another and then to her death, while the men with whom she was involved could not care less about her and suffer no consequences from their casual relationships. Madan's internalization of the ideal of women's chastity culminates with her death as she leaps into the sea. She is a "shooting star" whose ebullience is extinguished by her inability to fully embrace the sexual freedoms enjoyed by the men around her. Her death is depicted as a wasteful resolution to a woman's search for happiness. In defiance of officially sponsored rhetoric and a weighty regulatory framework, the female protagonists in both "Bang" and "Yuantian de liuxing" willingly engage in, and thoroughly enjoy, sexual activity outside of marriage. This literature is critical of ideals of chastity that unfairly privilege men while destroying women.

The destructive potential ascribed to sexual double standards is integral to Wu Ying's critiques of traditional mores, which she condemns for ruining the lives of both women and men. In "Xin youling," the uneducated, bound-foot Chun Huasao condemns her husband's affairs with "fashionable women [who] aren't women; they live like prostitutes ... born with cheap bones."[92] Chun castigates "modern" women for being sexually active and stealing her husband away. Her marriage is destroyed by her husband's lack of respect for her and his philandering, phenomena so prevalent that the narrator observes: "Women could all kill, men are all unfaithful."[93] This novella argues the inhumanity of arranged marriages that create sexually voracious men and women who yearn for vengeance. In the short story "Nü pantu" (Woman Rebel), Wu Ying depicts Li Ping as the epitome of the "fashionable women" that Chun Huasao condemns: a "woman rebel" who "can't get rid of her kind of craving for comfort from the opposite sex."[94] Li pursues men as sexual conquests, despite her female colleagues' pleadings for her to stop. Li's relationships leave her unfulfilled and ultimately result in her death during a botched abortion. Her failure to find fulfilment does not reflect negatively on her but rather on ideals of chastity that alienated her from her friends and drove her to a deadly abortion. Both Chun and Li are depicted as victims of ideals that denied women autonomy while allowing men to conduct relationships with few apparent restraints.

Wu Ying even more forcefully challenges women's lack of control over their bodies in "Yu" (Lust), a short story recounting the marriage of a grief-stricken, nameless widow to Wang Muxiang.[95] "Yu" revolves around the widow's refusal to have sex with her new husband. Her refusal to consummate their marriage serves as the vehicle through which the author critiques the subjugation of an unnamed woman, who becomes the sexual property of her new husband. The destructiveness assigned to the woman's lack of agency is vividly illustrated by the image accompanying "Yu" (Figure 5.2).[96] A phallic

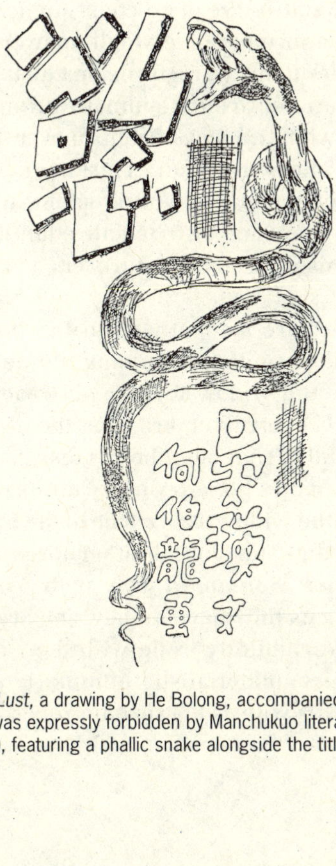

5.2 *Lust*, a drawing by He Bolong, accompanied a short story of the same name. Although writing about lust was expressly forbidden by Manchukuo literary regulations, Wu Ying published a short story titled "Yu" (Lust), featuring a phallic snake alongside the title.

snake, moving to bite the word "lust" (*yu*), represents the sexual tension that consumes the widow's life. The snake symbolizes the male protagonist's lust, which is portrayed as dangerous, fearful, and animalistic. Wu's negative depiction of the remarriage of widows would have appealed to social conservatives who advocated their chastity, although popular custom in the region militated against it. But the woman's utter rejection of her husband's sexual advances flew in the face of constructs of obedient good wives, wise mothers. Significantly, both the widow and her new husband, from different perspectives, stress the importance of sex and *not* national duty in marriage. "Yu" thus seemingly accords with the officially sanctioned ideal of the chastity of widows while violating the Eight Abstentions' prohibition of the discussion of women's sexuality, in both the work's title and content.

In "Yu," Wu Ying reveals the consequences of Wang Muxiang's unrequited sexual demands. Wang is described as an overbearing, insensitive brute whose violent behaviour wreaks havoc on the lives of the widow and her "too pitiful" (*tai kelian*) daughter.[97] Wang regards his new wife as a piece of property that he is entitled to use as he pleases. When he wants to have sex with her, she refuses. He yells at her, "Feel you up a little, you won't have any of it. If you won't let anyone love you, you might as well not be born a woman. What use are women if not for men's pleasure?"[98] According to Wang, his wife's feelings and desires – as well as the needs of the state – are of no consequence. In a drunken stupor, he argues with his wife and when she won't answer, he beats her and attempts, again, to subjugate her to his unreciprocated lust. The widow's silent refusal is manipulated by the author to elicit sympathy from the reader for her predicament. "Yu" condemns women's lack of control over their bodies and men's prioritization of their own "pleasure." Wang's lust has devastating consequences for the woman and her daughter, who is silent, withdrawn, and confused about her status in the new family. The entire family is victimized by the marital discord. Their misery fuels a controversy in the neighbourhood.

Not all of the female characters in "Yu" are sympathetic to the newly remarried widow's plight. Wu Ying gives voice to discord among the neighbourhood women, some of whom castigate the widow for her obstinacy. A long-haired, "grinning hideously" (*ningxiaozhe*) neighbour criticizes the widow for refusing to have sex with her new husband.[99] That neighbour's dissatisfaction with her own poverty-stricken husband makes her envy the widow's new, financially solvent husband. She argues that the widow's marriage to the hard-working, lusty Wang Muxiang is ideal and that she should either forget her former husband or make way for another woman to live with Wang. Reasoning that all men are the same, as long as they have money, she argues that sex is a commodity that women should rightfully trade with their husbands for financial stability. This neighbours' materialistic attitude is portrayed as negatively as Wang's perception of his wife as his sexual property. In

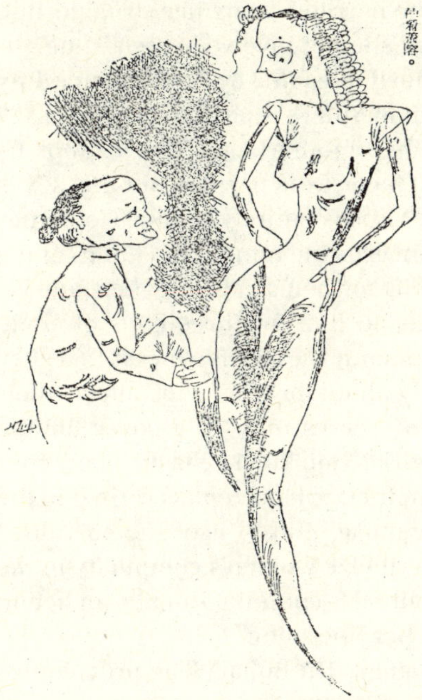

5.3 *Widow and Neighbour*, a drawing by He Bolong that accompanied the original publication of Wu Ying's short story "Yu" (Lust), shows a lurid-looking female neighbour contrasted with the long-suffering widow.

the illustrations accompanying the text, the female neighbour is depicted with a lurid appearance that vividly contrasts with the widow's submissive posture (Figure 5.3). The widow's miserable remarriage and her neighbour's favourable evaluation of it provide equally unflattering portrayals of women's lives in colonial Manchukuo.

Perhaps the harshest critiques of women's subjugation are associated with rape. In Mei Niang's "Luo Yan" (Fallen Yan), the title character's teaching career is destroyed after she is raped, while her attacker (a co-worker) is merely fined.[100] The writer contrasts Yan's exemplary behaviour as a model employee and a demure single woman with that of her Machiavellian colleagues, both women and men, to highlight the hypocrisy of officially sanctioned ideals of womanhood. Yan's behaviour is, according to conservative ideals, circumspect, but she is punished for being raped nonetheless. Her rapist is only lightly punished while other women pursue sexual relationships of their own. The "morality" applied to Yan is shown to be random and harsh and thus casts a pall over the nature of moral judgment in Manchukuo.

In two other stories, Zhu Ti links rape with the perilous state of the nation. In "Xiao Yinzi he ta de jiazu" (Little Yinzi and Her Relations), Yinzi, an orphaned girl, is raised by "adoptive parents" to attract men as a singing girl.

One night, as Yinzi is raped by her father, the narrator hears her struggle, but, cowed by her husband's admonishment that she not involve herself in neighbours' affairs, she abandons Yinzi to her "inevitable fate." By fulfilling her duty as an obedient wife, the narrator is complicit in Yinzi's rape, the seriousness of which is articulated by Yinzi's uncle, to her mother: "Ai! This cannot be blamed on my elder brother! As a matter of fact, sex is normal, but this sex is the most grievous. Ai, to talk about it, Little Yinzi is entirely wrong! No matter what, incest shouldn't happen! This, this concerns the future blood lines of the nation!"[101] Yinzi's uncle blames the young girl for being raped by her father – in order to persuade her mother to sell her to him for three bolts of cloth. Yinzi's "relations" stand in solidarity to condemn the girl for incest that they instigated. They care not about her, but only about how her rape affects their own self-interest. Reference to "the nation" serves only as a cover for the uncle's ambitions to gain ownership of the girl. "Xiao Yinzi he ta de jiazu" concludes as the narrator weeps to learn that another girl has replaced Yinzi in the adoptive household, thus perpetuating the abuse. Zhu Ti uses the narrator's passive reaction to Yinzi's rape and sale to criticize women's complicity in the perpetuation of their subjugation. Yinzi eventually commits suicide, an action represented as the only possible means for her liberation.

Rape is also a dominant theme in the story "Du Bohai." The protagonist, Mother, is raped en route to Manchukuo and then again after she arrives. Jailed for murdering her second rapist, she refuses to speak. From her cell, she watches the sun rise and fall, "thinking of the humiliation of Bohai, the mainland's famine, and savagery and rape."[102] Zhu Ti thus links the woman's rape with the subjected condition of China. In each of these instances, rape reflects a decline of morality directly linked to the state of society and the nation.

Several works also transgress Manchukuo's literary regulations by depicting employment in the sex industry as a viable, albeit regrettable, option that springs from financial necessity and that should not reflect negatively on a woman's character. Women, valued only for their bodies, were deprived of the means to achieve their full potential: as Dan Di observes, "Prostitutes are not mean and low; prostitutes are the sufferers of life."[103] In Wu Ying's story "Cui Hong," the title character, a former prostitute, refuses to view the selling of sex as degrading, solidly affixing blame on the men who forced her into the business. She argues with her pretentious middle-class critics that her labour is the same as any other: "Isn't [work] all just to eat?"[104] Cui's sentiments are echoed in Zuo Di's short story "Zhai xiang" (Narrow Alley), in which the female narrator responds to her brother's denigration of dancing girls and prostitutes by firmly asserting that "theory can't be used to judge everything."[105] The narrator refuses to view the women as shameful, as they are denied other means of employment. Their plight is illustrated in Lan Ling's poem "Xiao xiang de chuxi" (New Year in a Small Alley), in which a young starving widow is forced onto the streets:

she cannot steal,
she dare not rob,
she can only think of using her starving body,
to trade for little scraps of food.[106]

Lan Ling suggests that in Manchukuo even a devoted widowed mother was valued only for her body, which could not even be "trade[d] for little scraps of food." The poem ends with the woman collapsing on New Year's Eve in an abandoned street lit by fireworks, presumably to die as her starving baby lies abandoned in an empty, dark apartment. Her fatal decision to try to sell her body rather than to steal or to rob implies a prioritization of honesty over chastity, thus slighting the supposed "cornerstone" of women's virtue in Manchukuo.

The writers of this study contravened Manchukuo's literary regulations by depicting women's participation in, and enjoyment of, sex outside of marriage in a positive manner. This literature criticizes women's victimization under patriarchal ideals that allowed men to expel them from their families, to rape them, or to force them into prostitution. The sexual double standards inherent in *Wangdao* ideology are subverted through the authors' demands for women's access to equitable relationships and autonomous control over their bodies. Manchukuo's cultural functionaries may have promoted chastity for women, but these writers emphasized women's integrity in their work.

This chapter has highlighted the critiques of patriarchal society that prevailed in the literature produced by Manchukuo's most prolific Chinese women writers. The writers responded to official demands for women to cultivate chastity, obedience, and submission with clarion calls for women's emancipation. They stressed the importance of women's individual control over their own bodies, in relationships premised upon mutual love and respect. The construct of ideal womanhood that emerges from these writings – strong, independent women in control of their bodies – stands in contrast to constructs of *Wangdao* good wives, wise mothers who were beholden to men, their families, the state, and the nation. From the early 1930s, Manchukuo officials publicly denounced the evils of communism, Western materialism, and individualism. But these women, even at the height of the Sacred War, remained engaged in their own battle against what they perceived to be the most threatening force in their midst – "male-centred society" and the Manchukuo modernity that they believed embodied its worst excesses. These writers were driven by their own perceptions of modern Chinese womanhood to defy the imposition of what they perceived to be regressive constructs that resulted in the impoverishment, rape, and sale of women. Manchukuo's patriarchal foundations lay at the heart of the writers' remarkably wide-ranging critiques of the colonial state and its cultural agenda.

6

Contesting Colonial Society

I AM AFRAID I WILL BE SUFFOCATED BY THIS NORTHERN COUNTRY'S ATMOSPHERE.

– *Yang Xu, Wo de riji (My Diary)*

The suffocating atmosphere that Yang Xu fears is omnipresent in the portraits of Manchukuo society by all seven writers under discussion. Each of the women established her career through the production of literature that was highly critical of Manchukuo society even while she benefited in her professional life from opportunities provided by Manchukuo institutions. The writers' critiques of patriarchal society, as recounted in the preceding chapter, are integral to the their portraits of Manchukuo, which transgress its dense network of literary regulations on many levels. Despite official demands that writers align themselves with a distinct, positive "Manchukuo" identity, each of these women disdained the regime's *Wangdao* ideals, deploying May Fourth constructs of individual emancipation in her work. Collectively, their literary legacies reveal the inability or unwillingness of Manchukuo officials to provide the levels of proper governance, peace, and stability requisite for the realization of Manchukuo modernity.

Four tropes are especially relevant to reconstructing the writers' critiques of contemporary society: darkness, pessimism, disorder, and destitution. As discussed in Chapter 3, such writing was proscribed by Manchukuo's literary regulations, which were applied with increasing vigour following the launch of the Sacred War in 1941. While portraits of disorder and destitution may not have been explicitly prohibited, their prominence in this literature undermines Manchukuo legitimacy by highlighting the contrast between official proclamations and the lived experience of the state's Chinese subjects. In Zuo Di's 1942 story "Liu Qi," the female protagonist argues, with explicit reference to a novel by Johann von Goethe, that Chinese people must be counted, with Jews and "Negroes," among the "downtrodden in the world."[1] This bold assertion directly challenged claims by officialdom that Manchukuo had freed the people of the region and that the Sacred War would liberate the rest of the people of Asia. As is demonstrated below, Manchukuo's legitimacy was consistently affronted by these writers through setting, plot, and vocabulary, all of which were manipulated to expose the subjugation of the downtrodden Chinese. In 1943, Yang Xu wrote, "God has gone blind, God has lost his sense of fairness."[2] This chapter reveals various means through which the loss of God's "sense of fairness" is depicted in the Chinese-language literature of Manchukuo.

Darkness

> THE PEOPLE CATCHING CRABS ON THE SHIP ARE HANGING UP LAMPS, CRABS RUN TOWARD THE LIGHT, THEN THE CRABS FALL INTO THE PREPARED NETS.
>
> – *Mei Niang, Xie (Crabs)*

The title of the 1986 volume of short fiction by Manchukuo's women writers, *Changye yinghuo* (*Fireflies of the Long Night*), juxtaposes the writers with the oppressive environment in which they forged their careers: the writers are posited to be small sparks of light hovering within a long night of Japanese occupation. This imagery – however slighting it may be – reflects the ambition

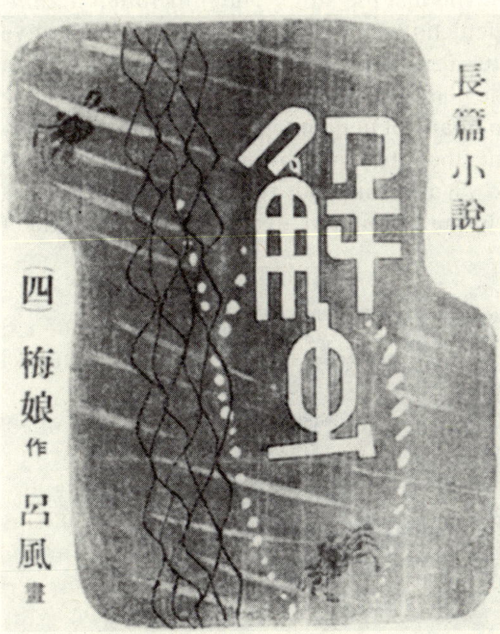

6.1 *Crabs*, a drawing by Lü Feng from the original publication of Mei Niang's *Xie* (*Crabs*) features two crabs, representative of the novel's female protagonists, who are threatened in dark waters by a net that lies between them.

of the volume editor, Liang Shanding, that the writers' legacies be recognized as a positive cultural feat achieved within the darkness of foreign occupation. The title also underlines the darkness that dominates this literature: darkness both frames the setting and conjures the mood of much of this writing, and the plots often climax during the night. Darkness is essential to this literature, casting long shadows through it. Whether the dark is "repulsive as a bottomless black pit,"[3] or as threatening as a "black-coloured net,"[4] it characterizes the writers' portraits of Manchukuo society. The dangers of the dark are portrayed in the drawing that accompanies the original publication of Mei Niang's *Xie* (*Crabs*) (Figure 6.1). Two crabs, representing the two young female protagonists, dart dangerously close to a net, which is set between them. The net divides and traps its victims in the murky water, vividly illustrating the author's depiction of the dangers facing women in Manchukuo.

Works of fiction by these women often begin with direct reference to the dark. Dan Di's award-winning novella, *Andi he Mahua* (*Andi and Mahua*), opens with a sentence that alludes to the loss of Chinese sovereignty in Manchuria in September 1931: "At the end of August, the sun sank into the west."[5] She subverts the symbolic rising sun of Japanese propaganda to imply that the Japanese invasion did not usher the light of civilization into the region but rather darkened it instead. The setting sun reflects the novella's dark tone and underlines the confrontational stance adopted by Dan Di; she was renowned for "singing the worries of people who lost the sun."[6] The illustration accompanying *Andi he Mahua*, with its depiction of islands, is also highly suggestive of Japan, the invading power (Figure 6.2). This work is explicitly critical of the invasion's impact on the lives of the poorest members of society. Dan Di's style may be more forthright than that of many of her contemporaries, but her work is representative of the dark tone that they all share. Zuo Di's "Nü nan" (Women's Difficulty), for example, also begins with reference to the dark, as the pregnant narrator is dragged to the hospital to give birth in the middle of

6.2 *Andi and Mahua*, a drawing by Lu Wang from the original publication of Dan Di's *Andi he Mahua* (*Andi and Mahua*), features a group of islands suggestive of the invading power that destroys the lives of the title characters.

the night with "evil spirits whirling" all about her.[7] Throughout much of this literature, the dark heralds suffering.

Darkness is often accentuated through connections with autumn, to "make people have a kind of strangely alone and strangely melancholic feeling."[8] Autumn commonly serves as a metaphor for a world in decline, and in this literature subverts Manchukuo propaganda, which stressed regional renewal. Lan Ling's poem "Zai jingjing de yulinli" (In a Quiet Forest) unfolds one "deep autumn evening / [as] dusk covers a lonely Buddhist nunnery."[9] The stark cold that envelopes the quiet, darkening forest is symbolic of the empty life of a young orphaned novice, who dreams of a future in which she is blessed with a warm family life. The despair that grips her is common to women throughout this literature, as female characters wistfully compare their lives to the dead and drifting autumn leaves that fall to the ground and are swept away by the wind: "Isn't [life] the same as fallen leaves drifting around?"[10] Yang Xu, in her writings, notes the melancholic power of the red leaves of autumn. Yang associates them with the passing of time and with restrictions on Chinese life in Manchukuo; she expresses her dismay at the ban on Chinese access to the park at the Zhaoling imperial tombs in Fengtian, which were open to the public in the 1920s, before the establishment of Manchukuo.[11] The melancholy evoked by autumn is illustrated by the stance of the woman in the drawing accompanying the original publication of Zhu Ti's "Meng yu qingchun" (Dreams and Youth) (Figure 6.3). Holding onto a branch bereft of leaves, a woman gazes

6.3 *Dreams and Youth* represents the young female protagonist in Zhu Ti's short story "Meng yu qingchun" (Dreams and Youth), who mourns her dreams and youth as they pass her by like the boat and the river's waters.

on a passing ship on the water, above which appears the title, "Dreams and Youth." Zhu Ti's short story is a reflection on the ephemeral nature of dreams and youth in a society that denies young women the opportunity to realize their potential.

Darkness underlines the authors' apprehensions regarding contemporary life and the future in Manchukuo. A dramatic use of dark imagery can be found in Zuo Di's "Yi ge huise de meng" (A Grey-Coloured Dream), in which the protagonist inches along a path alone in the night, terrified by shapes that she knows surround her yet cannot be seen, wondering if they are "a person, a beast, or a devil."[12] In Zhu Ti's essay "Bangwan de shiye" (Dusk's Field of Vision), the narrator looks outside a classroom window to view the capital's skyline, which is partly obliterated by an "oppressive grey-coloured sky."[13] Xinjing's newly constructed skyline appears "ancient" (*gulao*) in the "rotten and weak dusk."[14] Zhu describes Manchukuo's citadels of modernity as the antithesis of colonial rhetoric, which trumpeted them as the height of modern civilization. When the lights in the room are turned on at the start of the evening class, the narrator is blinded to the world outside, a thinly veiled critique of contemporary education.

Stormy weather is often employed to amplify the dark's effect. A blustery storm provides the backdrop for the inner turmoil that tears Fen, the female protagonist in Mei Niang's "Yu," apart: "There is so much rain and the wind is blowing so hard, as if to blow the house down. The thunder is bellowing in my ears. I'm afraid, I have no courage by myself."[15] The storm raging outside her home causes an electrical blackout in which Fen is freed to vent her pent-up anger. In the dark, she forces her lover to listen to her recounting the subjugation she has experienced from the men in her life; the dark, stormy weather mirrors Fen's emotional state and emboldens her to reject the status quo. In Dan Di's poem "Meng yu guqin" (Dreams and an Old Qin), the narrator's mournful spirit is accentuated by the weather:

> Outside
> that pitch-black night
> the windy, rainy night
> snuffs out the candle
> striking down the white-coloured flower petal![16]

The stormy night, the candle extinguishing, and the fall of the white flower stir the author to compose a verse on the melancholy reflected in her surroundings. Dan Di deploys storm imagery even more dramatically in her short story "Feng" (Wind). A storm dominates the narrative as it destroys the characters' lives: "The sky is an evil yellow, and the sun emits only a pale white light. All is as if dead, at a standstill."[17] Strong winds force dark, thick clouds over a fishing village, creating a storm: "The waves are like the side of a black wall, angrily, threateningly rolling up."[18] The sea claims the lives of the local fishermen, leaving the pregnant protagonist widowed and prostrate with grief. At the end of the story, she gives birth to her baby, alone, on the dirt floor of her home. Thus, storms are symbolic of the pressures bearing on women in Manchukuo.

Darkness, misery, and stormy weather all undermine Manchukuo propaganda of a paradise-like land. This literature not only denigrates such an assertion but commonly links overcoming contemporary misery with future happiness. In Yang Xu's story "Ye zhi ge" (Song of the Night), a note inspires the narrator, "I just need the wind to stop and the rain to cease. I am ever awaiting the dawn."[19] The narrator reads this message of hope aloud to a small group of friends who are discussing how bleak their lives have become in recent years. Their negative reflection on Manchukuo, a veritable "song of the night," gives voice to the author's own hopes for the future. The preface to Lan Ling's "Yehang" (Night Navigators) evokes a similar longing:

> Discarded by life
> are those people with discarded lives.
> Oh, the hardships of the night navigators,
> tightening their grip on the oar of life.
> You must firmly paddle ahead.
> Adjoining the dark night
> is the brink of daylight.[20]

Lan Ling urges that the "dark night" enveloping those "discarded by life" not deter them from grasping "the oar of life" to deliver them to a brighter future. "Yehang" is a critique of patriarchal jealousies that restrict a young woman's social circle and destroy her otherwise happy marriage. The oppressive nature of women's lives is suggested by the prison-like appearance of the ship in the drawing accompanying "Yehang" (Figure 6.4), which does not actually have a nautical theme. Both the illustration and the title of this work, "Night Navigators," accentuate the darkness of the story's content.

These writers manipulated the extensive focus on the dark to subvert Japanese sun-centred propaganda. The rising sun was symbolic of imperial Japan as well as being the physical embodiment of masculinity (*yang*), thus serving as a tool for the criticism of imperialism and patriarchy. A superb illustration of the subversion of sun symbolism is found in Zhu Ti's work "Du Bohai" (Crossing the Bohai Sea), in which the female protagonist is imprisoned for murdering her rapist. From her prison cell, she watches the sun rise and set and recalls the horrifying events that devastated her life. In her poem "Jimo de shengyin" (The Sound of Loneliness), Yang Xu sighs,

> Seeing the sun circle around,
> again gazing at the moon's rise and fall,
> this universe paints a very sad picture.
> I bow my head, speechless.[21]

6.4 *Night Navigators.* The forbidding appearance of the ship in the illustration by Bi Ya that accompanied the original publication of Lan Ling's "Yehang" (Night Navigators) underlines the dark and oppressive circumstances of the female protagonist's life.

Yang links the sun with her submission, silence, and a "very sad picture" of the universe. (Elsewhere, Yang cites Rabindranath Tagore's inspiration for her characteristic description of life as an illusion: "Everything is smoke."[22] She ascribes an illusory nature to life that underlines Chinese vulnerability in Manchukuo.) Dan Di likened the "northern winter's sun [to] a melancholy goddess, shining a melancholy light in the grey sky, spreading across the great land, without a rosy cloud."[23] At the end of Mei Niang's award-winning novella *Xie*, the female protagonist, Ling, is inspired by the setting sun to escape her family and seek a new life elsewhere. Edward Gunn, Jr. has argued that "since Japanese propagandists made much of their symbol of a rising sun, Mei Niang's choice of a setting sun to symbolize hope shows at least a marked indifference or insensitivity to, if not actual rejection of, Japanese propaganda themes and symbols."[24] Mei Niang further defied Manchukuo ideals by sympathetically portraying a woman who was prepared to abandon her family for her own well-being, which had been destroyed by the patriarchal ideals that she identified with Japanese occupation. While the motivation can never be known with certainty, the critical acclaim accorded to *Xie* in the final year of the empire testifies to the endurance of Chinese cultural criticism throughout the Japanese occupation. *Xie* is an unambiguously negative portrait of life in Manchukuo that reflects Mei's personal experiences in her own birth family.

Darkness is a defining element of this literature. The writers' consistent engagement with dark imagery, and the negativity ascribed to the sun, directly violated Manchukuo's literary regulations. Over time, this darkness became an abiding concern of censors, who only began in the final stage of Manchukuo to pay strict attention to the literature produced by these women.

Pessimism

> Shaxia only felt life is a kind of threat, is a kind of hateful existence.
>
> – *Zhu Ti, "Meng yu qingchun" (Dreams and Youth)*

The predominance of the dark is accentuated in this literature by a pessimism explicitly proscribed by Manchukuo officials. As discussed in Chapter 1, Liu Aihua has detailed Dan Di's manipulation, in *Andi he Mahua*, of over two dozen different words to voice emotions such as bitterness, disappointment, and pessimism to compound the negativity of the novel's narrative.[25] Dan Di's work is reflective of that of the other writers, who, as Yang Xu plainly stated in 1944, "stepped onto the road of pessimism" (*maizai beiguanlu shang*) in direct contravention of literary regulations such as the Eight Abstentions.[26] Despite demands by colonial officials for the production of paeans to Manchukuo modernity, these writers revelled in a pessimism that reflected poorly on *Wangdao* ideology.

The pessimism in this literature is captured in the illustration that accompanies Yang Xu's poem "Piaoling de xin" (Forsaken Heart) (Figure 6.5).[27] The woman's posture, with her head lowered submissively, fit well with constructs of submissive good wives, wise mothers, but it is also suggestive of the tone of Yang's written work – the woman bows her head not just in submission but in sadness. In "Xin de tiaodong" (Fluttering of the Heart) Yang declares:

> Yes, all of us are studying death
> studying how to walk into a tomb.
> But who can believe
> the lessons of death can be this difficult.[28]

Yang's contention that "all of us are studying death," and that the lessons are more difficult than need be, is a blatant criticism of contemporary life. Yang Xu was not alone in such frank expression of pessimism. In the essay "Fuchen de xinyu" (Drifting Words from the Heart), Wu Ying also describes her depressed state: "My spirit is not enough to resist the oppression of an attack from outside."[29] Lamenting the "unbearable tyranny" that she suffers, Wu ascribes a burden to her torment that far surpasses the pain one might associate with

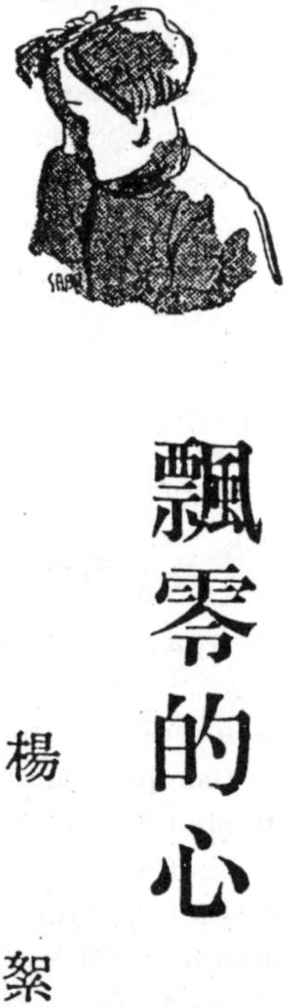

6.5 *Forsaken Heart,* a drawing from the original publication of Yang Xu's "Piaoling de xin" (Forsaken Heart), captures the melancholic spirit that dominates her writings.

academic study, the topic that the essay ostensibly describes.[30] In the early 1940s, Dan Di jotted in her diary, "at the end of September, illusions, despair, vexation. Bitter smile. Shaking, war aims, tears, blurred."[31] As recounted earlier, Dan Di also, and more publicly, expresses her disappointment in life in the Japanese metropole, grieving in the essay, "Yiguo" (Foreign Country), "Left to myself, all is desolate."[32] Manchukuo literature is replete with such pessimistic reflections on contemporary life.

In the short story "Wo he wo de haizimen" (Me and My Children), Zhu Ti furthers her critique of Manchukuo education, as the protagonist, a teacher, avers that she must teach her students how to overcome the pressures that "crushed [her generation] under the wheel and axle of life."[33] The teacher dreams that her students will be able to study to the best of their ability, despite her fear that "in today's environment, they have lost all opportunities for advanced studies."[34] A letter from a former student inspires her: "You use your wisdom, use your hot enthusiasm, use your great humanitarian heart to stretch out your hands to save thousands of the little people from the contagious poisons in the common world."[35] A teacher who mourns for her students, who in turn praise her for saving them from "contagious poisons," does little to enhance perceptions of contemporary life for youth in Manchukuo.

The mental anguish that dominates this literature is magnified by the depiction of physical pain, as characters are variously mistreated, beaten, and bloodied. In Dan Di's short story "Jie" (Warning), the unmarried female protagonist, Little Qin, is drenched in blood after giving birth alone in a forest. Qin's mother is frantic over her unwed daughter's future, but both women live in fear of Qin's father, who blames his daughter for her seduction. After discovering Qin's pregnancy, her father drove her out of their home and beat his wife. Qin then gives birth to her baby alone in a field, drenched in blood with her life in tatters, "she is that kind of pitiful, she is finished."[36] Driven mad by the betrayal of every man in her life, Qin abandons her baby in the forest to return to her mother to beg for money; crying "like a cat," she makes three attempts before she is able to leave her baby.[37] Qin's desperation eventually drives her to a nunnery, in front of which she encounters an escaped convict who inspires her to persevere. On the threshold of the religious institution, he vows to her that with "no bending, no yielding, victory will certainly be ours," propelling Qin back to the forest, where she is unable to find her baby.[38] Qin is encouraged by a convict to resist her victimization. Her spirit resurrected, she sets off on "a pure and holy road" in search of a new life with dignity.[39] Dan Di sympathetically portrays a single unwed woman who forsakes her roles as a daughter and mother for a future that is revealed to her by a convict, who, with an unspecified criminal past, is the only man in the story with any morals. The unrelenting violence that characterizes the first half of "Jie" contrasts with the latter half in which Qin rejects her subjugated position. Manchukuo censors cited both the story's negativity and Qin's convict-inspired transformation as proof of Dan Di's anti-Manchukuo sentiment.[40]

Depiction of physical pain and persecution underlines the pessimistic ambiance of this literature. In Dan Di's "Huma he zhi ye" (Night on the Huma River) the pale, thin protagonist, Zhu Nixi, has a final meeting with her lover, Dai Xi, a writer who was banished and tortured for an essay he wrote.[41] The tubercular Nixi staggers miles from Harbin, coughing up blood, as she passes through a majestic mountain landscape, the beauty of which contrasts with the horror of her life. Since the couple was last together seventeen years before, Xi suffered exile as well as the amputation of both hands and his tongue. When Nixi rushes towards him, he can only communicate with her by writing with a pencil lodged in his nostril. "Like a wooden chicken," Nixi stands dumbstruck at the appearance of her once vital lover.[42] Happy at seeing Nixi again, Xi dies holding her in his arms. Nixi is buffeted by emotion upon his death, variously "a hurt cat" and a solemn "stone goddess."[43] She presides over his cremation before jumping to her own death in the Huma River. As Xi's fire burns out, the river's waters swallow Nixi and two lives are extinguished – a tragic loss on account of one essay. "Huma he zhi ye" is Dan Di's explicit recognition of the consequences of violating Manchukuo's literary regulations. The persecution of writers is also the focus of a short story published shortly after the collapse of Manchukuo, Zuo Di's "Buqu de renmin" (Indomitable People). Zuo Di details the "terrifying, darkly sad days" of a small group of writers in Manchukuo who live under an omnipotent "blood-stained" hand of oppression.[44] Despite the constant danger in which they operate, they pursue their literary ideals while decrying the abandonment of Manchukuo's masses by those who fled to join the resistance, an obvious justification by the author for her own activities during the occupation.

The pain of human life is reflected in, and exacerbated by, ties with the natural world.[45] In Zhu Ti's "Da Heilongjiang de youyu" (The Melancholy of the Mighty Black Dragon River), the protagonist, Mother, cries "Ah, mighty Black Dragon River! You pierce my chest!"[46] On the boat that carries her and her daughter away from Manchukuo back to her homeland (the Soviet Union), Yana develops a love-hate relationship with the Black Dragon River. Yana vows that she despises life in Manchukuo, from its political system to the "cities covered with a layer of opium smoke," its wretched food, and unattainable rice.[47] But gazing into the water, she sees her past or hears whispers from it; the sounds of the waves lapping against the side of the boat raise fond memories of Western dances, such as the Charleston, and the song "Spanish Nights."[48] She remembers that as a young girl, by listening to the quiet waves of the river, she could escape into her dreams with her whole body "bathed with warmth."[49] The waters transport Yana into another world that vividly contrasts with her tortured condition. The timeless, evocative, and nurturing nature of the environment that the travellers move within, but can't enjoy because of personal tragedies, all foment the "melancholy of the mighty Black Dragon River."

The bond between humans and nature is also prominent in Lan Ling's work. In the poem "Qiaopan" (The Side of the Bridge), "a little river, curls up in the dusk's embrace, weeping."[50] The author attributes to the river an empathy for human sadness that is evident in her other work as well. In her essay "Tongnian zhi chun" (Spring in Childhood), Lan Ling gazes upon her garden, reflecting on her passing youth: "When I am in this long, drawn-out journey of life, when I feel discontented and weary, can I be forbidden to return to that time's paradise?"[51] She contrasts her journey into adulthood with the carefree childhood that, incidentally, predated the Japanese occupation. She mourns the lost "paradise" (*leyuan*) of her childhood, a clear allusion to propaganda extolling Manchukuo as a "paradise land."[52] In this essay, Lan Ling lauds the rousing qualities of spring that she asserts chrysanthemums, widely regarded as the symbol of Japan's imperial family, do not possess.[53] Within the confines of this short essay, Lan Ling engages in two overtly negative reflections on key components of Japanese and Manchukuo propaganda.

This literature is permeated with pessimism to enhance the authors' portraits of a society so dehumanizing that they often compare humans to animals. The writers' consistent engagement with negativity is perhaps the literature's most defining characteristic. The dramatic effect of pessimism is further compounded by ceaseless descriptions of social turmoil.

Disorder

THE ENVIRONMENT DRIVES PEOPLE TO THE END OF THEIR TETHER.

– *Yang Xu, "Ji yu fu" (Mail and Response)*

The raison d'être of the Manchukuo regime, as articulated in official propaganda, was to bring stability to a region wracked by warlord rule, "banditry," and communist aggression. The regime promoted the Confucian-based *Wangdao* ideal as the most modern embodiment of Eastern and Western civilization, which would bring peace and harmony to a population situated at the crossroads of empire. But the inability of Manchukuo officials to fulfil their professed agenda is revealed in the literature written by the seven writers through an overwhelming degree of discord, as confrontations and displacement rend the social fabric. The consistent depiction of disorder highlights the authors' efforts to publicize the failings of Manchukuo and the alienation that vexed its Chinese subjects. As Wu Ying caustically observed in her 1940 essay "Lianzhe de youren" (Missing Friends), following the establishment of Manchukuo, her friends had "scattered about like the stars and the dead" (*xingsan he siwang*).[54] For all the official rhetoric of harmony, Manchukuo emerges from this literature as a deeply disruptive entity.

Social instability and dysfunctional societies are prominent throughout Wu Ying's fiction. In "Xiao jie" (Mixed-Up Street), poverty-induced violence tears a community apart. The inability of the adults to provide economic sustenance to their families pits all of the neighbours against one another, leaving the children to fend for themselves, with tragic consequences. The children's innocence is sacrificed to their parents' desperate schemes for survival, as the children try to emulate their parents, by learning about "adult's mysteries" (*daren de shenmi*).[55] The story climaxes with the entire community brawling in front of the local magistrate, who is unable to provide them any resolution. In "Wang xiang" (Gazing Homeward), the protagonist, Ming, returns home after a ten-year absence that resulted from an altercation in his youth. He is devastated by his best friend who, in his absence, has degenerated into an unemployed, alcoholic wife-beater. He is taken aback by the numbers of homeless people with whom he must share his rented accommodation; they move about "like worms."[56] The decline that has consumed his hometown is so overwhelming that he resolves to save himself by leaving again. Significantly, Ming's ten-year absence approximates the length of Manchukuo rule when the story was published in 1939.

Mei Niang also stresses disorder in her short story "Bangwan de xiju" (An Evening's Comedy), which climaxes with a street brawl. The matriarch of the family (who founded and operates the family laundry business), her inept husband, their respective lovers, their son, the apprentice, and neighbourhood children all fall upon each other, "twirling about like horse cart lights."[57] The wholly incompetent husband fosters a tumultuous environment that is dominated by aggression and jealousy; the author blames him for the demeaning position of his wife, mistress, and son. The matriarch has a Korean lover, who is denigrated by the other characters as a "turncoat" (*er taijun*), a term once used in reference to ministers in imperial China who worked for one dynasty and its successor.[58] As the neighbourhood descends into chaos, the Korean relaxes in comfort inside the business that is corrupted by his presence. In "Bangwan de xiju," Mei Niang criticizes the adult men (Chinese and Korean) for conduct that disrupts the social order; additionally, the depiction of the Korean provides a rare glimpse of widespread Chinese distrust of Korean cooperation with the Japanese in Manchukuo.

The disruptive influence of outsiders is featured in Dan Di's short story "Kancaifu" (Wood-chopping Women). Dan Di recounts the intrusion of two university students, "a pair of free mountain birds," into the lives of three generations of poor women wood gatherers.[59] The women live "like pitiful squirrels" in a majestic mountain setting, in constant fear of punishment for illegally collecting the wood that affords them a subsistence-level existence.[60] Each of the three women has a different reaction to the intruders: the grandmother acts stiffly towards them, the mother is haunted by memories of her dead husband and responds awkwardly to them, and the starving granddaughter innocently accepts their offer of an orange. As the students merrily walk away, their mood contrasts with the women's misery as the young girl accidentally drops the orange, chases it, falls into a ravine, and breaks her arm. The students inadvertently devastate the lives of the impoverished women, who are in no position to secure medical treatment for the injury. "Kancaifu" is a thinly veiled parable that warns of the risks inherent to interaction with outsiders, who, even with the best of intentions, cannot help but inflict damage on locals who are forced to live in fear of outsiders.

Urban decadence, and the dislocation stemming from it, is evident in Lan Ling's work. In the play *Da di de ernü* (*Sons and Daughters of the Great Land*) a son's highly anticipated return to his family's farm is recounted. His aged parents resuscitate their dream of making their fallow farm prosper again as they aspire to marry him off to a woman in order to produce heirs to plough "the great land of Asia" (*Ya de da di*).[61] This work ostensibly celebrates rural life and the concept of "Greater Asia," but it does not reveal why the son originally left the farm, what was so "foul" (*wuzhuo*) about urban life that compelled his return, or why his parents' lives had fallen to ruin in his absence.[62] When *Da di de ernü* was published, at the peak of war censorship in April 1944, it would not only have been illegal for Lan Ling to explain in detail the characters' misfortune, it would have been redundant as well, as dissatisfaction with Manchukuo was so widespread. In the short story "Paomo" (Bubbles), the female protagonist, Ying, for reasons not clearly defined, is "fed up with the noisiness of the city."[63] Hoping for a better life in a small town, she is disappointed to discover that the people there have been "too changed by society" (*tai shehui huale*), a distinctly negative attribute.[64] Ying is disillusioned by her ex-boyfriend's newly materialistic and self-centred character and is appalled by the increasing focus on money rather than integrity. Disheartened, she returns to the big city. Her illusions of small-town purity shattered, she comes to recognize that the larger cities might provide employment opportunities even if not the moral environment that she sought.

The disorder that these writers ascribed to life often inspires physical flight. In the poem "Zhuiqiu" (The Pursuit), as the narrator gazes into the distance, hesitating at a crossroads, she notes: "One dark night, that shore of the little river was brightened a little by a light, / and a voice floated in the evening air, / 'Come! Cross the little river, just reach the other side!'"[65] The "dark night," the light in the distance, and the beckoning call to the "other side" are all suggestive of the anti-Japanese resistance. In Lan Ling's 1944 short story "Richu" (Sunrise), the protagonist refuses to acquiesce to the submission that she believes ruined her mother's life, so she and her lover flee her arranged marriage. Her steely determination is evidenced in the illustration featuring her upright posture and clenched fist (Figure 6.6). Although the outcome of their flight (ironically, to Manchukuo) is not revealed, their desperation is palpable. In other fictional works, the search for a better life in Manchukuo meets

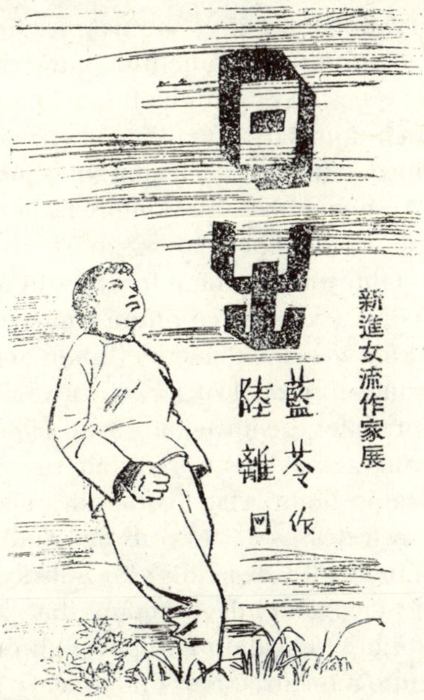

6.6 *Sunrise*, a drawing by Lu Li, shows a young woman's determined look and clenched fist, suggesting the personal strengths of the female protagonist who rejects an arranged marriage in Lan Ling's "Richu" (Sunrise).

with failure. In Mei Niang's *Xiao furen* (*Little Wife*), a young couple leaves their families in Beiping (the Republican name for Beijing) for the "virgin grasslands" of Manchukuo.[66] They are inspired to help youth there who are "hesitating [after the] big upheaval," stressing the ambiguous reception that the establishment of Manchukuo received.[67] It is unclear what assistance the young couple intend, but while attempting to survive dire poverty in Changchun, the "little wife" Phoenix becomes conscious of the power of money and regrets abandoning her wealthy family for a new life in Manchukuo.[68] Her dreams are dashed as she grows increasingly distant from her husband. Mei Niang's juxtaposition of life in Beiping and Changchun accentuates the importance of money in Manchukuo society, a critique that also informs her novella *Xie* and Lan Ling's "Paomo." Zhang Quan has argued that Mei Niang's use of Republican-era names for these cities, instead of their occupation-era names (Beijing and Xinjing respectively) underlines the author's subversive intent.[69] In "Du Bohai," Zhu Ti even more forcefully condemns life in the "strange land" of Manchukuo.[70] Mother leaves her native Shandong with son in tow, searching for her husband. The narrator notes that even though Mother's "love for her native soil is not less than others," she could not face life without her husband.[71] But from the moment she arrives at the pier to board a ship for Manchukuo, she is abused by men – "for the first time in her life she was measured up by a stranger";[72] her sequestered youth left her woefully unprepared for life in Manchukuo. When she tries to purchase tickets to cross the Bohai Sea, she is informed that women are not allowed to enter Manchukuo without an adult male escort. In her desperation, she hires the ticket seller's accomplice, who rapes her on the voyage. En route to Manchukuo, the boat becomes her 'prison on the sea' (*haishang de qiuyu*) as she is flung into the 'abyss of fate.'[73] When the boat docks in Manchukuo, customs officials seize her remaining silver money while the rapist absconds with her belongings, leaving her almost penniless. Her entrance to Manchukuo is marked by her utter subjugation, as she is repeatedly raped and robbed by Chinese men. Manchukuo is depicted as an entirely untenable environment for the woman.

The quest for security is portrayed as a dangerous yet common endeavour in this literature. In 1941, Dan Di's *Andi he Mahua* was lauded by Chinese critics for the author's portrayal of the devastating impact of foreign invasion. Andi and Mahua's downtrodden condition predates the invasion – Andi's father had been "defeated by life" in Manchuria during his twenty years there – but the invasion forces them into an even more perilous existence on the road.[74] The desperation of the times is articulated by a stranger who consoles Andi by observing that her father's death was not untimely: "To die in this year is lucky!"[75] Another woman mourns over the body of her dead child, weeping that "the dead are dead, but the living still have to suffer."[76] Escalating impoverishment and Andi's failing health pressure Mahua into a tortured decision to leave his family and join a Jewish man in a quest for work in an unnamed country (referred to only as "XXX" but presumably the Soviet Union); unwittingly,

Mahua embarks on a life that turns men into "savages" (*zhengning*).[77] He is tantalized by the stranger's promises of opportunity in the foreign land, contrasting prosperity there with the difficulty of living in Manchukuo. The Jewish man delivers the death blow to Andi and Mahua's relationship. His ethnicity and lack of local connections mark him as an outsider, but it is his unrealizable tales of prosperity elsewhere that make him most dangerous as he lures Mahua away from his family to his death in a country even more loathsome than Manchukuo. Andi remains with their son, poor but alive. She is shown to be more resilient than her husband and able to endure the turmoil because of bonds that kept her with family and co-workers.

In this literature, disorder exposes the dysfunctional nature of contemporary society. Manchukuo is shown to be utterly incapable of providing a healthy, safe, and prosperous environment for its Chinese subjects. These portraits of local life explicitly undermine Manchukuo propaganda and question the utility of *Wangdao* ideology.

Destitution

> Perhaps her own fate and that of her child has been predetermined, to starve to death on this piece of land east of the pass ...
>
> *– Zhu Ti, "Du Bohai" (Crossing the Bohai Sea)*

As outlined in Chapter 2, the opening of Manchuria to large-scale migration in the late Qing era made the region a magnet for ambitious migrants. Economic development, especially Japanese investment in the first half of the twentieth century, was transformative. But with the establishment of Manchukuo, the competitive nature of the regional economy evaporated, and the vast majority of the population sank into a subsistence existence, divorced from the benefits of economic growth. The writers discussed in this study, in their capacities as "custodians of the hearth" and active, articulate participants in the workplace, held a privileged space from which to reflect upon the living standards of the Chinese in Manchukuo. Their work memorializes the grinding poverty – as Lan Ling termed it, "the whip of life" – that structured life for the poor, including teachers, clerks, labourers, and sex workers, as well as rural farmers, fishers, and wood-gatherers.[78] The writers' depiction of widespread poverty not only describes the experience of much of the population in Manchukuo but also indicates the writers' more explicitly political agenda to expose the extent of Chinese subjugation.

Of the writers of this study, Dan Di has been most lauded for her focus on the lives of the poor.[79] In *Andi he Mahua*, foreign invasion forces a young couple to abandon the squalid shacks they live in for an even more precarious existence on the road. Their descent into abject poverty tears their family apart, explicitly linking the foreign presence with poverty, dislocation, and death. In the short story "Xuezu" (Flesh and Blood), published shortly after the fall of Manchukuo, Dan Di describes a young suburban man's pathetic attempt to halt his family's economic decline with a futile effort to raise chickens in his home.[80] Unlike his Japanese neighbours, who are oblivious to his plight, he has no idea how to raise healthy chickens. Frustrated by his inability to provide for his family, the man begins to physically abuse his wife and sister. His sister defends the misogynistic violence to their father, arguing that "the pressures of life result in this kind of meanness."[81] Dan shows that the pressures of Chinese life in Manchukuo have devastating consequences for families, and for women in particular. In addition, "Xuezu" provides a rare (albeit post-occupation) glimpse at the urban Japanese who lived in Manchukuo in relative affluence, oblivious to the desperation of the Chinese on their doorstep.

The decline of Manchukuo's Chinese upper classes is the focus of several celebrated works that highlight the socioeconomic costs of occupation. In Mei Niang's *Xie*, the foreign presence has a demonstrably negative influence on the Sun family, who, although fictional, significantly shared the same surname as Mei's paternal family. The Japanese, for the most part, remain at arm's length from the Chinese. All efforts by members of the once-prominent Sun family to ingratiate themselves with the Japanese, for financial gain, are unsuccessful. The novel reveals the Japanese work ethic, in particular, to be destructive in a Chinese context. The Japanese are aloof and do not speak Chinese. Third Uncle, for example, who is employed at the tax office, has no meaningful interactions with his Japanese bosses; his self-serving efforts to cultivate personal relationships with them fail miserably. In spite of his prominent position, he goes to work every day (according to a schedule), works long hours, and receives no gifts from clients. His family views these as marks of true failure, devaluing his work for the Japanese even further. The novel shows the Japanese occupation to be ruinous to the Chinese, especially in comparison to an earlier, relatively benign, Russian presence.

A central theme in *Xie* is the Manchukuo regime's inflation of the importance of money at the expense of personal relationships. Economic uncertainty forces Ling's stepmother to obsess over her stash of silver, which she begins to view as more important than life itself. Government demands to convert all silver to the new, worthless paper currency incapacitates her and robs the family of her steady, able control over their faltering finances. Cui's down-to-earth father, Sun Wangfu, loses all sense of propriety after he moves to the locus of Japanese domination, Changchun. He comes to view women as "a ready source of money" (*yaoqianshu*), to be bought and sold like commodities.[82] The protagonist, Cui, fears that her father will get drunk and sell her, or marry her into a rich family, with no concern for her well-being. She aspires to a "simple life" with a poor man, because she believes that when poor women like her marry into rich families they are treated abominably. *Xie* climaxes when Cui's father sells her to Third Uncle to gain control over the family businesses. Cui's betrayal by her "useless and emotionless" male relatives confirms Cui and Ling's worst fears.[83] Cui's innocence is sacrificed, women's lives become the stuff for barter, and the full impact of colonial misogyny shatters the family. Mei Niang's depiction of the fictional Sun family's decline reflects the dramatic changes that struck her own Sun family after the establishment of Manchukuo.

For its depiction of an upper-class family's slide towards economic ruin, Wu Ying's "Xuyuan" (Dilapidation) was awarded the top prize in a 1941 writing contest organized by the Manchukuo-China Arts Exchange.[84] The decline is manifested by the deaths of several children and the patriarch's futile attempts to maintain clan honour by rebuilding the family cemetery.[85] The entire family is traumatized by their ruination, which is especially vexing for the family's patriarch. He refuses to heed the advice of other family members, who caution that their scarce resources should be allocated to everyday essentials, not in pointless efforts to sustain an artificial social status. "Xuyuan" concludes with the breakup of the family. The patriarch's wife refuses to passively watch her family disintegrate, and she returns to her natal home with several of their children. In both *Xie* and "Xuyuan," women are affected by economic and moral decline, but they are generally hailed as more capable and resilient, and more distanced from the Japanese, than men. Indeed, men bring the full negativity of Manchukuo into the home, with catastrophic results.

The pressures bearing on the upper classes also proved disastrous for the middle and lower classes. In Lan Ling's "Guxiang de jia" (Native Place Home), a widow loses control over a family business to relatives who deal in opium. Her son, Ming, returns home to discover that she is overwhelmed by opium addiction, reduced to a mere pawn of his scheming aunt and her brother, who obtains illicit opium through his work at the Opium Monopoly. He learns how this entreprise darkened the family name and cost his sister, Yu, her fiancé because he refused to marry into a drug-dealing family. Ming's mother is aware of the family's predicament but contends that she is powerless – she would "rather go without food than give up opium."[86] Ming resolves to convince Yu to embark on a new life with him and send for their mother later. Although Ming questions whether his sister has "a man's bravery and courage" to forge a new life elsewhere, Yu proves ready, willing, and able to go; before Ming approaches her, Yu had already quit her job and packed.[87] There is no alternative but for them to flee for their lives. In Mei Niang's "Di'er dai" (The Second Generation), a group of children mimic the incessant, poverty-induced bickering of their parents; the children mourn, "God gives no way to live."[88] Raised in fractious surroundings, the children must beg for food. After one of them dies of poison inflicted by a Japanese fisherman who has tired of their constant begging, the neighbourhood is traumatized. The children are all victimized by the adults, Chinese and Japanese, who are so consumed with their own poverty that they are blinded to the devastating toll that their behaviour takes on the lives of their children.

Economic deprivation exacted devastating tolls, but the writers maintained that poverty need not breed immoral behaviour. In Lan Ling's "Duanwujie" (Dragon Boat Festival), a woman from Shandong who had migrated to Manchukuo with her husband for work raises her son alone and penniless after her husband's death on the job. She works tirelessly through the night, shedding bitter tears, starving and exhausted, in order to buy her son a *zongzi* to celebrate the Dragon Boat Festival.[89] Through hard work, self-denial, and devotion to her son, she hopes to inspire her son to believe that "poor people who have integrity are not poor."[90] In coping with the consequences of her husband's untimely death, the mother personifies the virtues essential to constructs of good wives, wise mothers. Significantly, the virtues that she promotes are not shown to be exclusive to women, but rather have application to her son as well. Perspicacity and integrity in the face of economic deprivation are consistent features in this literature, intended to inspire readers to overcome the difficulties that hampered contemporary life.

In this literature, the urban centres, the foci of Manchukuo modernity, are sunk in poverty, misery, and filth. In Zuo Di's short story "Zhai xiang" (Narrow Alley) urban filth is emblematic of Manchukuo life: "The mouth of the alley is piled with mountains and valleys of garbage, at the foot of the walls appear innumerable stains of feces and urine."[91] The increasing impoverishment of the once middle-class female narrator forces her to move to a narrow alley that is mired in squalor. Living among the poor, she acquires sympathy for her neighbours, who have eked out their entire lives. The alley is a setting defined by its filth, which denies inhabitants the ability to sustain economically sufficient, happy, and healthy lives. This depiction of urban deprivation is especially ironic because the capital of Manchukuo was widely publicized as one of the first Asian cities to be fitted with lavatories with running water and to emphasize modern hygiene as a symbol of enlightened *Wangdao* rule. In contrast, Zuo Di stresses the failings of Manchukuo to provide even the most basic benefits of socioeconomic development for its Chinese subjects.

Most of the writers of this study were raised in relative poverty, which they depict as a defining feature of Chinese life in Manchukuo. In their work, economic deprivation curses all classes. These portraits of destitution undermine Manchukuo's raison d'être of economic and moral development.

This chapter highlights the predominance of darkness, pessimism, disorder, and destitution in portraits of Manchukuo society. The writers deployed each of these tropes to expose reality in the most unflattering light. Their collective depiction of Manchukuo is that of a deeply dysfunctional society. The writers violated Manchukuo's dense body of literary regulations by establishing careers that enabled them to vividly articulate their alienation from the state and its cultural agenda. This literature depicts contemporary life with a negativity that was explicitly forbidden but that proved popular with Chinese and Japanese audiences.

It is worth reflecting on issues that are not directly addressed in this literature. Japanese people and their customs are rarely mentioned. Their absence underlines the racist, divisive nature of Manchukuo society. In Manchukuo, direct Chinese criticism of Japanese rule was impermissible. Nonetheless, as this study suggests, thinly veiled criticism was a motif across much of Chinese popular culture. Freely inspired, explicitly pro-Manchukuo Chinese-language literature was unlikely given that the state's militaristic, racist, and misogynistic nature constrasted so markedly with these writers' idealistic stances. Manchukuo state structures are mentioned only in passing and the monarchy only once, and pejoratively: in *Xie*, Mei Niang recounts the fear that struck the population of the capital when it was announced that the emperor was looking for concubines.[92] Neither Manchukuo nor Japanese customs are celebrated in any of these writings. Instead, melancholy, sorrow, and righteous indignation lay at the heart of this literature, in defiance of Manchukuo literary regulations.

The consistent denigration of Manchukuo society in these women's writings prompted official intervention only in the colony's twilight years. Until 1943, these writers skirted Manchukuo's regulatory framework, turning work opportunities and institutionalized misogyny to their advantage. While male writers lived under constant threat of persecution for engaging in social criticism, women writers were left relatively free to declare with impunity, like Yang Xu, that "life itself is evil."[93] Until the final years of Manchukuo, despite the prohibition of precisely the type of literature that these women produced, the writers issued forth critiques of Manchukuo that reflect their alienation from the state and its modernity project.

7

The Collapse of Empire and Careers

In the early 1940s, expanding official surveillance of Manchukuo's Chinese-language literary world bore serious ramifications for the region's writers. With the commencement of the Sacred War against Great Britain and the United States in 1941, the Chinese cultural resurgence that had been achieved, albeit within the confines of an onerous regulatory framework, faltered. Political persecution, in conjunction with Sacred War demands and paper shortages, nearly achieved the full submission of Chinese writers that colonial officials had long dreamed of. As the Japanese Empire verged on collapse, the local Chinese-language literary world quieted, as writers were forcibly or voluntarily silenced. But the near-suffocating environment that temporarily halted the careers of most Chinese writers in Manchukuo was merely a prelude to the tragedy of their post-liberation lives. Ironically, Chinese socialist liberation brought the writers more pressing persecution than they had ever experienced in Manchukuo.

The declaration of the Sacred War in 1941 triggered increasing demands on Chinese literati to accede loyally to the Manchukuo cultural agenda. Zhu Ti later noted that eventually even alluding to the "many difficulties in the people's livelihood" (*minsheng zhi duo jian*) could result in the state's refusal to publish work.[1] Of the writers discussed in this study, Wu Ying was the first to have her career sidelined by demands for greater cohesion between official regulations and Chinese cultural production.[2] In late 1942, she cited stomach problems and reduced her workload as editor at *Xin Manzhou*.[3] The following year, her short story "Ming" was sharply criticized by censors for its anti-patriarchal tone, which they perceived to be implicitly anti-Japanese and anti-Manchukuo. Censors noted in particular the following depiction of a couple's argument. The female protagonist curses her husband: "You, you are a dog. You plunder everything of mine, you occupy everything of mine ... Another time, you and my father were fighting, you ended the relationship between me and my father. You forbade me and my father to see each other, forbade any communication, making me separate from my own flesh and blood. Heavens! What kind of world is this!"[4] The vocabulary used and the relationships alluded to in this passage alerted censors to what they believed was the author's subversive intent. They argued that the characters personified contemporary Chinese political divisions: the female protagonist was Manchuria, her alienated father China, and her "dog" of a husband, Japan. Thus, Manchuria condemns Japan for an occupation that forced its division from its "flesh and blood," China. Wu Ying's short story, censors asserted, was not an innocent depiction of a woman's unhappy marriage; rather, they reported in a security dossier on her that the work constituted an attack on Japan and Manchukuo, disguised as feminist critique. As censors became more conscious of the implications of such criticism, the relative tolerance of women writers came to a halt.[5]

Shortly after the publication of "Ming," Wu Ying stopped writing fiction altogether, and in 1944 she resigned from *Xin Manzhou*, although her husband Wu Lang (who was also cited by censors in 1943 for two of his works) continued with his responsibilities as an editor for that publication.[6] In 1944, in open letters to Mei Niang and Liang Shanding printed in Beijing's *Funü zazhi* (*Ladies' Journal*), Wu Ying lamented the deterioration of life in Manchukuo: "Mei Niang, the world is basically cold."[7] Wu Ying decried the impact of her career on her personal life and urged Mei Niang as a new mother to focus on nurturing her motherly instincts. She asked: "Besides watching their children grow up, how else can women get comfort?"[8] Thus, in 1944, Wu Ying articulated the good wife, wise mother ideal that Manchukuo officials had long promoted, but she did so as officials in Japanese-occupied territories applied pressure on women to emulate European and North American women and join the workforce to replace the men, who were required for battle on the front lines. Wu Ying also publicly lauded Liang Shanding's relocation to the freer atmosphere of Beijing, to "resist the powers that block individual freedom," following publication of his novel *Lüse de gu*.[9] She noted that Manchukuo's deteriorating economic climate forced her to spend days standing in ration lines for oil and other essentials, and she contended that in January and February her home was too cold to do any work. In unequivocal terms, in Beijing-based media, Wu Ying expressed personal dissatisfaction with Manchukuo, and her career ended on this dismal note.

The shifting circumstances that contributed to the end of Wu Ying's career exemplifies the experience faced by other writers in the final years of Manchukuo.[10] By 1944, censors more thoroughly implemented the legal framework that they had painstakingly constructed. Of the women writers who remained in Manchukuo, the highest profile target was Yang Xu. She had achieved success as an entertainer and writer, but her second volume of collected writings, *Wo de Riji* (*My Diary*), was banned by Manchukuo censors for sexual content that violated every one of the Eight Abstentions. Yang Xu's explicit discussion of women's sexuality, her demands for individual emancipation, and her "wild horse character" were deemed utterly unacceptable as the empire was engaged in the Sacred War. Although *Wo de Riji* was published in Xinjing in 1944, its distribution was immediately halted. All copies that had not been distributed were recalled and destroyed. After liberation in 1945, the attempted republication of this volume was halted, this time by communist authorities, who condemned such work as too bourgeois for the revolution's needs. At present, only one copy of *Wo de Riji* is known to exist, in the Changchun Municipal Library.

In 1944, two of Zhu Ti's stories, "Du Bohai" (Crossing the Bohai Sea) and "Xiao Yinzi he ta de jiazu" (Little Yinzi and Her Relations), were banned. "Du Bohai" was submitted to *Xin Manzhou* for publication, but was rejected for its negative depiction of Manchukuo. The story climaxes with the realization by the much-abused heroine that she does not need a man to survive. In this story, Zhu Ti denigrated the good wife, wise mother ideal through an entirely negative depiction of women's lives in Manchukuo. "Du Bohai" was later renamed and included, as the title piece, in Zhu Ti's 1945 volume of collected works, *Ying* (*Cherry*). "Xiao Yinzi he ta de jiazu" was published in her collected works but was also, initially, banned for its depiction of the rape, sale, and suicide of a young girl. Both stories depicted a subjugation of women that censors rejected for implicitly anti-Manchukuo, if not anti-Japanese, intent.

Also in 1944, in Qiqihaer, the authorities twice interrogated Lan Ling for her writings.[11] Two investigators, one Japanese and one Chinese, were dispatched by the local authorities to question her regarding her relationship with the editors of Xinjing's popular journal *Qingnian bao* (*Youth Herald*), the purpose of her writings, and the nature of her political beliefs. Her husband, Hu Dounan, was interrogated at the same time. Lan Ling later recounted how, in addition to these overt intimidation tactics, their mail was tampered with or seized so that she did not always receive copies of her published work.[12] Lan Ling's mother, horrified by the risks inherent to cultural production in Manchukuo, pressured her to leave aside her writing ambitions and focus on raising her family. In the final year of the occupation, Lan Ling acquiesced, resumed teaching, and did not publish again until after liberation.

Such censorship and intimidation paled in comparison to the persecution experienced by Dan Di and Zuo Di. Dan Di returned to Manchukuo from study in Japan in 1942. A dossier detailing the dark and pessimistic tone of her writings in Japan preceded her. She was assigned to a teaching position in Kaiyuan, Liaoning, at the local Middle School for Women. After a term of teaching, she began to work at a local bookstore, in the editing pool for its publishing branch.[13] She then resumed writing, showing in her depiction of state persecution in "Huma he zhi ye" (Night on the Huma River), a hypercritical stance. In Manchukuo, she utilized her advanced education to secure employment in two sensitive cultural arenas, education and literary production. In 1943, her short story "Jie" was singled out by censors who interpreted its negative tone and questionable language to be thinly veiled criticisms of Japan and Manchukuo.

Dan Di's fame grew in conjunction with the desire of censors to silence her. In December 1943, Xinjing's Kaiming bookstore published her collected works, *Andi he Mahua*. Chinese critics acclaimed her Manchukuo's "most advanced woman writer" (*nü zuojia zhong qiancheng yaoyuan de yi shi*).[14] She was hailed as "ahead of her times" (*hou lai zhe ju*).[15] Such praise came with a price. In late 1943, Dan Di was jailed for a suspected plot to leave Manchukuo to join the anti-Japanese resistance; she was taken into custody by the military and held for trial.[16] Ironically, she later noted that this incarceration afforded her unimpeded access to jailed Communist Party members.[17] After six months of confinement, in June 1944, she was convicted of the "crime of being a fugitive" (*taowang zui*) and was sentenced to a further two years imprisonment.[18] But in the early fall, due to her failing health and consistent with contemporary legal practice in Japan, she was released from prison under the watchful eyes of guarantors, who were held accountable for her actions. Dan Di was remanded to house arrest in Xinjing. In compliance with the conditions of her probation, she was employed as an editor at the movie magazine *Manzhou yinghua* (*Manchukuo Movies*). Officials no doubt believed that her employment at a blatantly pro-Manchukuo gossip magazine was not only fitting work for an educated woman but also a particularly efficacious muzzle for an outspoken critic. She remained in this position until Japan's defeat in August 1945.

In 1943, Zuo Di's personal life was also devastated by state persecution. After she edited her husband Liang Shanding's serialized novel *Lüse de gu* (*The Green Valley*) for the *Datong bao* (*Great United Herald*), her family was targeted by the National State Publicity Department's investigation unit, the department that had first employed her when she moved to Xinjing in 1938. Publication of *Lüse de gu* was suspended. Following revisions, three more instalments were published, but the entire work was subsequently banned after the launch of an official investigation. In July, the family home was subjected to two searches by the Japanese military.[19] In September, Liang Shanding left Manchukuo for Beijing, where he lodged with Zuo Di's uncle, an eye doctor.[20] Ongoing investigations resulted in the destruction of their home in Xinjing in December, and Zuo Di fled with her daughter to Beijing. The family was reunited and lived throughout 1944 with a former classmate of Zuo Di's. Zuo Di stayed at home, caring for their daughter and writing children's stories.[21]

The persecution of writers in Manchukuo differs strikingly from the experience of writers in Beijing. The heavy hand of censorship in Manchukuo forced the relocation of prominent Manchukuo writers, including Liang Shanding, Mei Niang, and Yuan Xi, to Beijing. As writers in Manchukuo were subjected to increasing levels of surveillance and interrogation, in Beijing Mei Niang rose to the height of her popularity, for work that, had it been published in Manchukuo, would likely have been censured. In 1944, Mei Niang's *Xie*, a work highly critical Manchukuo, was recognized as Novel of the Year by the Greater East Asia Writers' Congress.

In August 1945, Japan's unconditional surrender and the collapse of Manchukuo brought liberation to the region, but at considerable cost to the local literary scene. Over the following years, cities alternated between Nationalist and Communist control, as decisive battles of the Chinese civil war were fought in the region. In the immediate aftermath of Manchukuo, almost all the fruits of industrial investment from the fourteen-year occupation were hauled off or destroyed by the Soviet occupation forces, the Nationalists, and the Communists. Most of Manchukuo's industrial complex was dismantled and shipped across the Soviet Union for reconstruction of the war-ravaged states in eastern Europe. As the physical symbols of Japanese imperialism were ripped away, the experience of living in Manchukuo was transformed into a silent spectre over the region, manipulated by an ultra-nationalist Chinese regime with a political agenda of its own and a population eager to relegate its contentious colonial heritage to the past. Significantly, after the collapse of Manchukuo, most of the writers did not flee the new order, which promised a revival of Chinese sovereignty and national pride. They believed that the progressive stances in their work evidenced their patriotism and zeal for reform.

In early September 1945, many writers, Dan Di among them, regained their freedom. The colonial capital, Xinjing, reverted to its former name, Changchun, and by October a raft of publications burst forth, revitalizing the literary scene that had been stifled during the last years of the war.[22] Writers who had stayed in Manchukuo throughout the Japanese occupation were joined by those who had fled, including Bai Lang, Liang Shanding, and Xiao Jun, who began to edit the journals *Dongbei wenyi* (*Arts of the Northeast*), *Caoyuan* (*Grasslands*), and *Wenhua bao* (*Culture Herald*), respectively.[23] On 1 December in Changchun, the first issue of *Dongbei wenxue* (*Northeastern Literature*) was published; edited by Li Zhengzhong, it featured Dan Di's "Yu zhong ji" (Notes from Jail), Lan Ling's "Yehai" (Night Sailing), and Zhu Ti's "Hanghai" (Sailing the Seas). The regional literary scene was revitalized within the context of the drive towards resolution of the civil war and the restoration of Chinese sovereignty.

Civil war dramatically changed several of the writers' lives. In Changchun, after attempts to republish *Wo de riji* were quashed by Communist authorities, Yang Xu completely abandoned her writing aspirations and immersed herself in family life; her family grew with the birth of two more children, in 1945 and 1949. Her husband, Zhang Hong'en, supported the family by working at a printing factory.[24] Also in Changchun, Zhu Ti worked as a teacher, while her husband, Li Zhengzhong, after editing *Dongbei wenxue* was persecuted for his Manchukuo-era work as a writer and a judge. In the spring of 1946 he was imprisoned by the Chinese Communist Party (CCP); Zhu Ti was forced to cope with work and a baby on her own.[25] Upon his release one year later, Li was encouraged by Li Lisan to join the Eighth Route Army and he left for Harbin. In 1948, Zhu Ti joined him as a soldier in Harbin. Within a few years of the end of Manchukuo, Zhu Ti and her husband had both traded pens for guns, fighting for a communist victory.

In the fall of 1945, Mei Niang and Zuo Di both relocated from Beijing to the Northeast. Mei and her family returned to the Sun family home in Changchun and lived there until 1948, when they moved to Shanghai and then to Taiwan. Following resolution of the civil war in 1949, Mei refused a job offer to teach in Osaka, and the couple determined to return to China to participate in national reconstruction. Tragically, Liu died en route, and the heartbroken widow, pregnant with their son, returned to the mainland with their two daughters; she gave birth to their son shortly thereafter. In Beijing, she supported her family by teaching. Also in Beijing, immediately after liberation, Zuo Di and her younger sister began publication of the short-lived journal *Funü shenghuo* (*Ladies' Life*) (1945); Zuo wrote articles, poems, and short stories, under various pen names, for the magazine. In November 1945, Zuo returned to Shenyang (the former Fengtian) to work as a pharmacist and, through Wu Ying's introduction, as an editor at the *Dongbei minbao* (*Northeast People's Herald*).[26] In 1948, Zuo Di's boss at the *Dongbei minbao* was alerted to local Nationalist officials' suspicions regarding her growing sympathy for the CCP and she fled to communist-held Harbin. Also in the far north, in Qiqihaer, Lan Ling taught at the Municipal Women's Middle School and began to write again; her husband, Hu Dounan, worked at the Second Middle School.[27]

Dan Di had experienced harsh persecution during the final years of Manchukuo, and with the collapse of Japanese rule she left the journal *Manzhou yinghua* (*Manchukuo Movies*) to work under CCP direction writing movie scripts at the Northeast Film Factory in Xingshan County, Heilongjiang; shortly thereafter she married a co-worker, Chen Zhiyuan.[28] The civil war era marks the second stage of her writing career, characterized by work that "boils with righteous ardour" (*feiteng de rexue*) against Japanese colonial rule.[29] In addition, Dan Di participated in Communist rearguard activities, including hospital work. In 1947, however, she was jailed by the Communists for suspected ties with the Guomindang. As a result, her husband immediately initiated divorce proceedings.[30] This second term of imprisonment, for eighteen months, caused serious deterioration of her health: she suffered from enlarged lymph nodes and tuberculosis.[31]

Only one couple was seemingly cognizant of the dangerous consequences of their Manchukuo careers. They quickly acted upon their fears. During the occupation, Wu Ying and Wu Lang had forged high-profile careers as writers, editors, and members of prominent literary organizations. Although Wu Ying curtailed her work schedule in the final years of the occupation, Wu Lang continued his work as an editor and even chaired the 1944 Greater East Asia Writers' Congress in Nanjing. In 1946, fearing the ruinous and potentially fatal consequences of their careers during the Japanese occupation, they moved south to Nanjing, where Wu Ying found work as a librarian at a cultural centre. Even though they had abandoned their colonial careers and fled for their lives, their reputations followed them to the south, and within a few years their political persecution began in earnest. They never returned to the Northeast, yet they were unable to escape their past.

The establishment of the People's Republic in 1949 ushered in a brief resurgence for the writers who had found fame in Manchukuo. In the early 1950s, several embarked upon careers that incorporated their Manchukuo experiences as writers, editors, and educators. The conclusion of the civil war was marked by a generally conciliatory spirit towards most who had lived in Manchukuo. The early Maoist period thus brought stability to most of the women's lives as they integrated into the new socialist order. They believed that their patriotism was clearly evidenced by their work and was unassailable. They did not view their Manchukuo-era activities as any more traitorous than those of the other thirty million Chinese who had lived and worked through the Japanese occupation. None of their writings praised Japan, Japanese cultural ideals, or Manchukuo. Nor did they praise conservative and anti-communist Republican policies such as the New Life Movement. Indeed, several viewed the CCP sympathetically as offering the best hope of reforming Chinese society. As the Communists routed the Nationalists in the late 1940s, none of these women left China, and two eventually joined the CCP: Lan Ling (1950) and Zuo Di (1962). The women were convinced that their legacies testified to their distaste for both foreign occupation and the Republic. They could not anticipate that a Chinese socialist regime would wreck more devastation on their lives than had the Japanese occupation.

Several of the women initially revived their writing ambitions in China's socialist literary world. Lan Ling and Zuo Di achieved the most notable success in this regard. In the early 1950s, Lan edited and wrote for journals such as *Dongbei jiaoyu* (*Northeast Education*) and *Jiaoshi bao* (*Educator's Herald*).[32] In the autumn of 1954, she moved to Beijing to edit *Renmin jiaoyu* (*People's Education*), at which she would work for over thirty years. Her husband, Qiu Jingshan, held prominent positions in the prestigious Foreign Languages Press. In September 1949, Zuo Di began work at several journals, including *Beifang wenxue* (*Northern Literature*), *Dongbei qingnian bao* (*Northeast Youth Herald*), *Mengya xue* (*Sprouts Studies*), and the *Shenyang bao* (*Shenyang Herald*).[33] From 1950 to 1954, she was chief editor at *Hao haizi* (*Good Children*), until she was transferred to Beijing's *Zhongguo shaonian bao* (*China Youth Herald*).[34] In 1959, she was promoted to assistant manager of the latter's literature department; her achievements in this position included interviewing China's president, Liu Shaoqi.[35] Two of the writers, Dan Di and Mei Niang, were inducted into their local Writers' Federations. Mei Niang was inducted into the Beijing Writers' Federation with such luminaries as Ding Ling, Lao She, Ma Feng, and Zhao Shuli.[36]

In the early 1950s, Dan Di, Mei Niang, Yang Xu, and Zhu Ti took advantage of their Manchukuo education and all secured teaching positions. Dan Di taught for several years in Qiqihaer. In 1951, Mei Niang began teaching at

Beijing's Agricultural Film Studio. Yang Xu and her husband taught in Shenyang. From 1949 to 1952, also in Shenyang, Zhu Ti worked as a teacher at the Northeast National Minorities Association. In 1953, she was transferred permanently to Liaoning Provincial Science Materials Company. Their family expanded with the birth of another daughter in 1952 and a son in 1955. Despite such activities, the post-liberation calm that the writers experienced was brief. Regardless of their critiques of the inequities of colonial society, they had not physically taken up arms against the colonial government, and for that reason their career achievements were deeply suspect. Additionally, their seeming focus on issues of particular relevance to them as women and not on national liberation per se enabled critics to tar them with charges of treason or conspiracy, or, even worse, with accusations that the writers were spies for the Japanese.

The political persecution of Manchukuo writers began in the 1950s and reached a crescendo in the late 1960s, with their youthful triumphs transforming into heavy burdens. The writers discussed in this study had assertively pursued and advocated ideals of womanhood that were personally empowering, potentially alienating, and, in the 1950s, utterly condemned as bourgeois. The high-profile nature of their careers in Manchukuo sealed their fate. People with foreign connections and alleged "bourgeois" characteristics were fodder for the political campaigns that ravaged Maoist China. These women proved perfect targets. By the advent of the Cultural Revolution, the writers of Manchukuo had been effectively silenced. The loss of their knowledge and professional experience can never be calculated, but the costs to their personal lives have been recorded in some detail, as the writers' families were torn apart for two decades during the Maoist era.

The first of the women to fall victim to the ceaseless political campaigns that marked the Maoist era was Yang Xu. At the end of 1951, she was sentenced to eight years imprisonment for her Manchukuo career. She was paroled after one year, twice the length of time that her husband, Zhang Hong'en, had spent in jail.[37] In 1952, Mei Niang was widely criticized for "degenerate bourgeois ideas," as feminism was denounced as a foreign import. In 1955, Zuo Di's husband, Liang Shanding, came under intense investigation. This was during the Hu Feng movement, a political campaign launched that year against writer Hu Feng and others accused of being counter-revolutionary and bourgeois. Fearing incarceration, Liang sent their son from the Northeast to Beijing to join Zuo Di and his sisters.[38] That same year, the state labelled Mei Niang a "suspected special agent of Japan" (*Riben tewu xianyi*).[39] The treatment accorded these high-profile targets set the stage for further persecution during periods of radicalism.

During the Anti-Rightist Campaign of 1957, most of Manchukuo's writers were denounced as "writers of the Enemy Occupation." Mei Niang, Yang Xu, and Liang Shanding were all labelled "Rightists" and subjected to various levels of persecution. Yang Xu was imprisoned again.[40] Zuo Di and Liang

Shanding immediately divorced so that his persecution would not taint the entire family. The following year, Liang was condemned as a "traitor to China" and was sentenced to ten years in prison, during which time Zuo Di died. Liang was estranged from his children, and the relationships were not mended before his own death. Despite the efforts of Wu Ying and Wu Lang to put their colonial careers behind them by physically removing themselves from the Northeast, they were also targeted during the Anti-Rightist Campaign. Wu Lang, unable to continue to face the unremitting persecution, committed suicide. Wu Ying died a few years later in 1961. For most, the Maoist era constituted the most repressive period of their lives. Those who survived the Anti-Rightist Campaign enjoyed a brief period of calm, during which most did not dare to continue their careers but rather busied themselves with their families and attempted to restore the dignity of their lives lost during the political persecution.

The Cultural Revolution began in 1966 with the professed ambition of reigniting the revolutionary spirit in China, to transform China into a socialist utopia. Anyone with foreign connections, suspect political allegiances, questionable family heritages, or even disagreeable personal characteristics was targeted for persecution. The Cultural Revolution was the high point of persecution for Dan Di, Mei Niang, Zhu Ti, and Zuo Di. Only two of the writers, Lan Ling and Yang Xu, weathered the turmoil in relative obscurity. As the Cultural Revolution gathered momentum, Dan Di was jailed for a third time, as a "literati traitor to China" (*Hanjian wenren*). Imprisoned for one and a half years for suspected ties with the Guomindang, she was then sentenced to labour in the countryside of Heilongjiang for the remainder of the Cultural Revolution; she was deprived of all rights for over a decade.[41]

Mei Niang's high profile during the Japanese occupation guaranteed her subsequent condemnation as a "literati traitor to China" during the Cultural Revolution.[42] Her assertive character and prominent achievements during the Japanese occupation cost her dearly.[43] For her, the Maoist era passed in a succession of imprisonment, forced labour (including bomb shelter and tunnel excavation in the capital), street cleaning, and work as a housekeeper.[44] During this extended period of hardship, her family shattered: amidst extreme poverty her youngest daughter and her son both died of illness; Mei was informed of the deaths by her eldest daughter, Liu Qing, during visits to the prison.[45] Facing a regime so preoccupied with narrow definitions of collaboration and resistance that it denied any validity to the other voices of dissent that had delegitimized Japan's imperial project from within, Mei endured over two decades of persecution by the Maoists. The assertive, independent character that had served her so well during the Japanese occupation became a hindrance when facing her Maoist accusers.

The Cultural Revolution was also the highpoint of persecution for Zhu Ti's family. Her husband, Li Zhengzhong, was condemned as an anti-revolutionary. At the peak of his persecution, he was forced to wear an "anti-revolutionary" badge on his clothing.[46] Li was sentenced to labour in rural Liaoning from 1969 to 1979; Zhu Ti and their three children accompanied him. Although Li earned nothing, Zhu was allotted a wage for her work, as she had not been convicted of any crime; her small wage packet supported the family of five for ten years.[47] While in retrospect both Li and Zhu admit that great friendships were forged in the countryside, the disruption to their careers and personal lives was devastating.

In 1966, Zuo Di lost her job when *Zhongguo shaonian bao* was closed down and she was investigated for "class" and "historical questions."[48] In 1969, she was sentenced to three months of labour and ended up spending the following six years labouring in rural Hunan, far from her family.[49] In 1970, she was stripped of all party and political rights, and her wages were downgraded three levels. The following year, she was diagnosed with tuberculosis but was forced to continue with labour of reform. In August 1973, although her earlier verdict was repealed, she was expelled from the CCP and her wages were lowered another level. In 1975, suffering from acute liver disease, she was transferred to Beijing for treatment. She died on 20 September 1976, the same day as Mao Zedong.[50]

Almost all of the Manchukuo writers were severely persecuted during the Maoist era. Their families shared in the misfortune. Of the seven couples, only two remained intact, despite separation by prison sentences, to endure into the twenty-first century: Yang Xu and Zhang Hong'en, and Zhu Ti and Li Zhengzhong. The children of all the writers suffered for the youthful ambitions of their mothers and fathers. Most experienced separation from, if not the incarceration of, their parents. Wu Ying's son was raised by his grandmother and was never reconciled with his parents. Mei Niang's elder daughter, Liu Qing, was forced to assume responsibility for her younger siblings when her mother was imprisoned, but the two younger children died in extreme poverty.[51] Dan Di's daughter resented her mother's relentless pursuit of a writing career in the face of ceaseless persecution. All of these children were tainted by their parents' persecution. Most of the writers had, as youths, forged careers in Manchukuo that lasted for less than a decade; they suffered the consequences for the rest of their lives. To this day, the children of Dan Di and Wu Ying refuse any association with their parents' careers.

Following the end of the Maoist era in 1976, socio-political reforms transformed the cultural landscape in China. In 1978, the political verdict against "writers of the enemy occupation" was repealed *in toto*. Since then, scholars in China have begun to reappraise their literary legacy as the writers who had survived struggled to restore their broken family lives and, for several, their careers. Manchukuo literature began to appear in anthologies of Chinese and regional literature, commemorative volumes for luminaries such as Xiao Jun, and in collected works of individual authors. In the 1980s, several of these women began to write again; most penned accounts of their early careers.

Almost unbelievably, upon the reversal of her political verdict, Dan Di resumed writing, to launch the fourth and final phase of her career in 1979. This activity further alienated her daughter, who disapproved of her mother's writing, which she argued had produced only misfortune. Dan Di's husband died in 1981, as she was beginning to resurrect her career. Since the 1980s, her novellas, poems, essays, and diary excerpts have been published in anthologies of modern Chinese literature and were featured in the 1986 volume of women's fiction from Manchukuo, *Changye yinghuo* (*Fireflies of the Long Night*). In 1987, Dan Di lauded Liang Shanding for his work in revising interpretations of her legacy, for "salvaging the withered flowers that had been cast into the bottom of the frozen river."[52] In 1990, Dan Di fell in love and married, moving with her husband to Zhejiang Province, where she penned her still unpublished memoirs, *San ru lianyu* (*Thrice into Purgatory*). She died in 1992.

Mei Niang also resumed writing in the 1980s. Now, seventy years after the publication of her first volume of collected writings, *Xiaojie ji*, she is still active in the literary world of Beijing.[53] She is again attracting critical attention, and her work has been featured in major Chinese literary anthologies and in *Changye yinghuo*. Over the past decade, numerous separate editions of Mei Niang's collected works have been published in Beijing and Hong Kong. In 2001 a volume of tributes from colleagues, scholars, friends, and family was published in Beijing. Her latest volume of collected works, *Mei Niang jin zuo ji shujian* (*Mei Niang: Recent Writings and Correspondence*), was published in 2005. But despite trends towards a less politicized approach to the history of Chinese lives and literature under Japanese occupation, Zhang Quan has warned that the denunciation in the Chinese press in 1996 of the prominent writer Zhang Ailing reveals the still contentious nature of the legacy of "writers of the enemy occupation."[54]

Lan Ling, who emerged from the Cultural Revolution unscathed, retired from *Renmin jiaoyu* in 1986 and remained active with family, archival work, and painting. Recognized as one of Qiqihaer's most famous writers of the twentieth century, she died in 2003. Yang Xu lived in semi-reclusion with her husband, Zhang Hong'en, in Shenyang until her death in 2004. Zhu Ti and Li Zhengzhong currently live in Shenyang; she is retired and he has revived his career as a prominent calligrapher.

Many of the writers who survived the Maoist era lived to see their literary legacies revisited by scholars who questioned the collaboration/resistance dichotomy in Manchukuo. But for all of the progress on the scholarly front, and political recognition by the CCP of the wrongful verdicts of the Maoist era, most Manchukuo writers continue to be written out of, or condemned by, popular memory. As new women and as women writers in Manchukuo, they were roundly criticized in anti-bourgeois, anti-Manchukuo, and anti-Japanese narratives. The construction of post-occupation historical narratives demanded their denunciation as political deviants, models of bourgeois recidivism, or traitors. Today, those few Chinese who still remember their names view them as relics of a past best forgotten. But their tenacious survival skills, despite all odds, and their determination to resume writing careers in the face of relentless persecution suggest the strengths that they relied on to survive Japanese occupation and the "liberations" that have swept China since the mid-1940s. Today in China, few want to think about Manchukuo. Even fewer want to acknowledge the cultural achievements of Manchukuo's most prolific Chinese women writers.

8

Resisting Manchukuo

"LIFE IS WOMEN'S, THE KINGDOM IS WOMEN'S; IT IS NOT HEAVY BUT IT IS A SYSTEM OF DESTRUCTION."

– *Zuo Di, "Nü nan" (Women's Difficulty)*

Manchukuo lasted fourteen years, from 1932 to 1945. Those years constitute an era in which one generation grew to maturity while the life courses of others were permanently altered. But despite the length of the occupation and its manifold ramifications for the people of the region, Manchukuo – especially its gendered foundations – remains for the most part unexamined. The dominant position of the Japanese, the militaristic and racist nature of the state, the Japanese-language publications that it produced, and later the condemnation of all Chinese "collaboration" with the Japanese have contributed to harshly critical evaluations of Manchukuo in most Chinese- and English-language historiography. At the same time, Japanese sources, while focusing on economic and military matters, have revealed little about Chinese cultural life.

The hegemonic position of Japan and Japanese-language sources in the reconstruction of the history of Manchukuo has long overshadowed the records left by the vast majority of the population, the Chinese. Although numerically superior, the Chinese in Manchukuo were thought by scholars to have bequeathed far fewer sources for historical study than the Japanese. Japanese-language publications, as well as statistics gathered and recorded by Japanese organizations, are undeniably valuable for the reconstruction of regional history. But this study argues that viable Chinese-language sources also exist, and I have focused on Chinese women's writings in the Chinese-language books, journals, and newspapers produced within Manchukuo's borders. Although many contemporary Japanese celebrated Manchukuo's Chinese population for "turning Japanese," the sources of this study suggest that significant numbers of women in Manchukuo were alienated from officially sanctioned Japan-centric ideals and that these women self-identified in ways that stressed their essential Chineseness. For these women, at least, May

Fourth–inspired cultural ideals proved stronger than Japan's cultural, economic, or military might.

Several factors have undermined the perceived value of the literature of the enemy occupation, in particular the writings of the women under discussion here, for understanding the Chinese experience of Japanese imperialism. In China, popular fiction was long thought to have little value, historical or otherwise. Confucian maxims that directed women to internal household matters meant that their writings, regardless of artistic merit, were believed to have little political relevance, a belief that Manchukuo's cultural functionaries appear to have embraced. But the May Fourth movement revolutionized literature, investing it with a power that continues to inform Chinese literary production and the interpretation of it. Since May Fourth, literary forms that have failed to meet prescribed political criteria have been dismissed or condemned by various political movements. In the Maoist era, popular literary styles of preliberation China, such as the Mandarin Duck and Butterfly schools, the "bourgeois" work produced by writers such as Ding Ling, and especially the literature of the enemy occupation, were all shunted aside. All literature produced in Manchukuo, after the departure of the exiled faction, was perceived as tainted by its "colonial" genesis and was removed from circulation. Today, Manchukuo's Chinese-language literary legacy remains largely forgotten. Lan Ling, Mei Niang, Yang Xu, and Zhu Ti have all reasoned that young people in China at the turn of the twenty-first century are more interested in economics than culture and are repelled by the supposedly maudlin nature of their work.[1] This study argues, however, that the legacies of Manchukuo's Chinese women writers have much to contribute to the understanding of Chinese experiences of Japanese imperialism. Their legacies also attest to the strengths of early Republican cultural ideals.

In Manchukuo, social realism emerged as the most favoured literary form, as it did in Japanese-occupied Taiwan. Social realism enabled writers to vent political frustration while exploring issues of personal identity. Exposing reality became a popular tool with which to entertain and influence readers, to question Japanese colonial authority, and to articulate individual ideals of modernity. If writers were to publish at all, they had to engage in cooperative relationships with colonial institutions. But such cooperation by no means guaranteed the writers' respect for colonial authority. Writers in Manchukuo and Taiwan were separated geographically, but they shared similar literary styles. In Taiwan, colonial literature embodied a renewed search for self-identity and a yearning for independence. In Manchukuo, the most prolific Chinese women writers engaged in similar critiques as they rejected the conservative Confucian ideals of womanhood advocated by officials in Manchukuo and in the Republic. Unwittingly, writers in both territories contributed to their own destruction by portraying contemporary society as unrelentingly oppressive, thereby throwing questionable light on their own successes. Remarkably, regardless of the critical nature of their writings and the different political contexts, writers in Manchukuo and Taiwan were condemned in the postliberation period as "traitors." Paradoxically, Japanese occupation allowed for a plurality of voices that for decades was not tolerated after liberation, whether by Chinese Communist Party or Guomindang administrations.

In many ways, the lives of Manchukuo's Chinese women writers parallel that of twentieth-century China's most famous woman writer, Ding Ling. In their youth, all pursued overtly independent paths, chose their own mates, and engaged in feminist critiques of contemporary society. By doing so, they chose not to conform to dominant social mores. But they did reflect the anxieties that stirred youth in Republican China during the May Fourth era to condemn patriarchy, social conservatism, and China's semi-colonial status. Feminist writings were later condemned by the Maoist state as bourgeois. Ding Ling, although acclaimed throughout the socialist world for her novel *Taiyang zhaozai sanggan he shang* (*The Sun Shines over the Sanggan River*) (1951), was sentenced to twenty years of labour reform in the Northeast. Although her work lauded socialism and she showed unassailable patriotism, the Maoist state persecuted her for bourgeois behaviour and declared her writing unfit for consumption. Thus Ding Ling, a vocal advocate of challenging the subordinate status of women, found herself, like her Manchukuo compatriots, on the front line of criticism. She was targeted by Leftists, social conservatives, and, indeed, anyone with a grudge to bear. During the Maoist period, May Fourth emphasis on the individual and feminist discourses were denounced as bourgeois. Those who had most vociferously pursued the ideals of women's emancipation saw their lives and careers fall to ruin.

The Chinese women writers who rose to prominence in Manchukuo consciously emulated Ding Ling and their self-exiled predecessor, Xiao Hong. All were raised in Manchuria, weaned on May Fourth ideals of women's emancipation, and fired by idealism. In their natal homes, they were nurtured by ideals and literary influences that reflected contemporary norms in the rest of China, the hardships of life in Manchuria, and a dominating Japanese presence. They were repulsed by the conservative constructs of the good wife, wise mother through which Manchukuo officials promoted their *Wangdao* vision of modernity. May Fourth renunciation of political autocracy, imperialism, and patriarchy predisposed the women to reject the conservative Confucian ideals of womanhood advocated both by the Manchukuo and Republican governments in the 1930s. My interpretation of their writings stresses the perseverance in Manchukuo of the May Fourth cultural criticism that had energized urban Republican society during the early 1920s. Gendered identities, girded by Chinese ideals of modernity, undermined Japanese efforts to sever ties between Chinese residing in Japanese-occupied areas and those in the rest of China. A direct correlation exists between the patriarchal foundations of Japan's imperial project and these women's alienation: they defined themselves as modern women within and, even more importantly, *against* the Manchukuo cultural agenda.

The women discussed in this study graduated from Manchukuo's education system, forged careers in Manchukuo's literary world, and worked closely with the Japanese, all the while repulsed by what they identified as the regime's male chauvinist, oppressive foundations. Yang Xu clearly articulated the "wild horse character" that propelled these women into their oppositional stances.[2] Dan Di, Lan Ling, Mei Niang, Wu Ying, Yang Xu, Zhu Ti, and Zuo Di deployed and were constituted by the May Fourth ideals that they espoused from within Manchukuo. These writers epitomized the new women that their conservative counterparts railed against. Each of them cooperated to some extent with the Japanese, but their work did not legitimate the Manchukuo state or its cultural agenda. The harsh nature of Manchukuo rule left little, if any, room for progressive-minded Chinese women to engage in the type of active "collaborationism" of which they were later accused in the Maoist era. Colonial officials promoted a conservative Confucianism that the women vociferously rejected even though they came to realize many of its essential elements. In their writings, they explicitly condemn not only Manchukuo's patriarchal foundations but also the subjugation of the masses. That they were allowed to engage in such critical discourses for most of the occupation is a testament to colonial officials' low regard for, and lax attitude towards, women writers and their activities.

Ties between the women intersected on many levels. While still in school, many met or learned of each other. In their respective writings, they strove for similar goals: to describe and expose the reality of women's lives in Manchukuo. At work, Wu Ying promoted younger women like Zuo Di, introducing her to various facets of literary production as well as to her future husband, Liang Shanding. Liang was a colleague of Dan Di, Mei Niang, Wu Ying, and Yang Xu. Mei Niang cultivated relationships with Dan Di, Lan Ling, Wu Ying, and Zhu Ti that lasted a lifetime. Their lives were structured by ideals of women's emancipation that entered public debate in Manchuria before the Japanese occupation began. Those ideals were also shared by sympathetic Japanese intellectuals, who lent Manchukuo's Chinese writers a legitimacy that in turn complicated the ways in which colonial officials could treat them. Manchukuo culture was greatly enriched by these women and their partners. Young Chinese writers in Manchukuo cultivated their careers with a flourish that challenges received interpretations of the colony as a cultural wasteland. But the professional successes that they achieved ultimately proved as injurious to them as the failings of officialdom did to the Manchukuo state.

The official denigration of new woman idealism in Manchukuo undermined the achievement of Manchukuo modernity. The conservative *Wangdao* ideal that colonial officials promised would deliver the region from the evils of warlordism, fascism, and communism through the creation of the most modern social order in the world was at odds with the most visible emblem of modernity in their midst, the new woman. This contradiction was not unique to Manchukuo. In Vichy France, too, state policies "seemed to disregard the realities of the professional, scholastic, and intellectual situation of French women in 1939 and that had evolved since the nineteenth century."[3] In Manchukuo, a retrogressive political platform precluded officialdom's acceptance of the new women's ideological stance or the accurate interpretion of their work. Manchukuo officials viewed male writers as potential troublemakers but their female counterparts as harmless. This misogynistic attitude enabled the women to engage in simultaneously cooperative and subversive intellectual activities. As young adults, they worked in close association with colonial institutions, which failed to adequately gauge the political implications of their work, thereby freeing the writers to engage in wide-ranging critiques of Manchukuo. Despite the development of a weighty regulatory framework and a commensurate bureaucratic apparatus to survey cultural production, officials in Manchukuo never gained the absolute control that they sought over the Chinese literary world. A constantly expanding framework of literary regulations, which was loudly trumpeted but achieved seemingly few results, had the unintended effect of encouraging even greater transgression by the most prolific Chinese women writers. As a result, Manchukuo's Chinese-language literary world has bequeathed a rich legacy that exposes weaknesses of Japanese colonial rule and the tenacity of Chinese new women ideals.

Manchukuo's state structure has long been described as both "fascist" (*faxisi*) and "bogus" (*wei*). These labels reveal a central contradiction in Japan's imperial project in Manchukuo: it was simultaneously overweening and undergirded. Japanese rule over the Chinese-language literary world in Manchukuo was uneven and compartmentalized. This unevenness produced an environment of fear and freedom for Manchukuo writers. As writers engaged in what they knew to be prohibited activities, none could be certain if or when the proverbial knock on the door would finish her or his career.[4] In Manchukuo, socially progressive Chinese writers whetted the appetite of the reading public for fundamental socioeconomic change. Women writers used the space relegated to them to denounce the inequities of colonial society, from within. In Manchukuo, as in Vichy France, women were "to be 'mobilized' but not given power."[5] Especially during the Sacred War, officialdom sought women's submission and orderly deployment. But the most prolific Chinese women writers demanded parity with men while struggling against a conservative cultural agenda that refused their fundamental equality. In the post-occupation period, the women were condemned for their focus on issues that were of direct relevance to them as women and individuals living in a patriarchal oppressive state – instead of on national subjugation or class warfare. Their outspoken, anti-patriarchal stances, and their seeming inability to live like most of their contemporaries, drew visceral reactions in the Maoist era. Ironically, the women who forthrightly discredited a misogynous Japanese colonial state that paid them little heed were silenced by a Chinese regime that was vociferously committed to women's liberation. Officials in Manchukuo did not credit women for the political power emanating from their pens, but their Maoist counterparts appreciated that writers, female *and* male, were potentially dangerous. Those who were most successful during the Japanese occupation thus became convenient lightning rods for the political forces that they had played no small part in unleashing.

The literary promise evident in the women's early careers was shattered during the Maoist era. Unlike Zhang Ailing, who spent her post-occupation life in Taiwan and the United States – and became known as one of the greatest Chinese writers of the twentieth century – these women were effectively silenced. Their careers were cut short by a Chinese regime that dictated control over historical narratives, and by a population that was eager to put the region's colonial heritage behind them. Their literary legacies were rejected as part of a humiliating colonial and bourgeois past. Both the historical context and content of Manchukuo literature has made such work less appealing than other contemporary work by authors such as Zhang Ailing, whose writings are perceived to be less "political." By working within Manchukuo institutions to reveal the dark reality of contemporary life, the women irreparably sullied their postcolonial reputations.

The final paradox of the legacies of Dan Di, Lan Ling, Mei Niang, Wu Ying, Yang Xu, Zhu Ti, and Zuo Di is that they enjoyed far greater freedom, personally and professionally, during Manchukuo than during the liberation of Maoist China. Their literary legacy reveals a freedom that belies both Manchukuo's substantial regulatory framework and the dark and negative content of their writing. This was the result not of magnanimous Japanese rule but rather of ineffectual and misogynistic colonial practices. By tolerating their writings, or viewing them as inconsequential, colonial officials effectively encouraged the women to flourish as cultural critics. Their success was not to be repeated. Yet though their literary legacy is largely forgotten, it retains relevance for Chinese society. Their portraits of society in tumult, of the menacing power of money and foreigners, and of the continued, inexplicable devaluation of women all strike a responsive, albeit bleak, chord more than half a century after the collapse of Manchukuo. In the twenty-first century, as the People's Republic of China looks for tools to bridge divides between Chinese regions and heal the wounds of the twentieth century, the literary legacy of women writers during the Japanese occupation of Manchuria has much to offer.

Notes

Introduction

1 Mei Niang is the pen name of Sun Jiarui. Her other pen names include Fang Zi, Lao Xia, Liu Qingniang, Lu Yin, Min Zi, and Sun Minzi.

2 *Nan Ling bei Mei* was coined by Beijing's Madezeng and Shanghai's Yuzhoufeng bookstores after a contest to determine the most popular contemporary Chinese woman writer. Shangguan Yin, "Wo suo zhidao de Mei Niang" (All That I Know about Mei Niang) in Shangguan Yin, *Shu hua* (*Talking about Books*) (Changchun: Jilin renmin chubanshe, 2001), 33.

3 Manchukuo is the most common romanization of Manzhouguo and, after 1934, Manzhoudiguo; it is also spelled Manchoukuo. The name highlighted the state's regional distinction as a Manchu homeland and stressed its autonomy from the rest of China.

4 Edward Gunn Jr., *Unwelcome Muse: Chinese Literature in Shanghai and Peking, 1937-45* (New York: Columbia University Press, 1980), 279n92.

5 Dan Di is one of the pen names of Tian Lin. She also went by An Di, Luo Li, Ma'dini, Ma'erhua, Maruo, Shan Ying, Tian Xiang, Xi Xi, and Xiao Xi.

6 Lan Ling is one of the pen names of Zhu Zhenhua. She also went by Ah Hua and Li Suo.

7 Wu Ying is one of the pen names of Wu Yuying. She also went by Xiao Ying and Yingzi.

8 Yang Xu is one of the pen names of Yang Suanzhi. She also went by Ah Jiao and Jiao Fei.

9 Zhu Ti is the pen name of Zhang Xingjuan; others include Xingzi.

10 Zuo Di is the pen name of Zuo Xixian; others include Ba'er, He Qi, Hong Ping, Jin Tanzhi, Luo Mai, Yue Di, Zuo Xin, and Zuo Yi.

11 Margaret Atwood, *Survival: A Thematic Guide to Canadian Literature* (Toronto: Anansi, 1972), 18-19.

12 For a contemporary analysis of this work, see Liang [Shan Ding], "Cong *Xiaojie ji* dao *Di'er dai*" (From *Young Lady's Collection* to *The Second Generation*) in Mei Niang, *Di'er dai* (*The Second Generation*) (Xinjing: Wencong han xinghui, 1940), 1-4.

Chapter 1: Chinese Women and Cultural Production in a Japanese Colonial Context

1 Fengtian, also known as Mukden, was the contemporary name of Shenyang. The term Manchuria is increasingly associated with foreign, imperialist designs on the region. See Gavin McCormack, *Chang Tso-lin in Northeast China, 1911-1928* (Stanford: Stanford University Press, 1977), 4. Manchuria is used in this work as the most common contemporary international term for the territory; the Northeast will be used in reference to the post-1945 period, when the term Manchuria fell into wide disfavour.

2 Yamamuro Shin'ichi, *Manchuria under Japanese Dominion*, trans. Joshua A. Fogel (Philadelphia: University of Pennsylvania Press, 2006), 4.

3 David D. Buck, "Railway City and National Capital: Two Faces of the Modern in Changchun," in *Remaking the Chinese City: Modernity and National Identity, 1900-1950*, ed. Joseph W. Esherick (Honolulu: University of Hawai'i Press, 2000), 86-7.

4 Lü Qinwen, "Dongbei lunxian qu de wailai wenxue yu xiangtu wenxue" (External and Local Literature of the Northeast Occupied Territories), in *Zhongri zhanzheng yu wenxue* (*Sino-Japanese War and Literature*), ed. Yamada Keizō and Lü Kangming (Changchun: Dongbei shifan daxue chubanshe, 1992), 152.

5 Timothy Brook, *Collaboration: Japanese Agents and Local Elites in Wartime China* (Cambridge, MA: Harvard University Press, 2005), 4, 7.

6 Ibid., 26.

7 Ibid., 12.

8 Ibid., 8.

9 David Barrett, "Introduction: Occupied China and the Limits of Accomodation," in *Chinese Collaboration with Japan, 1937-45: The Limits of Accommodation*, ed. David P. Barrett and Larry N. Shyu (Stanford: Stanford University Press, 2001), 17.

10 Ibid., 17.

11 Ibid., 8.

12 Ibid.

13 Ibid., 9, 10. Timothy Brook provides a more complete analysis of this term. Brook, *Collaboration*, 20.

14 Nicholas B. Dirks, "Introduction," in *Colonialism and Culture*, ed. Nicholas Dirks (Ann Arbor: University of Michigan Press, 1992), 2.

15 Werner Rings, *Life with the Enemy: Collaboration and Resistance in Hitler's Europe, 1939-1945*, trans. J. Maxwell Brownjohn (London: Weidenfeld and Nicolson, 1979), 11.

16 Ibid., 73, 86, 106, 128.

17 Ibid., 153, 162, 172, 189, 229.

18 Keith Schoppa, "Patterns and Dynamics of Elite Collaboration in Occupied Shaoxing County," in Barrett and Shyu, eds., *Chinese Collaboration*, 157.

19 Ibid., 178.

20 Ibid., 157, 158.

21 Ibid., 177.

22 Ibid., 179.

23 John Hunter Boyle, *China and Japan at War, 1937-1945: The Politics of Collaboration* (Stanford: Stanford University Press, 1972), 6.

24 Lo Jiu-jung, "Survival as Justification for Collaboration, 1937-1945," in Barrett and Shyu, eds., *Chinese Collaboration*, 130.

25 Cited in Boyle, *China and Japan at War*, 355.

26 James H. Carter, *Creating a Chinese Harbin: Nationalism in an International City, 1916-1932* (Ithaca, NY: Cornell University Press, 2002), 3.

27 Ibid.

28 For example, see Mitter's case study of Ma Zhanshan. Rana Mitter, *The Manchurian Myth: Nationalism, Resistance, and Collaboration in Modern China* (Berkeley: University of California Press, 2000), 203-24. Quotation from p. 3.

29 Ibid., 228.

30 Ibid., 225.

31 Prasenjit Duara, *Sovereignty and Authenticity: Manchukuo and the East Asian Modern* (Lanham, MD: Rowman and Littlefield, 2003), 59.

32 Ibid., 76.

33 Ibid., 3.

34 Michael Adas, "From Avoidance to Confrontation: Peasant Protest in Pre-Colonial and Colonial South-East Asia," in Dirks, ed., *Colonialism and Culture*, 116-17.

35 Cited in Margaret Weitz, *Sisters in the Resistance: How Women Fought to Free France* (New York: J. Wiley, 1995), 8.

36 Margaret Atack, *Literature and the French Resistance* (Manchester: Manchester University Press, 1989), 4-5.

37 Poshek Fu, *Passivity, Resistance, and Collaboration: Intellectual Choices in Occupied Shanghai, 1937-45* (Stanford: Stanford University Press, 1993), xiv.

38 Ibid., 10.

39 Poshek Fu, "Resistance in Collaboration: Chinese Cinema in Occupied Shanghai, 1941-1945," in Barrett and Shyu, eds., *Chinese Collaboration*, 197.

40 Ibid., 181.

41 Ibid., 183.

42 Ibid., 186.

43 Ibid., 197.

44 Margaret Rossiter, *Women in the Resistance* (New York: Praeger, 1986), 147; Xu Naixiang and Huang Wanhua, *Zhongguo kangzhan shiqi lunxianqu wenxue shi* (*History of the Literature of the Enemy-Occupied Territories during China's War of Resistance*) (Fuzhou: Fujian jiaoyu chubanshe, 1995), 5.

45 Triolet and Aragon were early members of the French Communist Party. Triolet won France's prestigious Goncourt prize for literature in 1945, and Aragon has been lauded as the premier poet of wartime France. Max Adereth, *Elsa Triolet and Louis Aragon* (Lampeter, UK: Edwin Mellen Press, 1994), 240.

46 Edward Gunn Jr., *Unwelcome Muse: Chinese Literature in Shanghai and Peking, 1937-45*, (New York: Columbia University Press, 1980), 50.

47 Ibid., 3.

48 Ibid., 5.

49 Ibid., 51.

50 Leo Ching, *Becoming Japanese: Colonial Taiwan and the Politics of Identity Formation* (Berkeley: University of California Press, 2001), 8.

51 Cited in ibid., 114.

52 "Kōmin" is a derivative of Japan's "kōminka" (imperialization) movement (1937-45) in Taiwan. Ching argues that the *kōminka* movement should be viewed as a radical departure from Japan's previous emphasis on *doka* (assimilation). Ibid., 89-91, 96, 176.

53 Ibid., 129.

54 Sheng Ying, *Ershi shiji Zhongguo nüxing wenxueshi* (*History of Twentieth-Century Chinese Women's Literature*) (Tianjin: Tianjin renmin chubanshe, 1995), 11.

55 Shangguan Ying, "Dongbei lunxian shiqi wenxue ceying" (Profile of the Northeast's Enemy-Occupied Territory's Literature), in Shangguan Ying, *Yiwen luantan* (*Random Notes on Literature and Art*) (Changchun: Shidai wenyi chubanshe, 1989), 102.

56 Zhang Quan, "Wei wanjie de huati: Luxianqu wenxue de zhengzhi pingjia" (Unfinished Conversation: Political Evaluation of Enemy-Occupied Territory Literature), in *Mei Niang xiaoshuo sanwen ji* (*Mei Niang's Collected Fiction and Essays*), ed. Zhang Quan (Beijing: Beijing chubanshe, 1997), 494.

57 Ibid.

58 Ibid., 493.

59 For example, *Nan Ling Bei Mei* (*The South Has Zhang Ailing, The North Has Mei Niang*) (1989); *Mei Niang xiaoshuo sanwen ji* (*Mei Niang's Collected Novels and Essays*) (1997); *Xunzhao Meiniang* (*Searching the World of Mei Niang*) (1998); *Mei Niang xiaoshuo: Huanghun zhi xian* (*Mei Niang's*

Short Stories: Dusk Offerings) (1999); *Mei Niang jin zuo ji shujian* (*Mei Niang: Recent Writings and Correspondence*)(2005); and Zuo Di's *Luo Mai xiaoshuo sanwen ji* (*Luo Mai's Collected Short Stories and Essays*) (1990).

60 Liang Shanding, "Dai xue chong han zhe nen huang" (Carrying Snow, Dashing into the Cold, Turning Yellow), in *Changye yinghuo* (*Fireflies of the Long Night*), ed. Liang Shanding (Shenyang: Chunfeng wenyi chubanshe, 1986), 1-2, 5-6.

61 For example, Feng Weiqun, Wang Jianzhong, Li Chunyan, and Li Shuquan, eds., *Dongbei lunxian shiqi wenxue guoji xueshu yantaohui lunwenji* (*Collection of Papers from the International Symposium on Literature of the Enemy-Occupied Northeast*) (Shenyang: Shenyang Chubanshe, 1992).

62 Prasenjit Duara, "Local Worlds: The Poetics and Politics of Native Place in Modern China," *South Atlantic Quarterly* 99, no. 1 (2000): 31.

63 See Atack, *Literature and the French Resistance*, 23; Paula Schwartz, "Redefining Resistance: Women's Activism in Wartime France," in *Behind the Lines: Gender and the Two World Wars*, ed. Margaret Randolph Higonnet et al. (New Haven, CT: Yale University Press, 1987), 142-3.

64 Brook, *Collaboration*, 23.

65 Weitz, *Sisters in the Resistance*, 12; Xu and Huang, *Zhongguo kangzhan shiqi lunxianqu wenxue shi*, 5.

66 Miranda Pollard, *Reign of Virtue: Mobilizing Gender in Vichy France* (Chicago: University of Chicago Press, 1998), 33.

67 Ibid., 46; Wang Yeping, *Dongbei lunxian shisinian jiaoyushi* (*The History of Education in the Northeast's Fourteen Years of Enemy Occupation*) (Changchun: Jilin jiaoyu chubanshe, 1989), 114.

68 Francine Muel-Dreyfus, *Vichy and the Eternal Feminine: A Contribution to a Political Sociology of Gender*, trans. Kathleen A. Johnson (Durham, NC: Duke University Press, 2001), 311.

69 Pollard, *Reign of Virtue* 42.

70 Ibid.

71 Ibid., 49.

72 Ibid.

73 Ibid., 75.

74 Jennifer Milligan, *The Forgotten Generation: French Women Writers of the Inter-War Period* (Oxford: Berg, 1996), 212.

75 Muel-Dreyfus, *Vichy and the Eternal Feminine*, 32.

76 Mei Niang, personal interview, Beijing, 13 November 2000.

77 Cited in Liang, "Dai," 2.

78 Weitz, *Sisters in the Resistance*, 7.

79 Rey Chow, *Woman and Chinese Modernity: The Politics of Reading between West and East* (Minneapolis: University of Minnesota Press, 1991), 170.

80 Chow terms this "a dialectic of resistance-in-givenness that is constitutive of modernity in a non-Western, but Westernized context." Ibid.

81 Nicole Huang, *Women, War, Domesticity: Shanghai Literature and Popular Culture of the 1940s* (Leiden: Brill, 2005), 34.

82 Ibid., 19.

83 Ibid., 17.

84 Ibid., 21.

85 Lydia Liu, *Translingual Practice: Literature, National Culture, and Translated Modernity: China, 1900-1937* (Stanford: Stanford University Press, 1995), 290.

86 Lydia Liu, "The Female Body and Nationalist Discourse: Manchuria in Xiao Hong's *Field of Life and Death*," in *Body, Subject and Power*, ed. Angela Zito and Tani E. Barlow (Chicago: University of Chicago Press, 1994), 64.

87 Ibid., 66.

88 Xiao Hong has attracted the greatest scholarly attention in the West as well. For example, see Howard Goldblatt, *Hsiao Hung* (Boston: Twayne, 1976).

89 Zhang Yumao, "Ping *Changye yinghuo*" (A Critique of *Fireflies of the Long Night*), in Zhang Yumao, *Zhe tuan huo, zhe zhen feng* (*This Ball of Fire, This Gust of Wind*) (Shenyang: Shenyang chubanshe, 2000), 469.

90 For example, see Shangguan Yin, "Wo suo zhidao de Mei Niang" (All That I Know about Mei Niang), in *Shuhua (Talking about Books)* (Changchun: Jilin renbin chubansh, 2001), 33-6.

91 Xu and Huang, *Zhongguo kangzhan,* 5.

92 Ibid., 282.

93 Shen Dianhe and Huang Wanhua, *Dongbei lunxian shiqi wenxue shilun* (*Historical Discourses on the Literature of the Enemy Occupation of the Northeast*) (Harbin: Beifang wenyi chuabanshe, 1991), 70.

94 Liu Aihua, "Gudu de wudao: Dongbei luxian shiqi nüxing zuojia qunti xiaoshuo lun" (The Lonely Dance Floor: A Discussion of the Colonial Fiction of Women Writers from the Northeast Enemy Occupation Period) (PhD diss., Beijing shifan daxue, 1999), 137.

95 Feng Weiqun and Li Chunyan, *Dongbei lunxian shiqi wenxue xinlun* (*New Discourse on the Literature of the Northeast Occupation Era*) (Changchun: Jilin daxue chubanshe, 1991), 270.

Chapter 2: Foundations of Colonial Rule in Manchukuo and the "Woman Question"

1 Hsinking, Bureau of Information, ed., *An Outline of the Manchoukuo Empire, 1939* (Dairen: Manchoukuo Daily News, 1939), 22.

2 *Manchoukuo Yearbook: 1941* (Hsinking: Manchoukuo Yearbook Company, 1942), 136-7.

3 Louise Young, *Japan's Total Empire* (Berkeley: University of California Press, 1998), 92.

4 Kishi Nobosuke, cited in Yamamuro Shin'ichi, *Manchuria under Japanese Dominion,* trans. Joshua A. Fogel (Philadelphia: University of Pennsylvania Press, 2006), 4.

5 Toshio Tamura, "On Cultural Administration," *Manchoukuo Today*, no. 6. (1940): 2.

6 For a recent, concise explanation of Ishiwara's thought, see Yamamuro, *Manchuria*, 31-4.

7 Cited in Oka Yoshitake, *Konoe Fumimaro* (Tokyo: University of Tokyo Press, 1983), 2.

8 Cited in Prasenjit Duara, *Sovereignty and Authenticity: Manchukuo and the East Asian Modern* (Lanham, MD: Rowman and Littlefield, 2003), 62.

9 Young, *Japan's Total Empire*, 93, 106.

10 This image is featured in an advertisement entitled "Five Races United" in *Contemporary Manchuria* 3, no. 4 (1939): 22.

11 For example, see Yamamuro, *Manchuria*, 200.

12 For example, see *Outline of the Manchoukuo Empire*, 111-18. The use of "Manchoukuoan" is also discussed in James H. Carter, *Creating a Chinese Harbin: Nationalism in an International City, 1916-1932* (Ithaca, NY: Cornell University Press, 2002), 188-9.

13 Gavan McCormack, *Chang Tso-lin in Northeast China, 1911-1928* (Stanford: Stanford University Press, 1977), 7.

14 Diana Lary and Thomas Gottschang, *Swallows and Settlers* (Ann Arbor: University of Michigan Press, 2000), 134.

15 Ibid., 16.

16 Louise Young, "Imagined Empire: The Cultural Construction of Manchukuo," in *The Japanese Wartime Empire, 1931-45*, ed. Peter Duus, Ramon H. Myers, and Mark R. Peattie (Princeton, NJ: Princeton University Press, 1996), 88. Contemporary targets are outlined in *Sixth Report on Progress in Manchuria to 1939* (Dairen: South Manchuria Railway Company, 1939), 117.

17 Young, *Japan's Total Empire*, 45.

18 Ann Kinney, *Japanese Investment in Manchuria* (New York: Garland Publishing, 1982), 5.

19 Ann Kinney recounts how the majority of funding came from inflationary financing and Japanese investment; local investment in 1939 accounted for only 16 per cent. See ibid., 3-5, 93.

20 See Young, *Japan's Total Empire*, 196.

21 Kinney, *Japanese Investment in Manchuria*, 93.

22 Ramon H. Myers, "Creating a Modern Enclave Economy: The Economic Integration of Japan, Manchuria, and North China, 1932-45," in Duus et al., eds., *Japanese Wartime Empire*, 138.

23 *Japan Today and Tomorrow: 1938* (Osaka: Osaka Mainichi, 1939), 82.

24 A recent, concise account of Japanese attempts at integration can be found in Rana Mitter, *The Manchurian Myth: Nationalism, Resistance, and Collaboration in Modern China* (Berkeley: University of California Press, 2000), 72-81.

25 For an account of 1937 changes, see *Sixth Report on Progress in Manchuria to 1939*, 117. Mark Peattie has termed the Manchukuo regime "military fascist." Mark Peattie, *Ishiwara Kanji and Japan's Confrontation with the West* (Princeton, NJ: Princeton University Press, 1975), 253-4.

26 Duara, *Sovereignty*, 73.

27 This organization was created to organize the wives of the senior army and government officials. Liu Jinghui, *Minzu, xingbie yu jieceng* (*Nation, gender and social stratum*)(Beijing: Shehui kexue xenxian chubanshe, 2004), 21-2.

28 For a contemporary account, see *Outline of the Manchoukuo Empire*, 22-4. A recent examination can be found in Yamamuro, *Manchuria*, 78-80.

29 H.G.W. Woodhead notes the vehement reaction against the "Three People's Principles" that occurred in interviews with colonial officials in Xinjing in 1932. See H.G.W. Woodhead, *A Visit to Manchukuo* (Shanghai: Mercury Press, 1932), 23.

30 Austin Fulton, *Through Earthquake, Wind, and Fire* (Edinburgh: Saint Andrew Press, 1967), 19.

31 Ichiro, *Oriental Lullaby*, in *Concordia and Culture in Manchoukuo* (Xinjing: Manchuria Daily News, 1938), 31.

32 Ibid., 18.

33 Liu, *Minzu, xingbie yu jieceng*, 6-7.

34 Duara, *Sovereignty*, 147.

35 Owen Lattimore, *Manchuria: Cradle of Conflict* (New York: Macmillan, 1935), 312.

36 Jin Xunmin argues that there is a connection between their "dark" writings and *Wangdao* ideals. See Jin Xunmin, "Zuo ri de huang hua, 'Qiutu' de beige: Dongbei lunxian shiqi wenxue zai renshi" (Yesterday's Yellow Flowers, the Sad Melody of "Prisoners": Understanding Again the Literature of the Northeast Enemy Occupation Era), in *Dongbei lunxian shiqi wenxue guoji xueshu yantaohui lunwenji* (*Collection of Papers from the International Symposium on Literature of the Enemy-Occupied Northeast*), ed. Feng Weiqun, Wang Jianzhong, Li Chunyan, and Li Shuquan (Shenyang: Shenyang chubanshe, 1992), 27-40.

37 Pamela Crossley, *The Manchus* (Cambridge, MA: Blackwell, 1997), 27.

38 Young, "Imagined Empire," 91.

39 Kazeta Eiki, "Wei Manzhouguo wenyi zhangye de fazhan" (The Development of Bogus Manchukuo's Literary Rules and Regulations), in Feng et al., eds., *Dongbei lunxian shiqi wenxue guoji xueshu yantaohui lunwenji*, 37.

40 For women, education stressed morality, patriotism, and hygiene. See Liu, *Minzu, xingbie yu jieceng*, 32.

41 Fulton, *Through Earthquake, Wind, and Fire*, 90.

42 *Manchoukuo Yearbook: 1941*, 682-3.

43 Cited in Yamamuro, *Manchuria*, 177.

44 Fulton, *Through Earthquake, Wind, and Fire*, 86.

45 Christina Gilmartin, *Engendering the Chinese Revolution: Radical Women, Communist Politics, and Mass Movements in the 1920s* (Berkeley: University of California Press, 1995), 19.

46 Sally Borthwick, "Changing Concepts of the Role of Women from the Late Qing to the May Fourth Period," in *Ideal and Reality: Social and Political Change in Modern China, 1860-1949*, ed. David Pong and Edmund Fung (Lanham, MD: University Press of America, 1985), 75.

47 Gilmartin, *Engendering the Chinese Revolution*, 22.

48 Wang Zheng, *Women in the Chinese Enlightenment: Oral and Textual Histories* (Berkeley: University of California Press, 1999), 4.

49 Leo Oufan Lee, "Modernity and Its Discontents: The Cultural Agenda of the May Fourth Movement," in *Perspectives on Modern China: Four Anniversaries*, ed. Kenneth Lieberthal et al. (Armonk, NY: M.E. Sharpe, 1991), 158-9, 165.

50 Yü Ying-shih, "Neither Renaissance nor Enlightenment," in *The Appropriation of Cultural Capital: China's May Fourth Project*, ed. Milena Dolezelova-Velingerova and Oldrich Kral (Cambridge, MA: Harvard University Press, 2001), 307.

51 Vera Schwarcz, *The Chinese Enlightenment: Intellectuals and the Legacy of the May Fourth Movement of 1919* (Berkeley: University of California Press, 1986), 6.

52 Ibid., 83, 84.

53 Luo Jialun, "Reply to Mr. Zhang Puquan," cited in ibid., 94.

54 Yü, "Neither Renaissance nor Enlightenment," 320.

55 The "Enlightenment" was sparked by the December Ninth incident (1935) and lasted throughout 1936-7. Ibid., 303.

56 Schwarcz, *Chinese Enlightenment*, 226.

57 Ibid., 231.

58 Ibid., 117.

59 Wang, *Women in the Chinese Enlightenment*, 20.

60 Cited in Schwarcz, *Chinese Enlightenment*, 116.

61 Cited in Wang, *Women in the Chinese Enlightenment*, 45.

62 Schwarcz, *Chinese Enlightenment*, 218.

63 Ibid., 114.

64 Ibid., 115.

65 Wang, *Women in the Chinese Enlightenment*, 16.

66 Ibid., 128.

67 Ibid., 121.

68 Cited in Liu, *Minzu, xingbie yu jieceng*, 256.

69 Vera Mackie, *Creating Socialist Women in Japan: Gender, Labour, and Activism, 1900-1937* (Cambridge: Cambridge University Press, 1997), 162.

70 Ibid.

71 Ibid., 28.

72 Patricia Tsurumi, "Visions of Women and the New Society in Conflict: Yamakawa Kikue versus Takamure Itsue," in *Japan's Competing Modernities: Issues in Culture and Democracy, 1900-1930*, ed. Sharon A. Minichiello (Honolulu: University of Hawai'i Press, 1998), 342.

73 Ibid., 93.

74 Ibid., 144.

75 Carter, *Creating a Chinese Harbin*, 62-3.

76 This is evident throughout the transcript of a women's conference in Xinjing, 2 August 1941. "Nimen zhidao ma? Qingnian nüxing de lixiang huoban shi jianchuan nüxing de xin keti" (Do You Know? Women's Ideal Partner Is a Healthy Women's New Topic), *Xin Manzhou* 3, no. 10 (1941): 55.

77 Duara, *Sovereignty*, 160.

78 Xiu Wen, *Butong de nüxing* (*Different Women*), in *Xin Manzhou* 2, no. 4 (1940): 155.

79 Bai Wu, "Funü yu wenhua" (Women and Culture), *Daban Huawen meiri* 8, no. 8 (7 December 1941): 29.

80 *Ershi shiji de guniang* (*Twentieth-Century Girl*), in *Xin Manzhou* 2, no. 2 (1940): 148.

81 *Qiuhun* (*Marriage Offer*), in *Xin Manzhou* 3, no. 10 (1941): 115.

82 These illustrations are from a series of articles on officially sanctioned ideals of women in *Qingnian wenhua* 1, no. 3 (1943): 32-6.

83 *Manchoukuo Yearbook: 1941*, 677.

84 Wang Yeping, *Dongbei lunxian shisinian jiaoyushi* (*The History of Education in the Northeast's Fourteen Years of Enemy Occupation*) (Changchun: Jilin jiaoyu chubanshe, 1989), 114.

85 *Manchoukuo Yearbook: 1941*, 678.

86 D. de Penfentenyo, *Manuel de Père de Famille*, cited in Miranda Pollard, *Reign of Virtue: Mobilizing Gender in Vichy France* (Chicago: University of Chicago Press, 1998), 75.

87 Shimoda's efforts are outlined in Duara, *Sovereignty*, 134-35.

88 Pollard, *Reign of Virtue*, 80.

89 "Shidai xiaojiemen" (Contemporary Girls), *Datong bao*, 5 November 1936, 7.

90 "Xiandai jiating zhong" (In Today's Households), *Datong bao*, 5 November 1936, 7.

91 Wei Zhonglan, "Xin Zhongguo nüxing de dongjing" (Sounds of the New Chinese Women's Movement), *Qingnian wenhua* 1, no. 3 (1943): 34.

92 Bai, "Funü yu wenhua," 30.

93 Takebe Utako, "Dadongya zhanzheng xia qingnian funü de juewu" (Young Women's Consciousness under the Greater East Asia War), *Qingnian wenhua* 1, no. 3 (1943): 16.

94 Xi Yi, "Manzhou funü suixiang" (Casual Thoughts on Women in Manchukuo), *Qingnian wenhua* 1, no. 3 (1943): 31.

95 Duara, *Sovereignty*, 147.

96 Xi, "Manzhou funü suixiang," 38.

97 Ibid., 37.

98 Shi Xiuwen, "Zhiyu funü yu jiating funü" (Professional Women and Household Women), *Daban Huawen meiri* 9, no. 7 (1942): 30.

99 Mochizuki Yuriko, "Zai Man-Ri xi nüxing tan" (Discussion of Feminism in Manchukuo and Japan), *Qingnian wenhua* 1, no. 3 (1943): 35-6.

100 Ibid., 36.

101 Ibid.

102 Cited in Wei, "Xin Zhongguo nüxing de dongjing," 33.

103 Cited in ibid., 34.

104 Bai, "Funü yu wenhua," 30.

105 Ibid.

106 Wei, "Xin Zhongguo nüxing de dongjing," 35.

107 Ibid.

108 Takebe, "Dadongya zhanzheng xia qingnian funü de juewu," 16.

109 Ibid., 17-18. See also, "Nimen zhidao ma?" 56.

110 Takebe, "Dadongya zhanzheng xia qingnian funü de juewu," 17.

111 For example, see ibid., 18; Xi, "Manzhou funü suixiang," 38.

112 Takebe, "Dadongya zhanzheng xia qingnian funü de juewu," 18.

113 See Xi, "Manzhou funü suixiang," 38. These are reminiscent of early-twentieth-century and May Fourth comparisons of women's status in Europe, Japan, and the United States. See Borthwick, "Changing Concepts of the Role of Women," 73, 85.

114 Shi, "Zhiyu funü yu jiating funü," 29.

115 Duara outlines the main goals of the Morality Society in *Sovereignty*, 149-62.

116 Ibid, 153.

117 Ibid.

118 Ibid.

119 Prasenjit Duara, "Of Authenticity and Woman," in *Becoming Chinese: Passages to Modernity and Beyond*, ed. Yeh Wen-hsin (Berkeley: University of California Press, 2000), 359.

120 Ibid., 353.

Chapter 3: Manchukuo's Chinese-Language Literary World

1 For details, see Dong Xingquan, "'Wu si' yundong yu Dongbei lunxian qu wenxue" ("May Fourth" Activities and the Literature of the Northeast Enemy-Occupied Territories), in *Dongbei lunxian shiqi wenxue guoji xueshu yantaohui lunwenji* (*Collection of Papers from the International Symposium on Literature of the Enemy-Occupied Northeast*), ed. Feng Weiqun, Wang Jianzhong, Li Chunyan, and Li Shuquan (Shenyang: Shenyang chubanshe, 1992), 107-19.

2 Zhang Yumao and Yan Zhihong, "Lun Dongbei lunxian shiqi xiaoshuo" (Discussing Novels of the Northeast Enemy Occupation Era) in ibid., 2.

3 For more in-depth discussion of foreign influences, see Lü Qinwen, "Dongbei lunxian qu de wailai wenxue yu xiangtu wenxue" (External and Local Literature of the Northeast Occupied Territories) in *Zhongri zhanzheng yu wenxue* (*Sino-Japanese War and Literature*), ed. Yamada Keizō and Lü Kangming (Changchun: Dongbei shifan daxue chubanshe, 1992), 127-59.

4 See Wang Qiuying, "Zhide tantao de ji ge wenti" (Several Questions Worthy of Inquiry), *Dongbei wenxue yanjiu shiliao* (*Historical Research Materials of Northeast Literature*), no. 3 (September 1986): 182-9.

5 Prasenjit Duara, *Sovereignty and Authenticity: Manchukuo and the East Asian Modern* (Lanham, MD: Rowman and Littlefield, 2003), 145.

6 Xu Naixiang and Huang Wanhua, *Zhongguo kangzhan shiqi lunxianqu wenxue shi* (*History of the Literature of the Enemy-Occupied Territories during China's War of Resistance*) (Fuzhou: Fujian jiaoyu chubanshe, 1995), 39.

7 Wang Yeping, *Dongbei lunxian shisinian jiaoyushi* (*The History of Education in the Northeast's Fourteen Years of Enemy Occupation* (Changchun: Jilin jiaoyu chubanshe, 1989), 23-9.

8 Kazeta Eiki, "Wei Manzhouguo wenyi zhangye de fazhan" (The Development of Bogus Manchukuo's Literary Rules and Regulations), in Feng et al., eds., *Dongbei lunxian shiqi wenxue guoji xueshu yantaohui lunwenji*, 37.

9 For details, see Sun Zhongtian, "Lishi de jiedu yu shenmei quxiang" (Towards a History of Interpretation and Aesthetics), in *Dongbei lunxian shiqi wenxue xinlun* (*New Discourse on the Literature of the Northeast Occupation Era*), ed. Feng Weiqun and Li Chunyan (Changchun: Jilin daxue chubanshe, 1991), 2.

10 Jie Xueshi, "Ri wei shiqi de wenhua tongzhi zhengce" (State Policies of Cultural Domination during the Japanese Occupation), in Feng et al., eds., *Dongbei lunxian shiqi wenxue guoji xueshu yantaohui lunwenji*, 190-1.

11 Feng Zengyu argues linkages between Lu Xun and the development of native place literature in Manchuria. See Feng Zengyu, "Dongbei lunxian qi xiangtu wenxue yu Zhongguo xiandai wenxue shi shang xiangtu wenxue zhi bijiao" (A Comparison of Native Place Literature from the Enemy Occupation of the Northeast and Native Place Literature in Contemporary Chinese Literature), in Feng et al., eds., *Dongbei lunxian shiqi wenxue guoji xueshu yantaohui lunwenji*, 70-4.

12 Cited in Duara, *Sovereignty and Authenticity*, 223.

13 Ibid., 145.

14 For recent analysis of these main groups, see Qian Liqun, ed., *Zhongguo lunxianqu wenxue daxi. Shiliao juan* (*Compendium of the Literature of China's Enemy-Occupied Territories. Volume of Historical Data*), 11 vols. (Nanling, Guangxi: Guangxi jiaoyu chubanshe, 2000), 11: 557-67.

15 Ibid., 11: 1.

16 Ibid., 11: 9.

17 Ibid., 11: 72.

18 *Manchoukuo Yearbook: 1941* (Hsinking: Manchoukuo Yearbook Company, 1942), 703-4.

19 Liu Huijuan and Xu Qian, "Zhongguo xiandai wenxue shi shang bu ke queshao de pianzhang: Jianshu Dongbei lunxian shiqi zuoyi wenxue huodong" (Writings That the History of Contemporary Chinese Literature Cannot Lack: A Brief Account of Left-Wing Literary Activities during the Northeast's Enemy Occupation Era), in Feng et al., eds., *Dongbei lunxian shiqi wenxue guoji xueshu yantaohui lunwenji*, 84-5.

20 Zhang Yumao, ed., *Dongbei xiandai wenxue daxi, 1919-1949*, vol. 14, *Ziliao suoyin* (*Compendium of Modern Northeastern Literature, 1919-1949*, vol. 14, *Data Index*) (Shenyang: Shenyang chubanshe, 1996), 57.

21 Xu and Huang, *Zhongguo kangzhan shiqi lunxianqu wenxue shi*, 1.

22 Payment rates are rarely listed, but two prominent journals provide the following information: in 1940, the *Daban Huawen meiri* posted the following rates: novellas, 200 yen, and general articles, 30-50 yen; *Daban Huawen meiri* 5, nos. 1-4 (1940); in 1942, *Xin Manzhou* paid 50-500 yen per novella or 1.5-10 yen per thousand characters, 20 yen per thousand characters for theses and articles, and 1.5-10 yen per thousand characters for articles on family life and society.

23 Cited in Kazeta, "Wei Manzhouguo wenyi zhangye de fazhan," 160.

24 Ibid.

25 Xu and Huang, *Zhongguo kangzhan shiqi lunxianqu wenxue shi*, 80.

26 Yang Xu, "Gongkai de zuizhuang" (Open Indictment), in Yang Xu, *Wo de riji* (*My Diary*) (Xinjing: Kaiming tushu gongsi, 1944), 97.

27 Wang Qiuying, "Wo suo zhidao de dongbei lunxianqi Shengyang wenxue" (All I Know about Shenyang Literature from the Era of the Enemy Occupation of the Northeast), *Dongbei wenxue yanjiu shiliao* (*Historical Research Materials on Northeastern Literature*), no. 6 (1987): 114.

28 Xu and Huang, *Zhongguo kangzhan shiqi lunxianqu wenxue shi*, 77.

29 Cited in ibid., 82.

30 Hiroshi Takama, "New Culture in Manchoukuo," *Manchoukuo Today*, no. 6 (1940): 40.

31 For example, see Sun Zhongtian, Feng Zengyu, Huang Wanhua, and Liu Aihua, *Liaokao xia de Miu Si: Dongbei lunxian qu wenxue shigang* (*The Shackled Muse: Historical Outline of the Literature of the Northeast Occupied Territories*) (Changchun: Jilin daxue chubanshe, 1999), 102.

32 For analysis of Gu Ding's work, see ibid., 126-45.

33 Yang Yi, "Dongbei lunxianqu xiaoshuo" (Novels of the Northeast Enemy-Occupied Territory), *Dongbei wenxue yanjiu shiliao* (*Historical Research Materials on Northeastern Literature*), no. 6 (December 1987): 6.

34 Zhang and Yan, "Lun Dongbei lunxian shiqi xiaoshuo," 13. See also Sun et al., *Liaokao*, 145-60.

35 The various influences on these writers are recounted in Zhang and Yan, "Lun Dongbei lunxian shiqi xiaoshuo," 12-13. See also Sun et al., *Liaokao*, 160-72.

36 Wang Qiuying, "Yijiusiling nian qian de dongbei wenyi qingkuang" (The Condition of the Arts in the Northeast before 1940), *Dongbei xiandai wenxue shiliao* (*Historical Materials of the Northeast's Modern Literature*), no. 1 (March 1980): 85-6.

37 Zhang, ed., *Dongbei xiandai wenxue daxi*, 14: 68.

38 For example, see Li Chunyan, "Zai anye li ranshaozhe de huohua: Tan Wang Qiuying zai Dongbei lunxian shiqi de xiaoshuo chuangzuo" (Burning Sparks in the Dark Night: Discussion of Wang

Qiuying's Production of Fiction during the Northeast Occupation), *Dongbei wenxue yanjiu shiliao* (*Historical Research Materials of Northeast Literature*) no. 3 (September 1986): 26.

39 These comments are cited in an addendum to the 1941 Eight Abstentions. See Yu Lei, trans., "Ziliao" (Data) in Feng et al., eds., *Dongbei lunxian shiqi wenxue guoji xueshu yantaohui lunwenji*, 181.

40 For a description of their contemporary impact, see Lü Qinwen, "Dongbei lunxian shiqi de wenxue shetuan" (The Literary Mass Organisations during the Northeast Occupation), in *Zhongguo xiandai wenxue shetuan liupai* (*Mass Organization Factions in Chinese Modern Literature*), ed. Jia Zhifang (Nanjing: Jiangsu jiaoyu chuban she, 1989), 1000.

41 For a recent discussion of the uses of native place writing, see Prasenjit Duara, "The Poetics and Politics of Native Place in Modern China," *South Atlantic Quarterly* 99, no. 1 (2000): 13-45.

42 Lü Qinwen, "Dongbei lunxian qu de wailai wenxue yu xiangtu wenxue" (External and Local Literature of the Northeast Occupied Territories), in *Zhongri zhanzheng yu wenxue* (*Sino-Japanese War and Literature*), ed. Yamada Keiz? and Lü Kangming (Changchun: Dongbei shifan daxue chubanshe, 1992), 146.

43 Prasenjit Duara notes that the state approved of native place literature. See Duara, "Poetics and Politics of Native Place," 34.

44 Shinichi Yamaguchi, "Contemporary Literature in Manchuria," *Concordia and Culture in Manchoukuo* (Xinjing: Manchuria Daily News, 1938), 27.

45 Feng Weiqun and Li Chunyan, *Dongbei lunxian shiqi wenxue xinlun* (*New Discourse on the Literature of the Northeast Occupation Era*) (Changchun: Jilin daxue chubanshe, 1991), 49.

46 Kazeta, "Wei Manzhouguo wenyi zhangye de fazhan," 160.

47 Hiroshi Takama, "New Culture in Manchoukuo," 40.

48 Duara, *Sovereignty and Authenticity*, 224.

49 These are outlined in Jie, "Ri wei shiqi de wenhua tongzhi zhengce," 196, 266.

50 Kazeta, "Wei Manzhouguo wenyi zhangye de fazhan," 160-2.

51 Ibid., 162.

52 See Gregory Kasza, *The State and Mass Media in Japan, 1918-45* (Berkeley: University of California Press, 1988).

53 Duara, *Sovereignty and Authenticity*, 224.

54 The Eight Abstentions are reproduced in Yu, "Ziliao," 181.

55 Duara, *Sovereignty and Authenticity*, 224.

56 Cited in Kazeta, "Wei Manzhouguo wenyi zhangye de fazhan," 164.

57 The Artistic Guidelines are reproduced in Yu, "Ziliao," 174-8.

58 Cited in Xu and Huang, *Zhongguo kangzhan shiqi lunxianqu wenxue shi*, 267.

59 Ibid., 269.

60 Zhu Ti and Li Keju, "1942 yu 1945 nian dongbei wenyijie" (A Glimpse of the World of Arts in the Northeast, 1942-1945) in Feng et al., eds., *Dongbei lunxian shiqu wenxue guoji xueshu yantaohui lunwenji*, 408.

61 For comparison with the literary worlds of Beijing and Shanghai, see Poshek Fu's *Passivity, Resistance, and Collaboration: Intellectual Choices in Occupied Shanghai, 1937-45* (Stanford: Stanford University Press, 1993) and Edward Gunn's *Unwelcome Muse: Chinese Literature in Shanghai and Peking, 1937-45* (New York: Columbia University Press, 1980).

62 Kazeta, "Wei Manzhouguo wenyi zhangye de fazhan," 164.

63 Ibid., 161-2.

64 Ibid., 162.

65 See Wang, "Wo suo zhidao de dongbei lunxianqi Shenyang wenxue," 38; Kazeta, "Wei Manzhouguo wenyi zhangye de fazhan," 162.

66 Kazeta, "Wei Manzhouguo wenyi zhangye de fazhan," 165.

67 Li Zhengzhong, personal interview, Shenyang, 28 July 2005.

68 Li Zhengzhong, personal interview, Vancouver, 23 September 2001.

69 For more information on this journal, see Feng and Li, *Dongbei lunxian shiqi wenxue xinlun*, 141.

70 See Zhang, ed., *Dongbei xiandai wenxue daxi*, 14: 84.

71 Ibid., 63.

72 Xu and Huang, *Zhongguo kangzhan shiqi lunxianqu wenxue shi*, 266.

73 For details, see Sun et al., *Liaokao*, 64-5.

74 Xu and Huang, *Zhongguo kangzhan shiqi lunxianqu wenxue shi*, 1.

75 Chen Ti, personal interview, Harbin, 29 August 2003. For an outline of this incident, see Feng Weiqun, "Shi Hanjian wenxue haishi kang-Ri wenxue" (Is it the Literature of Traitors to China or Literature of the anti-Japanese Resistance?) in Feng et al., eds., *Dongbei lunxian shiqi wenxue guoji xueshu yantaohui lunwenji*, 102.

76 These were eventually amalgamated, in May 1944, into the *Manri*. See Zhang, ed., *Dongbei xiandai wenxue daxi*, 14: 91.

77 Ibid., 93.

78 Xu and Huang, *Zhongguo kangzhan shiqi lunxianqu wenxue shi*, 17.

79 Ibid.

80 Details of this Congress can be found in Gunn, *Unwelcome Muse*, 32-3.

81 Their activities are cited in ibid., 32.

82 *Hong Kong News*, 29 October 1942, 1, cited in ibid., 32-3.

83 Ibid., 31.

84 Mei Niang, personal interview, Vancouver, 10 May 2001.

85 Wu Ying, "Chuxi Dadongya wenxuezhe da hui suo gan" (Feelings about Attending the Greater East Asia Writers' Congress), *Qilin* (*Unicorn*) 3, no. 2 (1943): 49-50.

86 Xu and Huang, *Zhongguo kangzhan shiqi lunxianqu wenxue shi*, 264.

87 Ibid.

88 It is notable that no women members are mentioned in the membership lists of these groups. For lists, see Kazeta, "Wei Manzhouguo wenyi zhangye de fazhan," 165, 173-4, 180.

89 Feng and Li, *Dongbei lunxian shiqi wenxue xinlun*, 47-8; see also Sun et al., *Liaokao*, 108.

90 Yuan Xi is the pen name of Li Keyi. Zhang, ed., *Dongbei xiandai wenxue daxi*, 14: 87. Mei Niang recounts this incident in "Wo yu Riben" (Me and Japan), in *Xunzhao Mei Niang* (*Searching for the World of Mei Niang*), ed. Zhang Quan (Brampton, ON: Mirror Books, 1998), 145-6.

91 Xu and Huang, *Zhongguo kangzhan shiqi lunxianqu wenxue shi*, 269.

92 For Liang's activities, see ibid., 267.

93 Cited in ibid., 268.

94 See Duara, *Sovereignty and Authenticity*, 227.

95 Cited in Gunn, *Unwelcome Muse*, 36.

96 Cited in Kazeta, "Wei Manzhouguo wenyi zhangye de fazhan," 169.

97 Cited in Xu and Huang, *Zhongguo kangzhan shiqi lunxianqu wenxue shi*, 267.

98 Wang, "Wo suo zhidao de dongbei lunxianqi Shenyang wenxue," 38.

99 Gunn, *Unwelcome Muse*, 41-3.

100 Edward Gunn notes that Mei Niang received her award and a cash prize of twenty thousand yen. Ibid., 41-3, 279n92.

101 Wei Changming, "Dongbei Wenxue fakan qianhou" (Before and after the Publication of Northeast Literature), *Dongbei wenxue yanjiu shiliao* (*Historical Research Materials of Northeast Literature*), no. 3 (September 1986): 107.

102 For example, a reporter sent to interview Wu Ying was unable to obtain a copy of her collected works *Liang ji* because it had sold out. See Yi Bing, "Nü zuojia Wu Ying shi fangwen ji" (Notes from an Interview with Female Writer Wu Ying), *Qilin* (*Unicorn*), no. 8 (1943): 137.

Chapter 4: Forging Careers in Manchukuo

1 Diana Lary and Thomas Gottschang, *Swallows and Settlers* (Ann Arbor: University of Michigan, 2000), 10.

2 Fu Shangkui, "Fang nüzuojia Tian Lin" (Searching for Woman Writer Tian Lin), *Dongbei xiandai wenxue shiliao* (*Historical Materials of Modern Literature of the Northeast*), no. 5 (1982): 212.

3 Zhu Ti, personal correspondence, 6 July 2000.

4 Mei Niang's early life is outlined in Mei Niang, "Wo de qingshao nian shiqi: 1920-1938" (My Childhood, 1920-1938) in *Xunzhao Mei Niang* (*Searching for the World of Mei Niang*), ed. Zhang Quan (Brampton, ON: Mirror Books, 1998), 97-9.

5 Ibid., 99.

6 Lan Ling, "Nan wang de baojia hutong yi hao" (Unforgettable Baojia Hutong Number One), *Qiqiqhaer ribao: Chuanghan* (*The Qiqihaer Daily: Achievements in Publication*) (Qiqihaer: Qiqihaer ribao, 1985), 71; Zhu Ti, personal correspondence, 6 July 2000.

7 Yang Xu, "Tu yao ou'ji" (Casual Notes Illuminating the Land), in Yang Xu, *Luoying ji* (*Collection of Fallen Petals*) (Xinjing: Kaiming tushu gongsi, 1943), 102.

8 Wu Ying, "Fangwen juezhan xia Uda furen de yu'er" (Interviewing Madame Uda about Raising Her Son with War Resolve), *Xin Manzhou* 6, no. 10 (1944): 65-6.

9 See Prasenjit Duara, "Local Worlds: The Poetics and Politics of Native Place in Modern China," *South Atlantic Quarterly* 99, no. 1 (2000): 35.

10 For example, see Wu Ying, "Wo zenyang xie de 'Xuyuan'" (How I Wrote 'Dilapidation'"), *Yiwenzhi* 1, no. 1 (1943): 89-93, repr. in *Dongbei xiandai wenxue daxi, 1919-1949*, vol. 10, *Sanwen juan* (*Compendium of Modern Northeastern Literature, 1919-1949*, vol. 10, *Essays*), ed. Zhang Yumao (Shenyang: Shenyang chubanshe, 1996), 568; Yang Xu had several elder siblings, a mother who protected and coddled her, and a father who was already over sixty years old when she was born. Yang Xu, "Gongkai de zuizhuang," (Open Indictment) in Yang Xu, *Wo de riji* (*My Diary*) (Xinjing: Kaiming tushu gongsi, 1944), 91.

11 Lan, "Nan wang de baojia hutong yi hao," 70.

12 Mei, "Wo de qingshao nian shiqi," 99.

13 Luo Ping and Luo Ling, "Shenqie de huainian" (Fond Memories), in *Luo Mai xiaoshuo sanwen ji (Luo Mai's Collected Short Stories and Essays)*, ed. Liang Shanding (Shenyang: Shenyang renmin chubanshe, 1990), 220-3, 230.

14 Fu, "Fang nüzuojia Tian Lin," 212.

15 Zhou Qinghe, "Tian Lin de wenxue chuangzuo qingxiong he yishu tesi" (The Production Tendencies and Artistic Characteristics of Tian Lin's Literature), *Dongbei wenxue yanjiu shiliao* (*Research Materials on Literature of the Northeast*), no. 6 (December 1987): 105; Lan Ling, "Yan" (Feast), *Daban Huawen meiri* 4, no. 4 (1940), repr. in Zhang, ed., *Dongbei xiandai wenxue daxi*, 10: 716-18.

16 Luo Ying and Luo Yan, "Luo Mai nianbiao" (Luo Mai's Chronological Table), in Liang, ed., *Luo Mai xiaoshuo sanwen ji*, 229.

17 Mei, "Wo de qingshao nian shiqi," 97-9.

18 Ibid., 102.

19 Yang, "Gongkai de zuizhuang," 90.

20 Zhu Ti, "Xu" (Preface), in Zhu Ti, *Ying* (Xinjing: Guomin tushu zhushi huishe, 1945), 2.

21 Mei, "Wo de qingshao nian shiqi," 103.

22 Fu, "Fang nüzuojia Tian Lin," 212.

23 Lan Ling, personal correspondence, 10 February 2000; Wu, "Wo zenyang xie de 'Xuyuan,'" 566.

24 Lan Ling, personal correspondence, 10 February 2000.

25 Ibid.

26 Yang, "Gongkai de zuizhuang," 95.

27 Mei, "Wo mei kanjianguo niang de xiaolian" (I Never Saw Mother's Smiling Face), *Funü zazhi* (*Ladies' Journal*), November 1944, repr. in *Mei Niang xiaoshuo sanwen ji* (*Mei Niang's Collected Novels and Essays*), ed. Zhang Quan (Beijing: Beijing chubanshe, 1997), 512.

28 In the Chinese Buddhist pantheon, Yama is the King of Hell. Yang, "Tu yao ou'ji," 102-4.

29 Yang Xu, *Wo de riji* (*My Diary*) (Xinjing: Kaiming tushu gongsi, 1944), 148-9.

30 Mei, "Wo de qingshao nian shiqi," 118.

31 Mochizuki Yuriko, "Zai Man-Ri xi nüxing tan" (Discussion of Feminism in Manchukuo and Japan), *Qingnian wenhua* 1, no. 3 (1943): 36.

32 Mei Niang, *Xie* (*Crabs*), in Mei Niang, *Xie* (*Crabs*) (Beijing: Xinmin yinshuguan, 1944), repr. in *Dongbei xiandai wenxue daxi, 1919-49*, vol. 5, *Zhongpian xiaoshuo juan* (*Compendium of Modern Northeastern Literature, 1919-49*, vol. 5, *Medium-Length Fiction*), ed. Zhang Yumao (Shenyang: Shenyang chubanshe, 1996), 134.

33 Wang, *Dongbei lunxian shisinian jiaoyushi*, 114.

34 Yang, *Wo de riji*, 147.

35 Mei, "Wo de qingshao nian shiqi," 123.

36 Mei, "Wo yu Riben," 143-5.

37 "Qiaomin" was published in *Xin Manzhou* 3, no. 6 (June 1941): 180-4.

38 Dan Di, "Yiguo" (Foreign Country), *Daban Huawen meiri* 4, no. 3 (1940): 39.

39 Dan Di, "Gan" (Feelings), *Daban Huawen meiri* (*Chinese Osaka Daily*) 5, no. 10 (1940): 44.

40 Ibid.

41 Dan Di, "Riji chao" (Taking Up a Diary), *Dongbei wenxue yanjiu shiliao* (*Research and Historical Materials on Literature of the Northeast*), no. 6 (December 1987): 173.

42 Ibid., 179.

43 Ibid.

44 Tian Lang, also a noted writer, organized a Lu Xun Study Group, for which he was arrested in 1944. He was tortured in jail and died shortly after his release. For details, see Xu Naixiang and Huang Wanhua, *Zhongguo kangzhan shiqi lunxianqu wenxue shi* (*History of the Literature of the Enemy-Occupied Territories during China's War of Resistance*) (Fuzhou: Fujian jiaoyu chubanshe, 1995), 170. Also see Mei Niang, "Jinian Tian Lin" (Remembering Tian Lin), in Zhang, ed., *Mei Niang xiaoshuo sanwen ji*, 595.

45 Mei, "Jinian Tian Lin," 595.

46 Dan, "Riji chao," 175.

47 Fu, "Fang nüzuojia Tian Lin," 214.

48 Mei Niang, "Songhua jiang de buyu" (The Nurturing Songhua River), in *Xiao Jun jinian ji* (*Commemorative Collection for Xiao Jun*), ed. Liang Shanding (Shenyang: Chunfeng wenyi chubanshe, 1990), 232-3.

49 Mei Niang, "Wo de qingshao nian shiqi," 127-8.

50 Yang, "Gongkai de zuizhuang," 104.

51 Their relationship is outlined in ibid., 93.

52 Yang Xu, "Huainian" (Longing), in Yang, *Wo de riji*, 49-51.

53 Yang Xu, "Yi di shu" (Letters from Different Places), in ibid., 22.

54 Ibid.

55 Li, a prominent Manchukuo writer as well, has published under more than forty pen names including Wei Changming. See Qian, ed., *Zhongguo lunxianqu wenxue daxi*, 11: 395-6.

56 Yi Bing, "Nü zuojia Wu Ying shi fangwen ji" (Notes from an Interview with Woman Writer Wu Ying), *Qilin,* no. 8 (1943): 138.

57 Lan Ling, "Nan wang de baojia hutong yi hao" (Unforgettable Baojia Hutong Number One), *Qiqiqhaer ribao: Chuanghan* (*The Qiqihaer Daily: Achievements in Publication*) (Qiqihaer: Qiqihaer ribao, 1985), 71-2.

58 Qian, ed., *Zhongguo lunxianqu wenxue daxi,* 11: 437.

59 Lan Ling, personal correspondence, 30 July 2000.

60 Liang Shanding, "Shi nian shengsi liang mangmang: Zuo Di shisi shi zhou nian" (Ten Years in the Vastness of Life and Death: The Ten Year Anniversary of Zuo Di's Death), in Liang, ed., *Luo Mai xiaoshuo sanwen ji,* 209.

61 Qian Liqun, ed., *Zhongguo lunxianqu wenxue daxi. Shiliao juan* (*Compendium of the Literature of China's Enemy-Occupied Territories. Volume of Historical Data*), 11 vols. (Nanling, Guangxi: Guangxi jiaoyu chubanshe, 2000), 11: 437.

62 Zhu Ti earned sixty yuan teaching primary school while her husband earned three hundred yuan per month as a lower court judge, where his activities were confined to trying cases of petty crime and violence among the Chinese population. Li Zhengzhong, personal interview, Vancouver, 23 September 2001.

63 Dan, "Riji chao," 173-80; Lan, "Nan wang de baojia hutong yi hao," 71.

64 Zhu Ti, "Wo he wo de haizimen" (Me and My Children) in Zhu Ti, *Ying,* 80.

65 Lan, "Nan wang de baojia hutong yi hao," 70.

66 Yang, "Gongkai de zuizhuang," 96.

67 Ibid., 97.

68 Ibid., 99.

69 Ibid., 101; Qian, ed., *Zhongguo lunxianqu wenxue daxi,* 11: 346.

70 Yang, "Gongkai de zuizhuang," 101.

71 Ibid., 104.

72 Yang Xu, "Wo yu huaju" (Me and Drama), in Yang, *Luoying ji,* 75-7; Yang Xu, "Wo yu gechang" (Me and Singing), in ibid., 10-13.

73 Yang Xu, "Fu Xian shi yan zaji" (Jottings on the Facts of the Performance in Korea), in ibid., 90-8.

74 Yang Xu, personal interview, Shenyang, 12 November 1999.

75 For example, see Yang Xu, "Wo yu gechang" (Me and Singing), in *Manzhou yinghua* (*Manchukuo Movies*) 5, no. 1 (1941): 46-7; "Gechang" (Singing), *Xin Manzhou* (*New Manchukuo*) 5, no. 1 (1943): 54-5.

76 Li Zhengzhong, personal interview, Oxford, 31 October 2004.

77 Kazeta Eiki, "Wei Manzhouguo wenyi zhangye de fazhan" (The Development of Bogus Manchukuo's Literary Rules and Regulations), in *Dongbei lunxian shiqi wenxue guoji xueshu yantaohui lunwenji* (*Collection of Papers from the International Symposium on Literature of the Enemy-Occupied Northeast*), ed. Feng Weiqun, Wang Jianzhong, Li Chunyan, and Li Shuquan (Shenyang: Shenyang chubanshe, 1992), 160.

78 Qian, ed., *Zhongguo lunxianqu wenxue daxi,* 11: 437. For the role of the CCP, see Li Chunyan, "Wenxue de lunxian yu lunxian de wenxue: Dongbei lunxian shiqi wenxue de ji ge xianzhu tedian" (The Enemy Occupation of Literature and the Literature of the Enemy Occupation: Several Notable Characteristics of the Literature of the Northeast Enemy Occupation Era), in *Dongbei lunxian shiqi wenxue guoji xueshu yantaohui lunwenji* (*Collection of Papers from the International Symposium on Literature of the Enemy-Occupied Northeast*), ed. Feng Weiqun, Wang Jianzhong, Li Chunyan, Li Shuquan (Shenyang: Shenyang chubanshe, 1992), 43-5.

79 Tian Lin, "Huiyi *Wutian* yu Ba Lai" (Recollecting *Grassland* and Ba Lai), *Dongbei wenxue yanjiu shiliao* (*Historical Research Materials of Northeast Literature*), no. 3 (September 1986): 168-9.

80 Han Hu, "*Di'er dai* lun" (Discussion of *The Second Generation*) (Dalian: Datong bao wenyi, 1943), repr. in Zhang, ed., *Dongbei xiandai wenxue daxi,* 10: 454.

81 Qian, ed., *Zhongguo lunxianqu wenxue daxi,* 11: 346.

82 Lan, "Nan wang de baojia hutong yi hao," 71.

83 Dan, "Riji chao," 180.

84 Wu Ying's anticipated second collection of fiction, *Baigu* (*White Bones*) was never published. See Yi Bing, "Nü zuojia Wu Ying shi fangwen ji," 138.

85 Mei Niang's *Yu* went through six publications.

86 See Jia Ren, "Zhi Yang Xu nüshi" (To Madame Yang Xu), *Xin Manzhou* 5, no. 2 (1943): 96.

87 Mei Niang's earliest still extant writings (under the pen name Lian Jiang) can be found in the *Funü* page of the *Datong bao*, nos. 1655 and 1656 (1936), 7.

88 The editorial staff of *Xin Manzhou* included her husband and underground CCP, Xia Hang and Gao Liang. See Zhang Yumao, ed., *Dongbei xiandai wenxue daxi, 1919-1949,* vol. 14, *Ziliao suoyin* (*Compendium of Modern Northeastern Literature, 1919-1949,* vol. 14, *Data Index*) (Shenyang: Shenyang chubanshe, 1996), 64.

89 Qian, ed., *Zhongguo lunxianqu wenxue daxi,* 11: 354.

90 Luo and Luo, "Luo Mai nianbiao," 231.

91 Qian, ed., *Zhongguo lunxianqu wenxue daxi,* 11: 346.

92 A critical evaluation of this work can be seen in Wei Changming, "Dongbei nüxing wenxue shisi nian shi" (A History of Fourteen Years of Northeastern Women's Literature), *Dongbei wenxue* (*Northeast Literature*) 1, no. 4 (1946), repr. in *Dongbei xiandai wenxue daxi, 1919-1949,* vol. 1, *Pinglun juan* (*Compendium of Modern Northeastern Literature, 1919-1949,* vol. 1, *Critical Evaluation*), ed. Zhang Yumao (Shenyang: Shenyang chubanshe, 1996), 344.

93 Zuo Di, "Xu" (Preface) in Zuo Di, ed., *Nüzuojia chuangzuoxuan* (*Selected Writings of Women Writers*) (Xinjing: Wenhuashe, 1943), repr. in Liang, ed., *Luo Mai xiaoshuo sanwen ji,* 30-1.

94 Wu Ying, "Chuxi Dadongya wenxuezhe da hui suo gan" (Feelings about Attending the Greater East Asia Writers' Congress), *Qilin* 3, no. 2 (1943): 49.

95 Cited in Xu and Huang, *Zhongguo kangzhan shiqi lunxianqu wenxue shi,* 285.

96 Ibid.

97 Her novella was published in Beijing's *Chinese Arts* (*Zhongguo wenyi*). See Qian, ed., *Zhongguo lunxianqu wenxue daxi,* 11: 355; Yi, "Nü zuojia Wu Ying shi fangwen ji," 137. The prize of two hundred yuan was worth approximately two months' wages as an editor. Li Zhengzhong, personal interview, Vancouver, 23 September 2001.

98 Wu Ying, "Manzhou nüxing wenxue de ren yu zuopin," 347-8.

99 Shangguan Ying, "Dongbei lunxian shiqi wenxue ceying" (Profile of the Northeast's Occupied Territory's Literature), in Shangguan Ying, *Yiwen luantan* (*Random Notes on Literature and Art*) (Changchun: Shidai wenyi chubanshe, 1989), 109.

100 Han, "*Di'er dai* lun," 456-7.

101 Yoshikawa is cited in Gunn, *Unwelcome Muse,* 37.

102 Guo, "Mei Niang: Bu shi yong mei sheng yong mei" (Mei Niang: This Isn't an 'Ode to the Plum,' It's Better Than an 'Ode to the Plum'), in Zhang, ed., *Xunzhao Mei Niang,* 53.

103 *Xie* was published in serial form in the *Daban Huawen meiri* in 1941 and included in her collected works, *Xie* (1944). Edward Gunn asserts that Mei Niang received the prize based on her husband's high profile. See *Unwelcome Muse,* 41-3.

Chapter 5: Disrupting the Patriarchal Foundations of Manchukuo

1 Mei Niang, personal interview, Beijing, 23 November 2000.

2 Zuo Di, "Liu Qi" (Liu Qi), *Qilin* (*Unicorn*) 2, no. 10 (1942): 75-8, repr. in *Changye yinghuo* (*Fireflies of the Long Night*), ed. Liang Shanding (Shenyang: Chunfeng wenyi chubanshe, 1986), 77.

3 Yang Xu, "Ji" (Mail), in Yang Xu, *Luoying ji* (*Collection of Fallen Petals*) (Xinjing: Kaiming tushu gongsi, 1943), 130.

4 Yang Xu, "Zixu" (Author's preface) in Yang Xu, *Wo de riji* (*My Diary*) (Xinjing: Kaiming tushu gongsi, 1944), 1.

5 Ibid.

6 Mei Niang, "Wo de qingshao nian shiqi: 1920-1938" (My Childhood, 1920-1938), in *Xunzhao Mei Niang* (*Searching for the World of Mei Niang*), ed. Zhang Quan (Brampton, ON: Mirror Books, 1998), 127.

7 Mei Niang, "Yu" (Fish) in Mei Niang, *Yu* (*Fish*) (Beijing: Xinmin yinshuguan, 1943), 27-74, repr. in *Mei Niang xiaoshuo sanwen ji* (*Mei Niang's Collected Novels and Essays*), ed. Zhang Quan (Beijing: Beijing chubanshe, 1997), 70-1.

8 Mei Niang, "Ji Wu Ying shu" (Mailing a Letter to Wu Ying), *Qingnian wenhua* (*Youth Culture*) 1, no. 1 (1943): 84.

9 Yang Xu, "Gongkai de zuizhuang" (Open Indictment), in Yang Xu, *Wo de riji* (*My Diary*) (Xinjing: Kaiming tushu gongsi, 1944), 107.

10 Ibid.

11 Ibid., 102.

12 Jia Ren, "Zhi Yang Xu nüshi" (To Madame Yang Xu), *Xin Manzhou* 5, no. 2 (1943): 97.

13 Ibid., 96.

14 Ibid.

15 Ibid.

16 Shang Qiuhe, "Ji Yang Xu xiaojie" (Notes on Miss Yang Xu), in Yang Xu, *Wo de riji* (*My Diary*) (Xinjing: Kaiming tushu gongsi, 1944), 183.

17 It is implied that the film is European. Zhu Ti, "Xiao Yinzi he ta de jiazu" (Little Yinzi and Her Relations), *Dongbei wenxue* (*Northeast Literature*) 1, no. 1 (1945), repr. in Liang Shanding, ed., *Changye yinghuo* (*Fireflies of the Long Night*) (Shenyang: Chunfeng wenyi chubanshe, 1986), 484.

18 Zuo, "Liu Qi," 392.

19 Shopenhauer's work is cited in ibid., 395.

20 Mei Niang, "Wo de qingshaonian, 1920-38" (My Childhood, 1920-38), in Zhang, ed., *Xunzhao Mei Niang*, 105.

21 Dan Di, "Riji chao" (Taking Up a Diary), *Dongbei wenxue yanjiu shiliao* (*Research and Historical Materials on Literature of the Northeast*), no. 6 (December 1987): 180; Yang Xu, *Wo de riji*, 137.

22 Wu Ying, "Ming" (Howl), *Qingnian wenhua* 1, no. 3 (1943): 94.

23 Ibid., 92.

24 Ibid.

25 For a contemporary censor's report, see Sun Zhongtian, Feng Zengyu, Huang Wanhua, and Liu Aihua, *Liaokao xia de Miu Si: Dongbei lunxian qu wenxue shigang* (*The Shackled Muse: Historical Outline of the Literature of the Northeast Occupied Territories*) (Changchun: Jilin daxue chubanshe, 1999), 64-5.

26 Zhu Ti, "Du Bohai" (Crossing the Bohai Sea), repr. in Liang, ed., *Changye yinghuo*, 493.

27 Ibid., 498.

28 Lan Ling, "Richu" (Sunrise), *Xin Manzhou* 6, no. 10 (1944), repr. in Liang, ed., *Changye yinghuo*, 355.

29 Mei, "Yu," 108.

30 Zuo Di, "Nü nan" (Women's Difficulty), *Qingnian wenhua* 1, no. 3 (1943): 87.

31 For example, see Wu Ying, "Gan miao hui" (Dashing to the Temple Meeting), *Simin* (*This People*), July 1934, 13.

32 Wu Ying, "Cui Hong" (Cui Hong), *Wenxuan* (*Literary Selections*), no. 1 (1940), repr. in Liang, *Changye yinghuo*, 308.

33 Yang Xu, "Yidian chunzhen ji guren" (A Little Sincerity Mailed to an Old Friend), in Yang, *Luoying ji*, 8.

34 Lan Ling, "Yehang" (Night Navigators), *Daban Huawen meiri*, August 1942, repr. in Liang, *Changye yinghuo*, 385.

35 Yang, "Gongkai de zuizhuang," 102.

36 Yang Xu, "Jiyi shi ge canren de du chong" (Memory Is a Cruel Poisonous Insect), in Yang Xu, *Luoying ji*, 31.

37 Yang Xu, "Ji," 129-30.

38 Yang Xu, *Wo de riji*, 151.

39 Yang Xu, "Fangfu shi yi chang wennuan de meng" (As If It's a Warm Dream), in Yang Xu, *Luoying ji* (*Collection of Fallen Petals*) (Xinjing: Kaiming tushu gongsi, 1943), 17.

40 Yang Xu, "Yi di shu" (Letters from Different Places), in Yang, *Wo de riji*, 20.

41 Ibid.

42 Ibid., 16.

43 Ibid., 20.

44 Zuo, "Liu Qi," 78.

45 Wu Ying, "Xin youling" (New Ghost), in Wu, *Liang ji*, 2.

46 Ibid., 16.

47 Ibid., 22.

48 Mei Niang, *Ye he hua kai* (*Flowers That Blossom in the Night*) (1943), repr. in *Mei Niang xiaoshuo sanwen ji* (*Mei Niang's Collected Novels and Essays*), ed. Zhang Quan (Beijing: Beijing chubanshe, 1997), 415.

49 Mei, "Yu," 100.

50 Ibid., 94.

51 Mei Niang, "Bang" (Clam), in Mei Niang, *Yu* (*Fish*) (Beijing: Xinmin yinshuguan, 1943), repr. in *Changye yinghuo* (*Fireflies of the Long Night*), ed. Liang Shanding (Shenyang: Chunfeng wenyi chubanshe, 1986), 194.

52 Ibid., 191-4.

53 Ibid., 173.

54 Zhu Ti, "Xu," (Author's preface), in Zhu Ti, *Ying* (*Cherry*) (Xinjing: Guomin tushu zhushi huishe, 1945), 2-3.

55 For example, see the 1941 Eight Abstentions. Yu Lei, trans., "Ziliao" (Data), in *Dongbei lunxian shiqi wenxue guoji xueshu yantaohui lunwenji* (*Collection of Papers from the International Symposium on Literature of the Enemy-Occupied Northeast*), ed. Feng Weiqun, Wang Jianzhong, Li Chunyan, and Li Shuquan (Shenyang: Shenyang chubanshe, 1992), 181.

56 Zhu, "Du Bohai," 158.

57 Zhu Ti, "Da Heilongjiang de youyu" (The Melancholy of the Mighty Black Dragon River), in *Funü huabao* (*Ladies Pictorial*) (1943), repr. in Liang, ed., *Changye yinghuo*, 468.

58 Wu, *Liang ji*, 118.

59 Ibid., 121.

60 Zuo Di, "Meiyou guang de xing" (A Lustreless Star) (1943), repr. in Liang, ed., *Changye yinghuo*, 437.

61 Ibid.

62 Ibid., 442.

63 Another example is Wu Yuying, "Furen qianghou huodong zhi chengzhi" (Accomplishments of Women behind the Gun), *Xin Manzhou* (*New Manchukuo*) 2, no. 5 (1940): 61-6, which she also published under her real name.

64 Wu Yuying, "Zhangfu fushi" (Serving Husbands), *Xin Manzhou* (*New Manchukuo*) 2, no. 2 (1940): 70-2.

65 Ibid., 71.

66 Zuo, "Nü nan," 87.

67 Wu Ying, "Qian sipo" (Fourth Sister-in-law Qian), in Wu, *Liang ji*, 64.

68 Ibid., 65.

69 Wu, "Ming," 93.

70 Zuo, "Nü nan," 86.

71 Ibid.

72 Wu, "Ming," 94.

73 Lan Ling, "Zai jingjing de yulinli" (In a Quiet Forest), *Qingnian wenhua* (*Youth Culture*) 2, no. 2 (1944): 83-5, repr. in *Dongbei xiandai wenxue daxi, 1919-1949*, vol. 12, *Shige juan* (*Compendium of Modern Northeastern Literature, 1919-1949*, vol. 12, *Poetry*), ed. Zhang Yumao (Shenyang: Shenyang chubanshe, 1996), 834.

74 Dan Di, "Jie" (Warning), *Qingnian wenhua* (*Youth Culture*) 1, no. 3 (1943): 83.

75 Ibid.

76 Yang, "Gongkai de zuizhuang," 111.

77 All of these are fairly common topics among the writers under discussion, but homosexuality (*tongxinglian*) is explicitly raised only once in this literature, in Yang Xu's "Dang wo tai xinkao pengyou de shihou" (When I Trusted My Friend Too Much), in Yang, *Luoying ji*, 107.

78 Mochizuki Yuriko, "Zai Man-Ri xi nüxing tan" (Discussion of Feminism in Manchukuo and Japan), *Qingnian wenhua* 1, no. 3 (1943): 36.

79 Yang, "Fangfu shi yi chang wennuan de meng," 17.

80 Yang, "Gongkai de zuizhuang," 102.

81 Yang notes that this description is inspired by a description she read in a newspaper article. Yang, *Wo de riji*, 146.

82 Ibid.

83 Mei, "Yu," 98.

84 Yoshikawa is cited in Edward Gunn Jr., *Unwelcome Muse: Chinese Literature in Shanghai and Peking, 1937-45* (New York: Columbia University Press, 1980), 37.

85 Mei, "Yu," 73.

86 Ibid., 109.

87 Mei Niang, "Bang" (Clam), repr. in Liang, ed., *Changye yinghuo*, 173-4.

88 Ibid., 187.

89 Zhu Ti, "Yuantian de Liuxing" (A Shooting Star in a Faraway Sky), *Xin chao* (*New Tide*) 1, no. 7 (1943), repr. in Zhu Ti, *Ying* (*Cherry*) (Xinjing: Guomin tushu zhushi huishe, 1945), 92.

90 Ibid., 95.

91 Ibid.

92 Wu, "Xin youling," 18.

93 Ibid., 22.

94 Wu Ying, "Nü pantu" (Woman Rebel), in Wu, *Liang ji*, 31.

95 Wu, "Yu," 90.

96 He Bolong, *Widow and Neighbour*, in *Qilin* (*Unicorn*) 2, no. 10 (1942), 88.

97 Wu, "Yu," 92.

98 Ibid., 91.

99 Ibid., 92.

100 Mei Niang, "Luo Yan" (Fallen Yan), in Mei, *Di'er dai* (Xinjing: Wencong han xinghui, 1940), 188-9.

101 Zhu, "Xiao Yinzi he ta de jiazu," 488.

102 Zhu, "Du Bohai," 510.

103 Dan Di, "Shou xuezhe" (The Blood Donors) (1942), repr. in *Changye yinghuo* (*Fireflies of the Long Night*), ed. Liang Shanding (Shenyang: Chunfeng wenyi chubanshe, 1986), 234.

104 Wu, "Cui Hong," 307.

105 Zuo Di, "Zhai xiang" (Narrow Alley), *Dongbei minbao* (*Northeast People's Herald*), no. 1 (1946), repr. in Liang, ed., *Changye yinghuo*, 410.

106 Lan Ling, "Xiao xiang de chuxi" (New Year in a Small Alley), *Xin shige* (*New Poetry*), no. 1 (1940), repr. in Zhang Yumao, ed., *Dongbei xiandai wenxue daxi*, 12: 808.

Chapter 6: Contesting Colonial Society

1 Zuo Di cites Goethe despite official demands for cultural development to be based on Japanese, not Western, models. See Zuo Di, "Liu Qi" (Liu Qi), *Qilin* (*Unicorn*) 2, no. 10 (1942): 75-8, repr. in *Changye yinghuo* (*Fireflies of the Long Night*), ed. Liang Shanding (Shenyang: Chunfeng wenyi chubanshe, 1986), 393.

2 Yang Xu, "Luo hua shijie" (The Season of Fallen Flowers), in Yang Xu, *Luoying ji* (*Collection of Fallen Petals*) (Xinjing: Kaiming tushu gongsi, 1943), 64.

3 Zuo Di, "Zhai xiang" (Narrow Alley), *Dongbei minbao* (*Northeast People's Herald*), no. 1 (1946), repr. in Liang, ed., *Changye yinghuo*, 406-7.

4 Zhu Ti, "Meng yu qingchun" (Dreams and Youth), *Daban Huawen meiri* 10, no. 7 (1943): 42.

5 Dan Di, *Andi he Mahua* (*Andi and Mahua*), *Daban Huawen meiri* (*Chinese Osaka Daily*) 6, nos. 1, 2 (1940), repr. in Liang, ed., *Changye yinghuo*, 242.

6 Dan Di, "Yiguo" (Foreign Country), *Daban Huawen meiri* 4, no. 3 (1940): 39.

7 Zuo Di, "Nü nan" (Women's Difficulty), *Qingnian wenhua* 1, no. 3 (1943): 86.

8 Yang Xu, "Xiangfeng xin yi jiu" (Meeting Again, the Heart Is as Before), *Qilin* 2, no. 10 (1942): 74.

9 Lan Ling, "Zai jingjing de yulinli" (In a Quiet Forest), *Qingnian wenhua* (Youth Culture) 2, no. 2 (1944), repr. in *Dongbei xiandai wenxue daxi, 1919-49*, vol. 12, *Shige juan* (*Compendium of Modern Northeastern Literature, 1919-49*, vol. 12, *Poetry*), ed. Zhang Yumao (Shenyang: Shenyang chubanshe, 1996), 83.

10 Yang Xu, "Xiangfeng xin yi jiu," 77.

11 Yang Xu, "Yiqi Zhaoling" (Recalling the Zhao Mausoleum), *Qilin* 2, 10 (1942), repr. in *Dongbei xiandai wenxue daxi, 1919-1949*, vol. 10, *Sanwen juan* (*Compendium of Modern Northeastern Literature, 1919-1949*, vol. 10, *Essays*), ed. Zhang Yumao (Shenyang: Shenyang chubanshe, 1996), 542-4.

12 Zuo Di, "Yi ge huise de meng" (A Grey-Coloured Dream), *Qilin* 2, no. 4 (1942), repr. in Zhang, ed., *Dongbei xiandai wenxue daxi*, 10: 113.

13 Zhu Ti, "Bangwan de shiye" (Dusk Field of Vision), *Daban Huawen meiri* 11, no. 12 (1944): 31.

14 Ibid.

15 Mei, "Yu," 29.

16 A *qin* is a stringed musical instrument. Dan Di, "Meng yu guqin" (Dreams and an Old Qin), *Daban Huawen meiri* 6, no. 9 (1941), repr. in Zhang, ed., *Dongbei xiandai wenxue daxi*, 12: 519-20.

17 Dan Di, "Feng" (Wind), *Daban Huawen meiri* 4, no. 6 (1940), repr. in Liang, ed., *Changye yinghuo*, 219.

18 Ibid., 220.

19 Yang Xu, "Ye zhi ge" (Song of the Night), in Yang Xu, *Luoying ji*, 47.

20 Lan Ling, "Yehang" (Night Navigators), *Daban Huawen meiri* (1942), repr. in Liang, ed., *Changye yinghuo*, 3.

21 Yang Xu, "Jimo de shengyin" (The Sound of Loneliness), in Yang, *Luoying ji*, 3.

22 Yang Xu, "Yi qie dou shi yan" (Everything Is Smoke), in Yang, *Luoying ji*, 132.

23 Dan Di, "Kuangye li de gushi" (A Story in the Wilderness), *Huawen Daban Meiri* (*Chinese Osaka Daily*) 11, no. 5 (1944): 30.

24 Gunn, *Unwelcome Muse*, 42.

25 Liu Aihua, "Gudu de wudao: Dongbei luxian shiqi nüxing zuojia qunti xiaoshuo lun" (The Lonely Dance Floor: A Discussion of the Colonial Fiction of Women Writers from the Northeast Enemy Occupation Period) (PhD diss., Beijing shifan daxue, 1999), 136.

26 Yang Xu, *Wo de riji*, 144.

27 Yang Xu, "Piaoling de xin" (Forsaken Heart), in Yang Xu, *Luoying ji*, 145.

28 Yang Xu, "Xin de tiaodong" (Fluttering of the Heart), in Yang Xu, *Luoying ji*, 151-2.

29 Wu Ying, "Fuchen de xinyu" (Drifting Words from the Heart), *Qilin* 2, 4 (1942): 110, repr. in Zhang, ed., *Dongbei xiandai wenxue daxi*, 10: 110-11.

30 Ibid., 111.

31 Dan Di, "Riji chao" (Diary Excerpts), *Dongbei wenxue yanjiu shiliao* (*Research Materials on Literature of the Northeast*), no. 6 (December 1987): 173.

32 Dan, "Yiguo," 39.

33 Zhu Ti, "Wo he wo de haizimen" (Me and My Children), in Zhu Ti, *Ying* (*Cherry*) (Xinjing: Guomin tushu zhushi huishe, 1945), 76.

34 Ibid.

35 Ibid., 80.

36 Ibid.

37 Ibid.

38 Ibid., 84.

39 Ibid., 85.

40 A contemporary censor's report on "Jie" is reproduced in Yu Lei, trans., "Ziliao" (Data) in *Dongbei lunxian shiqi wenxue guoji xueshu yantaohui lunwenji* (*Collection of Papers from the International Symposium on Literature of the Enemy-Occupied Northeast*), ed. Feng Weiqun, Wang Jianzhong, Li Chunyan, and Li Shuquan (Shenyang: Shenyang chubanshe, 1992), 159.

41 The essay is not described in any detail. Dan Di, "Huma he zhi ye" (Night on the Huma River), *Daban Huawen meiri* 7, no. 4 (1941), repr. in Liang, ed., *Changye yinghuo*, 238.

42 Ibid., 240.

43 Ibid., 240-1.

44 Zuo Di, "Buqu de renmin" (Indomitable People), *Dongbei minbao* (*Northeast People*), no. 1 (1946), repr. in Liang, ed., *Changye yinghuo*, 427.

45 Wang Jianzhong notes linkages between the natural world and humans. See Wang Jianzhong, "Nü xing wenxue de jiao'ao: Ping *Changye yinghuo* de sixiang yishu chengjiu" (The Pride of Women's Literature: Appraising the Achievements in Ideological Artistry in *Fireflies of the Long Night*), in *Dongbei lunxian shiqi wenxue guoji xueshu yantaohui lunwenji* (*Collection of Papers from the International Symposium on Literature of the Enemy-Occupied Northeast*), ed. Feng Weiqun, Wang Jianzhong, Li Chunyan, Li Shuquan (Shenyang: Shenyang chubanshe, 1992), 275-7.

46 Zhu Ti, "Da Heilongjiang de youyu" (The Melancholy of the Mighty Black Dragon River), in *Funü huabao* (*Ladies Pictorial*) (1943), repr. in Liang, ed., *Changye yinghuo*, 477.

47 Ibid., 463.

48 Ibid., 460.

49 Ibid., 462.

50 Lan Ling, "Qiaopan" (Side of the Bridge), *Daban Huawen meiri* 4, no. 1 (1940): 46.

51 Lan Ling, "Tongnian zhi chun" (Spring in Childhood), *Daban Huawen meiri* 4, no. 4 (1940), repr. in Zhang, ed., *Dongbei xiandai wenxue daxi*, 10: 719.

52 Ibid.

53 Ibid.

54 Wu Ying, “Lianzhe de youren” (Missing Friends), *Daban Huawen meiri* 4, no. 3 (1940), repr. in Zhang, ed., *Dongbei xiandai wenxue daxi*, 10: 38.

55 Wu Ying, “Xiao jie (Mixed-Up Street),” *Wenxuan* (*Literary Selections*), no. 2 (1940), repr. in Liang, ed., *Changye yinghuo*, 318.

56 Wu Ying, “Wang xiang” (Gazing Homeward), in Wu, *Liang ji*, 136.

57 Mei Niang, “Bangwan de xiju” (An Evening’s Comedy), *Wenxuan* (*Literary Selections*), no. 1 (1940), repr. in *Mei Niang xiaoshuo sanwen ji* (*Mei Niang’s Collected Novels and Essays*), ed. Zhang Quan (Beijing: Beijing chubanshe, 1997), 10.

58 Ibid., 6.

59 Dan Di, “Kancaifu” (Wood-chopping Women), *Daban Huawen meiri* (1940), repr. in Liang, ed., *Changye yinghuo*, 227.

60 Ibid.

61 Lan Ling, *Dadi di de ernü* (*Sons and Daughters of the Great Land*), *Yiwenzhi* (*Chronicle of the Arts*) 1, no. 7 (1944): 118.

62 Ibid., 117.

63 Lan Ling, “Paomo” (Bubbles), *Dongbei wenxue* (*Northeast Literature*) 1, no. 1 (1945), repr. in *Dongbei xiandai wenxue daxi, 1919-1949*, vol. 4, *Duanpian xiaoshuo juan*, ed. Zhang Yumao (*Compendium of Modern Northeastern Literature, 1919-1949*, vol. 4, *Short Fiction*), 2082.

64 Ibid.

65 Lan Ling, “Zhuiqiu” (The Pursuit), *Xin shige* (*New Poetry*), no. 1 (1940), repr. in Zhang, ed., *Dongbei xiandai wenxue daxi*, 12: 812.

66 Mei Niang, *Xiao furen* (*Little Wife*), *Zhongguo wenxue* (*Chinese Literature*), no. 1 (1944), repr. in Zhang, ed., *Mei Niang xiaoshuo sanwen ji*, 330.

67 Ibid., 299.

68 For example, see ibid., 301, 331.

69 Zhang Quan, conference, Beijing, August 2005.

70 Zhu Ti, “Du Bohai,” 493.

71 Ibid.

72 Ibid., 494.

73 Ibid., 497-8.

74 Dan, *Andi*, 267.

75 Ibid., 276.

76 Ibid., 259.

77 Ibid., 287.

78 Lan, “Ke’erqin caoyuan de muzhe,” 819.

79 For example, see Zhou Qinghe, “Tian Lin de wenxue chuangzuo qingxiong he yishu tesi” (The Production Tendencies and Artistic Characteristics of Tian Lin’s Literature), *Dongbei wenxue yanjiu shiliao* (*Historical Research Materials on Northeastern Literature*), no. 6 (1987): 106-7. See also Fu Shangkui, “Minzu de beige, zhandou de haojiao: Lun Tian Lin xiaoshuo chuangzuo” (The Sad Melody of the Nation, the Bugle Call of Battle: A Discussion of Tian Lin’s Works of Fiction), *Dongbei xiandai wenxue shiliao* (*Historical Materials of Modern Literature of the Northeast*), no. 8 (1984): 219-20.

80 Dan Di, “Xuezu” (Flesh and Blood), *Dongbei wenxue* (*Northeastern Literature*) 1, no. 1 (1945), repr. in Zhang Yumao, ed., *Dongbei xiandai wenxue daxi, 1919-1949*, vol. 5, *Zhongpian xiaoshuo juan* (*Compendium of Modern Northeastern Literature, 1919-1949*, vol. 5, *Medium-Length Fiction*) (Shenyang: Shenyang chubanshe, 1996), 644-5.

81 Ibid., 674.

82 Ibid., 440. A *yaoqianshu* is a legendary tree that sheds coins when shaken.
83 Mei, *Xie*, 514.
84 The family was rumoured to have been Wu Ying's own family. See Wu Ying, "Wo zenyang xie de 'Xuyuan,'" 568-9.
85 Wu Ying, "Xuyuan" (Dilapidation), *Zhongguo wenyi* (*Chinese Arts*) 6, no. 5 (1942): 58.
86 Lan Ling, "Guxiang de jia" (Native Place Home), *Daban Huawen meiri* (*Chinese Osaka Daily*) 10, no. 1 (1943): 36.
87 Ibid., 37.
88 Mei Niang, *Di'er dai* (*The Second Generation*) (Xinjing: Wencong han xinghui, 1940), 20.
89 A *zongzi* is a dumpling made of glutinous rice wrapped in bamboo or reed leaves, a traditional dish associated with the Dragon Boat Festival. Lan Ling, "Duanwujie" (Dragon Boat Festival) (1937), repr. in Liang, ed., *Changye yinghuo*, 350.
90 Ibid.
91 Zuo, "Zhai xiang" (Narow Alley), 400.
92 Mei, *Xie*, 458-9.
93 Yang Xu, "Ye zhi ge," 46

Chapter 7: The Collapse of Empire and Careers

1 Zhu Ti, "Kugao de xinyuan shang saxia yipian yangguang" (Casting a Layer of Sunlight on Withered Dreams), *Dongbei wenxue yanjiu shiliao* (*Historical Research Materials of Northeast Literature*), no. 3 (September 1986): 171.
2 Yin Tiefen argues that Wu Ying's work, paralleling that of Lu Xun, sought to raise readers' consciousness of the shortcomings of contemporary society. See Yin Tiefen, "Wei nüren er zuo aishang zhi ge: Shilun Dongbei lunxian shiqi nüzuojia Wu Ying de xiaoshuo chuangzuo" (A Song of Sadness for Women: Tentative Views on the Fictional Works of Northeast Enemy Occupation Era Woman Writer Wu Ying), in *Dongbei lunxian shiqi wenxue guoji xueshu yantaohui lunwenji* (*Collection of Papers from the International Symposium on Literature of the Enemy-Occupied Northeast*), ed. Feng Weiqun, Wang Jianzhong, Li Chunyan, and Li Shuquan (Shenyang: Shenyang chubanshe, 1992), 319.
3 Yi Bing, "Nü zuojia Wu Ying shi fangwen ji" (Notes from an Interview with Female Writer Wu Ying), *Qilin* (*Unicorn*), no. 8 (1943): 137.
4 Wu Ying, "Ming" (Howl), *Qingnian wenhua* (*Youth Culture*) 1, no. 3 (1943): 90-1. For a censor's report on this work, see Yu Lei, trans., "Diwei mijian" (Secret Documents of the Enemy and Puppet Regime), *Dongbei wenxue yanjiu shiliao* (*Historical Research Materials of Northeastern Literature*), no. 6 (December 1987): 158-9; See also Sun Zhongtian, Feng Zengyu, Huang Wanhua, and Liu Aihua, *Liaokao xia de Miu Si: Dongbei lunxian qu wenxue shigang* (*The Shackled Muse: Historical Outline of the Literature of the Northeast Occupied Territories*) (Changchun: Jilin daxue chubanshe, 1999), 64-5.
5 Censors' reports were also issued for work by "left-wing" writers Dan Di, Jue Qing, Shan Ding, Shi Jun, Wu Lang, Yang Guangzhong, and Ye Li. See Li Chunyan, "Wenxue de lunxian yu lunxian de wenxue: Dongbei lunxian shiqi wenxue de ji ge xianzhu tedian" (The Enemy Occupation of Literature and the Literature of the Enemy Occupation: Several Notable Characteristics of the Literature of the Northeast Enemy Occupation Era), in Feng et al., eds., *Dongbei lunxian shiqi wenxue guoji xueshu yantaohui lunwenji*, 54-6.
6 As Wu Ying's "Ming" was being investigated for subversive content, Wu Lang had a poem and an essay similarly evaluated by censors. For details, see Feng Weiqun and Li Chunyan, *Dongbei lunxian shiqi wenxue xinlun* (*New Discourse on the Literature of the Northeast Occupation Era*) (Changchun: Jilin daxue chubanshe, 1991), 58.

7 Wu Ying, "Fu Mei Niang shu" (Responding to Mei Niang's Letter) *Funü zazhi* (*Ladies' Journal*) 5, no. 4 (1944): 20.

8 Ibid.

9 Wu Ying, "Ji Shan Ding shu" (Mailing Shan Ding a Letter), *Funü zazhi* (*Ladies' Journal*) 5, no. 4 (1944): 21.

10 For example, see Li Zhengzhong, "Liming qian zui hei'an de niandai" (The Darkest Time before the Dawn), *Dongbei wenxue yanjiu shiliao* (*Historical Research Materials of Northeast Literature*), no. 3 (September 1986): 170-1.

11 Lan Ling, "Ganxiang yu xinwang" (Reflections and Wishes), ibid., 166.

12 Zhu Zhenhua [Lan Ling], "Xi er dao jie shi hao de dong xiangfang" (The East Wing of Number Ten on West Second Street), *Qiqiqhaar ribao: Chuanghan* (*The Qiqihaar Daily: Achievements in Publication*) (Qiqihaar: Qiqihaar ribao, 1985), 92.

13 Fu Shangkui, "Fang nüzuojia Tian Lin" (Searching for Woman Writer Tian Lin), *Dongbei xiandai wenxue shiliao* (*Historical Materials of Modern Northeastern Literature*), no. 5 (1982): 214.

14 Cited in Xu Naixiang and Huang Wanhua, *Zhongguo kangzhan shiqi lunxianqu wenxue shi* (*History of the Literature of the Enemy-Occupied Territories during China's War of Resistance*) (Fuzhou: Fujian jiaoyu chubanshe, 1995), 289.

15 Cited in Shangguan Yin, "Dongbei lunxian shiqi wenxue ceying" (Profile of the Northeast Occupied Territory's Literature), in Shangguan Yin, *Yiwen luantan* (*Random Notes on Literature and Art*) (Changchun: Shidai wenyi chubanshe, 1989), 109.

16 The details of this imprisonment are recounted in Tian Lin, "San ru lianyu" (Thrice into Purgatory), manuscript, 116-233.

17 Fu, "Fang nüzuojia Tian Lin," 214.

18 Ibid.

19 Wang Jianzhong and Li Shuquan, "Wu cai binfen de nüxing shijie yu shao'er shijie: Ping nüzuojia Luo Mai de *Luo Mai shiwen ji*" (A Riot of Colour in Women's World and Young Men's World: Evaluating Woman Writer Luo Mai's *Collection of Luo Mai's Writings*), in Feng et al., eds., *Dongbei lunxian shiqi wenxue guoji xueshu yantaohui lunwenji*, 326.

20 Liang Shanding, "Shi nian shengsi liang mangmang: Zuo Di shisi shi zhou nian" (Ten Years in the Vastness of Life and Death: The Ten-Year Anniversary of Zuo Di's Death), in *Luo Mai xiaoshuo sanwen ji*, ed. Liang Shanding (Shenyang: Shenyang renmin chubanshe, 1990), 209-10.

21 Luo Ying and Luo Yan, "Luo Mai nianbiao" (Luo Mai's Chronological Table), in Liang, ed., *Luo Mai xiaoshuo sanwen ji*, 232.

22 See Wei Changming,"*Dongbei Wenxue* fakan qianhou" (Before and After the Publication of *Northeastern Literature*), *Dongbei wenxue yanjiu shiliao* (*Historical Research Materials of Northeastern Literature*), no. 3, (1986): 107-11.

23 Liang Shanding, "Shou huanying de Miao Si" (The Welcomed Muse), *Dongbei wenxue yanjiu shiliao* (*Research Materials on Literature of the Northeast*), no. 6 (December 1987): 133.

24 Yang Xu, personal interview, Shenyang, 12 November 1999.

25 Li Zhengzhong, personal interview, Vancouver, 23 September 2001.

26 Luo and Luo, "Luo Mai nianbiao," 232-3.

27 Lan Ling, personal correspondence, 30 July 2000.

28 Tian, "San ru lianyu," 257.

29 Zhou Qinghe, "Tian Lin de wenxue chuangzuo qingxiong he yishu tesi" (The Production Tendencies and Artistic Characteristics of Tian Lin's Literature), *Dongbei wenxue yanjiu shiliao* (*Historical Research Materials on Northeastern Literature*), no. 6, (1987): 107.

30 Tian, "San ru lianyu," 287-99.

31 Ibid.

32 Lan Ling, personal correspondence, 30 July 2000.

33 Luo and Luo, "Luo Mai nianbiao," 236.

34 Yu Yanbin, "Wo liuxiale beishang he xiyue: Shenqie huainian Luo Mai tongzhi" (I Cry Tears of Sadness and Joy: Heartfelt Memories of Comrade Luo Mai), in Liang, ed., *Luo Mai xiaoshuo sanwen ji*, 188-9. See also Luo and Luo, "Luo Mai nianbiao," 236.

35 For an account of her active life during this period, see Da Ting, "Huainian wo de muqin Luo Mai [Zuo Di]" (Cherishing the Memory of My Mother Luo Mai [Zuo Di]), *Dongbei wenxue yanjiu shiliao (Historical Research Materials of Northeast Literature)*, no. 5 (1987): 123-4.

36 Guo Daoyi, "Mei Niang: Bu shi yong mei sheng yong mei" (Mei Niang: This Isn't an "Ode to the Plum," It's Better Than an "Ode to the Plum"), in *Xunzhao Mei Niang* (*Searching for the World of Mei Niang*), ed. Zhang Quan (Brampton, ON: Mirror Books, 1998), 54.

37 Yang Xu, personal interview, Shenyang, 12 November 1999.

38 Luo and Luo, "Luo Mai nianbiao," 235.

39 Wang Qiuying, "Wo suo zhidao de dongbei lunxianqi Shengyang wenxue" (All I Know about Shenyang Literature from the Era of the Enemy Occupation of the Northeast), *Dongbei wenxue yanjiu shiliao* (*Historical Research Materials on Northeastern Literature*), no. 6 (1987): 21; Zhong Dazhong "Nan Ling Bei Mei de 'Mei'" (The "Mei" of the South Has Zhang Ailing, the North Has Mei Niang), in Zhang, ed., *Xunzhao Mei Niang*, 54.

40 Yang Xu, personal interview, Shenyang, 12 November 1999.

41 Fu, "Fang nüzuojia Tian Lin," 215.

42 Wang, "Wo suozhidao de Dongbei lunxian wenxue," 21; Zhong, "Nan Ling Bei Mei de 'Mei,'" 62.

43 Mei Niang noted personality clashes with her superior at the Agricultural Film Studio. Mei Niang, personal interview, Vancouver, 18 June 2001.

44 Yang Yong, "Caifang Mei Niang" (Interview with Mei Niang), in Zhang, ed., *Xunzhao Mei Niang*, 71.

45 Sheng Ying, *Ershi shiji Zhongguo nüxing wenxueshi* (*History of Twentieth-Century Chinese Women's Literature*) (Tianjin: Tianjin renmin chubanshe, 1995), 529; Liu Qing, personal interview, Vancouver, 18 June 2001.

46 Zhu Ti, personal interview, Shenyang, 14 February 2001.

47 Zhu Ti, personal interview, Oxford, 31 October 2004

48 Liang Dating, "Huainian wo de muqin" (Remembering My Mother), in Liang, ed., *Luo Mai xiaoshuo sanwen ji*, 213-14.

49 Luo and Luo, "Luo Mai nianbiao," 237.

50 Family members have speculated that upon hearing the news of Mao's death, Zuo Di passed out and never resumed consciousness. Liang, "Huainian wo de muqin," 216.

51 Sheng, *Ershi shiji Zhongguo nüxing wenxue shi*, 529; Liu Qing, personal interview, Vancouver, 18 June 2001.

52 Tian Lin, "Wei Changye yinghuo dansheng er huanhu" (Hailing the Birth of *Fireflies of the Long Night*), *Dongbei wenxue yanjiu shiliao* (*Historical Research Materials of Northeast Literature*), no. 5. (1987): 81.

53 Mei Niang published in journals such as *Lüyou* (*Travel*) and Hong Kong's *Dagong* (*Unity*).

54 Zhang Quan, "Wei wanjie de huati: Luxianqu wenxue de zhengzhi pingjia" (Unfinished Conversation: Political Evaluation of Enemy-Occupied Territory Literature), in Zhang, ed., *Xunzhao Mei Niang*, 493.

Chapter 8: Resisting Manchukuo

1 Personal interviews with Lan Ling and Mei Niang, Beijing, 15 November 1999 and with Yang Xu and Zhu Ti, Shenyang, 12 November 1999.

2 Yang Xu, *Wo de riji* (*My Diary*) (Xinjing: Kaiming tushu gongsi, 1944), 151.

3 Francine Muel-Dreyfus, *Vichy and the Eternal Feminine: A Contribution to a Political Sociology of Gender*, trans. Kathleen A. Johnson (Durham, NC: Duke University Press, 2001), 97.

4 In *Xie*, Mei Niang describes the sound of a car engine in the night as a source of panic for Xinjing's residents, who lived in fear of government officials. See Mei Niang, *Xie* (*Crabs*), in Mei Niang, *Xie* (*Crabs*) (Beijing: Xinmin yinshuguan, 1944), repr. in *Dongbei xiandai wenxue daxi, 1919-1949*, vol. 5, *Zhongpian xiaoshuo juan* (*Compendium of Modern Northeastern Literature, 1919-1949*, vol. 5, *Medium-Length Fiction*), ed. Zhang Yumao, (Shenyang: Shenyang chubanshe, 1996), 10-11.

5 Miranda Pollard, *Reign of Virtue: Mobilizing Gender in Vichy France* (Chicago: University of Chicago Press, 1998), 70.

Bibliography

Chinese-Language Sources

Bai Wu. "Funü yu wenhua" (Women and Culture). *Daban Huawen meiri* (*Chinese Osaka Daily*) 8, no. 8 (1941): 29-31.

Da Ting. "Huainian wo de muqin Luo Mai (Zuo Di)" (Cherishing the Memory of My Mother Luo Mai [Zuo Di]). *Dongbei wenxue yanjiu shiliao* (*Historical Research Materials of Northeastern Literature*), no. 5 (1987): 123-4.

Dan Di. *Andi he Mahua* (*Andi and Mahua*). Serialized novella. *Daban Huawen meiri* (*Chinese Osaka Daily*) 6, nos. 1-2 (1940). Reprinted in *Changye yinghuo* (*Fireflies of the Long Night*), ed. Liang Shanding, 242-302. Shenyang: Chunfeng wenyi chubanshe, 1986.

–. "Feng" (Wind). *Daban Huawen meiri* (*Chinese Osaka Daily*) 4, no. 6 (1940). Reprinted in *Changye yinghuo* (*Fireflies of the Long Night*), ed. Liang Shanding, 219-22. Shenyang: Chunfeng wenyi chubanshe, 1986.

–. "Gan" (Feelings). *Daban Huawen meiri* (*Chinese Osaka Daily*) 5, no. 10 (1940): 44.

–. "Huma he zhi ye" (Night on the Huma River). *Daban Huawen meiri* (*Chinese Osaka Daily*) 7, no. 4 (1941). Reprinted in *Changye yinghuo* (*Fireflies of the Long Night*), ed. Liang Shanding, 238-41. Shenyang: Chunfeng wenyi chubanshe, 1986.

–. "Jie" (Warning). *Qingnian wenhua* (*Youth Culture*) 1, no. 3 (1943): 83-5.

–. "Kancaifu" (Wood-chopping Women). *Daban Huawen meiri* (*Chinese Osaka Daily*) (1940). Reprinted in *Changye yinghuo* (*Fireflies of the Long Night*), ed. Liang Shanding, 223-8. Shenyang: Chunfeng wenyi chubanshe, 1986.

–. "Kuangye li de gushi" (A Story in the Wilderness). *Daban Huawen Meiri* (*Chinese Osaka Daily*) 11, no. 5 (1944): 29-30.

–. "Meng yu guqin" (Dreams and an Old Qin). *Daban Huawen meiri* (*Chinese Osaka Daily*) 6, no. 9 (1941). Reprinted in *Dongbei xiandai wenxue daxi, 1919-1949*. Vol. 12, *Shige juan* (*Compendium of Modern Northeastern Literature, 1919-1949*. Vol. 12, *Poetry*), ed. Zhang Yumao, 519-20. Shenyang: Shenyang chubanshe, 1996, 519-20.

–. "Riji chao" (Diary excerpts). *Dongbei wenxue yanjiu shiliao* (*Historical Research Materials on Northeastern Literature*), no. 6 (December 1987): 173-80.

–. "Shou xuezhe" (The Blood Donors) (1942). Reprinted in *Changye yinghuo* (*Fireflies of the Long Night*), ed. Liang Shanding, 229-37. Shenyang: Chunfeng wenyi chubanshe, 1986.

–. "Wo de ge" (My Song). *Daban Huawen meiri* (*Chinese Osaka Daily*) 6, no. 9 (May 1941). Reprinted in *Dongbei xiandai wenxue daxi, 1919-1949*. Vol. 12, *Shige juan* (*Compendium of Modern Northeastern Literature, 1919-1949*. Vol. 12, *Poetry*), ed. Zhang Yumao, 520-2. Shenyang: Shenyang chubanshe, 1996.

–. "Xuezu" (Flesh and Blood). *Dongbei wenxue* (*Northeastern Literature*) 1, no. 1 (1945): 4-31. Reprinted in *Dongbei xiandai wenxue daxi,*

1919-1949. Vol. 5, *Zhongpian xiaoshuo juan* (*Compendium of Modern Northeastern Literature, 1919-1949*. Vol. 5, *Medium-Length Fiction*), ed. Zhang Yumao, 635-77. Shenyang: Shenyang chubanshe, 1996.

–. "Yiguo" (Foreign Country). *Daban Huawen meiri* (*Chinese Osaka Daily*) 4, no. 3 (1940): 39. Reprinted in *Dongbei xiandai wenxue daxi, 1919-1949*. Vol. 10, *Sanwen juan*. (*Compendium of Modern Northeastern Literature, 1919-1949*. Vol. 10, *Essays*), ed. Zhang Yumao, 344-7. Shenyang: Shenyang chubanshe, 1996.

Dong Xingquan. "'Wu si' yundong yu Dongbei lunxian qu wenxue" ("May Fourth" Activities and the Literature of the Northeast Enemy-Occupied Territories). In *Dongbei lunxian shiqi wenxue guoji xueshu yantaohui lunwenji* (*Collection of Papers from the International Symposium on Literature of the Enemy-Occupied Northeast*), ed. Feng Weiqun, Wang Jianzhong, Li Chunyan, Li Shuquan, 107-19. Shenyang: Shenyang chubanshe, 1992.

Feng Weiqun. "Shi Hanjian wenxue haishi kang-Ri wenxue" (Is It the Literature of Traitors to China or Literature of the Anti-Japanese Resistance?). In *Dongbei lunxian shiqi wenxue guoji xueshu yantaohui lunwenji* (*Collection of Papers from the International Symposium on Literature of the Enemy-Occupied Northeast*), ed. Feng Weiqun, Wang Jianzhong, Li Chunyan, Li Shuquan, 91-106. Shenyang: Shenyang chubanshe, 1992.

Feng Weiqun and Li Chunyan. *Dongbei lunxian shiqi wenxue xinlun* (*New Discourse on the Literature of the Northeast Occupation*). Changchun: Jilin daxue chubanshe, 1991.

Feng Weiqun, Wang Jianzhong, Li Chunyan, Li Shuquan, eds. *Dongbei lunxian shiqi wenxue guoji xueshu yantaohui lunwenji* (*Collection of Papers from the International Symposium on Literature of the Enemy-Occupied Northeast*). Shenyang: Shenyang chubanshe, 1992.

Feng Zengyu. "Dongbei lunxian qi xiangtu wenxue yu Zhongguo xiandai wenxue shi shang xiangtu wenxue zhi bijiao" (A Comparison of Native Place Literature from the Enemy Occupation of the Northeast and Native Place Literature in Contemporary Chinese Literature). In *Dongbei lunxian shiqi wenxue guoji xueshu yantaohui lunwenji* (*Collection of Papers from the International Symposium on Literature of the Enemy-Occupied Northeast*), ed. Feng Weiqun, Wang Jianzhong, Li Chunyan, Li Shuquan, 63-74. Shenyang: Shenyang chubanshe, 1992.

Fu Shangkui. "Fang nüzuojia Tian Lin" (Searching for Woman Writer Tian Lin). *Dongbei xiandai wenxue shiliao* (*Historical Materials of Modern Northeastern Literature*), no. 5 (1982): 212-15.

–. "Minzu de beige, zhandou de haojiao: Lun Tian Lin xiaoshuo chuangzuo" (The Sad Melody of the Nation, the Bugle Call of Battle: A Discussion of Tian Lin's Works of Fiction). *Dongbei xiandai wenxue shiliao* (*Historical Materials of Modern Literature of the Northeast*), no. 8 (1984): 218-27.

Guo Daoyi. "Mei Niang: Bu shi yong mei sheng yong mei" (Mei Niang: This Isn't an 'Ode to the Plum,' It's Better Than an 'Ode to the Plum'). In *Xunzhao Mei Niang* (*Searching for the World of Mei Niang*), ed. Zhang Quan, 47-56. Brampton, ON: Mirror Books, 1998.

Han Hu. "*Di'er dai* lun" (Discussion of the *Second Generation*). Dalian: Datong bao wenyi, 1943. Reprinted in *Dongbei xiandai wenxue daxi, 1919-1949*. Vol. 10, *Sanwen juan* (*Compendium of Modern Northeastern Literature, 1919-1949*. Vol. 10, *Essays*), ed. Zhang Yumao, 453-58. Shenyang: Shenyang chubanshe, 1996.

Hu Lingzhi. "Shanghai, Huabei deng lunxian qu de wenxue shetuan" (Literary Mass Organisations of Shanghai, North China and Other Occupied Territories). In *Zhongguo xiandai wenxue shetuan liupai* (*Mass Organization Factions in Modern Chinese Literature*), ed. Jia Zhifang, 1059-84. Nanjing: Jiangsu jiaoyu chuban she, 1989.

Jia Ren. "Zhi Yang Xu nüshi" (To Madame Yang Xu). *Xin Manzhou* (*New Manchukuo*) 5, no. 2 (1943): 96.

Jie Xueshi. "Ri wei shiqi de wenhua tongzhi zhengce" (State Policies of Cultural Domination during the Japanese Occupation). In *Dongbei lunxian shiqi wenxue guoji xueshu yantaohui lunwenji* (*Collection of Papers from the International Symposium on Literature of the Enemy-Occupied Northeast*), ed. Feng Weiqun, Wang Jianzhong, Li Chunyan, Li Shuquan, 182-98. Shenyang: Shenyang chubanshe, 1992.

Jin Xunmin. "Zuo ri de huang hua, 'Qiutu' de beige: Dongbei lunxian shiqi wenxue zai renshi" (Yesterday's Yellow Flowers, the Sad Melody of 'Prisoners': Understanding again the Literature of the Northeast Enemy Occupation Era). In *Dongbei lunxian shiqi wenxue guoji xueshu yantaohui lunwenji* (*Collection of Papers from the International Symposium on Literature of the Enemy-Occupied Northeast*), ed. Feng Weiqun, Wang Jianzhong, Li Chunyan, Li Shuquan, 27-40. Shenyang: Shenyang chubanshe, 1992.

Kazeta Eiki. "Wei Manzhouguo wenyi zhangye de fazhan" (The Development of Bogus Manchukuo's Literary Rules and Regulations). In *Dongbei lunxian shiqi wenxue guoji xueshu yantaohui lunwenji* (*Collection of Papers from the International Symposium on Literature of the Enemy-Occupied Northeast*), ed. Feng Weiqun, Wang Jianzhong, Li Chunyan, Li Shuquan, 156-81. Shenyang: Shenyang chubanshe, 1992.

Lan Ling. "Da di de ernü" (Sons and Daughters of the Great Land). *Yiwenzhi* (*Chronicle of the Arts*) 1, no. 7 (1944): 112-18.

–. "Duanwujie" (Dragon Boat Festival) (1937). Reprinted in *Changye yinghuo* (*Fireflies of the Long Night*), ed. Liang Shanding, 349-53. Shenyang: Chunfeng wenyi chubanshe, 1986.

–. "Ganxiang yu xinwang" (Reflections and Wishes). *Dongbei wenxue yanjiu shiliao* (*Historical Research Materials of Northeastern Literature*), no. 3 (September 1986): 165-7.

–. "Guxiang de jia" (Native Place Home). *Daban Huawen meiri* (*Chinese Osaka Daily*) 10, no. 1 (1943): 34-8.

–. "Ke'erqin de muzhe" (The Shepherd of the Ke'erqin Plains). *Qingnian wenhua* (*Youth Culture*) 1, no. 3 (1944): 88-9. Reprinted in *Dongbei xiandai wenxue daxi, 1919-1949*. Vol. 12, *Shige juan* (*Compendium of Modern Northeastern Literature, 1919-1949*. Vol. 12, *Poetry*), ed. Zhang Yumao, 816-22. Shenyang: Shenyang chubanshe, 1996.

–. "Paomo (Bubbles)." *Dongbei Wenxue* (*Northeastern Literature*) 1, no. 1 (1945): 68-79. Reprinted in *Dongbei xiandai wenxue daxi, 1919-1949*. Vol. 4, *Duanpian xiaoshuo juan* (*Compendium of Modern Northeastern Literature, 1919-1949*. Vol. 4, *Short Fiction*), ed. Zhang Yumao, 2082-2101.Shenyang: Shenyang chubanshe, 1996.

–. "Qiaopan" (Side of the Bridge). *Daban Huawen meiri* (*Chinese Osaka Daily*) 4, no. 1 (1940): 46.

–. "Richu" (Sunrise). *Xin Manzhou* (*New Manchukuo*) 6, no. 10 (1944): 32-5. Reprinted in *Changye yinghuo* (*Fireflies of the Long Night*), ed. Liang Shanding, 354-62. Shenyang: Chunfeng wenyi chubanshe, 1986.

–. "Tongnian zhi chun" (Spring in Childhood). *Daban Huawen meiri* (*Chinese Osaka Daily*) 4, no. 4 (1940). Reprinted in *Dongbei xiandai wenxue daxi, 1919-1949*. Vol. 10, *Sanwen juan* (*Compendium of Modern Northeastern Literature, 1919-1949*. Vol. 10, *Essays*), ed. Zhang Yumao, 718-19. Shenyang: Shenyang chubanshe, 1996.

–. "Xiao xiang de chuxi" (New Year in a Small Alley). *Xin shige* (*New Poetry*), no. 1 (1940). Reprinted in *Dongbei xiandai wenxue daxi, 1919-1949*. Vol. 12, *Shige juan* (*Compendium of Modern Northeastern Literature, 1919-1949*. Vol. 12, *Poetry*), ed. Zhang Yumao, 808-11. Shenyang: Shenyang chubanshe, 1996.

–. "Yan" (Feast). *Daban Huawen meiri* (*Chinese Osaka Daily*) 4, no. 4 (1940). Reprinted in *Dongbei xiandai wenxue daxi, 1919-1949*. Vol. 10, *Sanwen juan* (*Compendium of Modern Northeastern Literature, 1919-1949*. Vol. 10, *Essays*), ed. Zhang Yumao, 716-18. Shenyang: Shenyang chubanshe, 1996.

–. "Yehang" (Night Navigators). *Daban Huawen meiri* (*Chinese Osaka Daily*) 9, no. 8 (1942).

Reprinted in *Changye yinghuo* (*Fireflies of the Long Night*), ed. Liang Shanding, 363-87. Shenyang: Chunfeng wenyi chubanshe, 1986.

–. "Zai jingjing de yulinli" (In a Quiet Forest). *Qingnian wenhua* (*Youth Culture*) 2, no. 2 (1944): 83-5. Reprinted in *Dongbei xiandai wenxue daxi, 1919-1949*. Vol. 12, *Shige juan* (*Compendium of Modern Northeastern Literature, 1919-1949*. Vol. 12, *Poetry*), ed. Zhang Yumao, 823-35. Shenyang: Shenyang chubanshe, 1996.

–. "Zhuiqui" (The Pursuit). *Xin shige* (*New Poetry*), no. 1 (1940). Reprinted in *Dongbei xiandai wenxue daxi, 1919-1949*. Vol. 12, *Shige juan* (*Compendium of Modern Northeastern Literature, 1919-1949*. Vol. 12, *Poetry*), ed. Zhang Yumao, 811-12. Shenyang: Shenyang chubanshe, 1996.

Li Chunyan. *Dongbei wenxue wenhua xinlun*. (*New Discourse on Northeastern Literary Culture*). Changchun: Jilin wenshi chubanshe, 2000.

–. "Wenxue de lunxian yu lunxian de wenxue: Dongbei lunxian shiqi wenxue de ji ge xianzhu tedian" (The Enemy Occupation of Literature and the Literature of the Enemy Occupation: Several Notable Characteristics of the Literature of the Northeast Enemy Occupation Era). In *Dongbei lunxian shiqi wenxue guoji xueshu yantaohui lunwenji* (*Collection of Papers from the International Symposium on Literature of the Enemy-Occupied Northeast*), ed. Feng Weiqun, Wang Jianzhong, Li Chunyan, Li Shuquan, 41-62. Shenyang: Shenyang chubanshe, 1992.

–. "Zai anye li ranshaozhe de huohua: Tan Wang Qiuying zai Dongbei lunxian shiqi de xiaoshuo chuangzuo" (Burning Sparks in the Dark Night: Discussion of Wang Qiuying's Production of Fiction during the Northeast Occupation). *Dongbei wenxue yanjiu shiliao* (*Historical Research Materials of Northeastern Literature*), no. 3 (September 1986): 24-9.

Li Zhengzhong. "Liming qian zui hei'an de niandai" (The Darkest Time before the Dawn). *Dongbei wenxue yanjiu shiliao* (*Historical Research Materials of Northeastern Literature*), no. 3 (September 1986): 170-1.

Liang Dating. "Huainian wo de muqin" (Remembering My Mother). In *Luo Mai xiaoshuo sanwen ji* (*Luo Mai's Collected Short Stories and Essays*), ed. Liang Shanding, 212-19. Shenyang: Shenyang renmin chubanshe, 1990.

Liang Shanding, ed. *Changye yinghuo* (*Fireflies of the Long Night*). Shenyang: Chunfeng wenyi chubanshe, 1986.

–. "Dai xue chong han zhe nen huang" (Carrying Snow, Dashing Into the Cold, Turning Yellow). In *Changye yinghuo* (*Fireflies of the Long Night*), ed. Liang Shanding, 1-6. Shenyang: Chunfeng wenyi chubanshe, 1986.

–. "Shi nian shengsi liang mangmang: Zuo Di shisi shi zhou nian" (Ten Years in the Vastness of Life and Death: Zuo Di Dead Ten Years). In *Luo Mai xiaoshuo sanwen ji* (*Luo Mai's Collected Short Stories and Essays*), ed. Liang Shanding, 198-211. Shenyang: Shenyang renmin chubanshe, 1990.

–. "Shou huanying de Miusi" (The Welcomed Muse). In *Dongbei wenxue yanjiu shiliao* (*Historical Research Materials on Northeastern Literature*), no. 6 (December 1987): 130-8.

Liu Aihua. "Gudu de wudao: Dongbei luxian shiqi nüxing zuojia qunti xiaoshuo lun" (The Lonely Dance: A Discussion of the Colonial Fiction of Women Writers from the Northeast Enemy-Occupation Period). PhD diss., Beijing shifan daxue, 1999.

Liu Huijuan and Xu Qian. "Zhongguo xiandai wenxue shi shang bu ke queshao de pianzhang: Jianshu Dongbei lunxian shiqi zuoyi wenxue huodong" (Writings That the History of Contemporary Chinese Literature Cannot Lack: A Brief Account of Left-Wing Literary Activities during the Northeast's Enemy-Occupation Era). In *Dongbei lunxian shiqi wenxue guoji xueshu yantaohui lunwenji* (*Collection of Papers from the International Symposium on Literature of the Enemy-Occupied Northeast*), ed. Feng

Weiqun, Wang Jianzhong, Li Chunyan, Li Shuquan, 75-90. Shenyang: Shenyang chubanshe, 1992.

Liu Jinghui. *Minzu, xingbie yu jieceng* (*Nation, Gender and Social Stratum*). Beijing: Shehui kexue xenxian chubanshe, 2004.

Lü Qinwen. "Dongbei lunxian qu de wailai wenxue yu xiangtu wenxue" (External and Local Literature of the Northeast Occupied Territories). In *Zhongri zhanzheng yu wenxue* (*Sino-Japanese War and Literature*), ed. Yamada Keizō and Lü Kangming, 127-59. Changchun: Dongbei shifan daxue chubanshe, 1992.

–. "Dongbei lunxian shiqi de wenxue shetuan" (The Literary Mass Organisations during the Northeast Occupation). In *Zhongguo xiandai wenxue shetuan liupai* (*Mass Organisation Factions in Chinese Modern Literature*), ed. Jia Zhifang, 1085-1118. Nanjing: Jiangsu jiaoyu chubanshe, 1989.

Luo Ping and Luo Ling. "Shenqie de huainian" (Fond Memories). In *Luo Mai xiaoshuo sanwen ji* (*Luo Mai's Collected Short Stories and Essays*), ed. Liang Shanding, 220-8. Shenyang: Shenyang renmin chubanshe, 1990.

Luo Ying and Luo Yan. "Luo Mai nianbiao" (Luo Mai's Chronological Table). In *Luo Mai xiaoshuo sanwen ji* (*Luo Mai's Collected Short Stories and Essays*), ed. Liang Shanding, 229-38. Shenyang: Shenyang renmin chubanshe, 1990.

Mei Niang. "Bang" (Clam). In Mei Niang, *Yu* (*Fish*). Beijing: Xinmin yinshuguan, 1943. Reprinted in *Changye yinghuo* (*Fireflies of the Long Night*), ed. Liang Shanding, 158-216. Shenyang: Chunfeng wenyi chubanshe, 1986.

–. "Bangwan de xiju" (An Evening's Comedy). *Wenxuan* (*Literary Selections*), no. 1 (1940): 75-81. Reprinted in *Mei Niang xiaoshuo sanwen ji* (*Mei Niang's Collected Novels and Essays*), ed. Zhang Quan, 1-12. Beijing: Beijing chubanshe, 1997.

–. "Di'er dai" (The Second Generation). In Mei Niang, *Di'er dai* (*The Second Generation*), 1-52. Xinjing: Wencong han xinghui, 1940.

–. "Ji Wu Ying shu" (Mailing a Letter to Wu Ying). *Qingnian wenhua* (*Youth Culture*) 1, no. 1 (1943): 84.

–. "Jinian Tian Lin" (Remembering Tian Lin). In *Mei Niang xiaoshuo sanwen ji* (*Mei Niang's Collected Novels and Essays*), ed. Zhang Quan, 594-6. Beijing: Beijing chubanshe, 1997.

–. "Luoyan" (Fallen Yan). In Mei Niang, *Di'er dai* (*The Second Generation*), 159-90. Xinjing: Wencong han xinghui, 1940.

–. "Qiaomin" (Expatriates). *Xin Manzhou* (*New Manchukuo*) 3, no. 6 (1941): 180-4.

–. "Songhua jiang de buyu" (The Nurturing Songhua River). In *Xiao Jun jinian ji* (*Commemorative Collection for Xiao Jun*), ed. Liang Shanding, 230-3. Shenyang: Chunfeng wenyi chubanshe, 1990.

–. "Wo de qingshaonian shiqi: 1920-1938" (My Childhood, 1920-1938). In *Xunzhao Mei Niang* (*Searching for the World of Mei Niang*), ed. Zhang Quan, 97-128. Brampton, ON: Mirror Books, 1998.

–. "Wo mei kanjianguo niang de xiaolian" (I Never Saw Mother's Smiling Face). *Funü zazhi* (*Ladies' Journal*), November 1944. Reprinted in *Mei Niang xiaoshuo sanwen ji* (*Mei Niang's Collected Novels and Essays*), ed. Zhang Quan, 511-12. Beijing: Beijing chubanshe, 1997.

–. "Wo yu Riben" (Me and Japan). In *Xunzhao Mei Niang* (*Searching for the World of Mei Niang*), ed. Zhang Quan, 143-6. Brampton, ON: Mirror Books, 1998.

–. *Xiao furen* (*Little Wife*). *Zhongguo wenxue* (*Chinese Literature*) (1944). Reprinted in *Mei Niang xiaoshuo sanwen ji* (*Mei Niang's Collected Novels and Essays*), ed. Zhang Quan, 296-393. Beijing: Beijing chubanshe, 1997.

–. *Xie* (*Crabs*). In Mei Niang, *Xie* (*Crabs*). Beijing: Xinmin yinshuguan, 1944. Reprinted in *Dongbei xiandai wenxue daxi, 1919-1949*. Vol. 5, *Zhongpian xiaoshuo juan* (*Compendium of Modern Northeastern Literature, 1919-1949*. Vol. 5, *Medium-Length Fiction*), ed. Zhang Yumao, 428-539. Shenyang: Shenyang chubanshe, 1996.

–. *Ye he hua kai* (*Flowers That Blossom in the Night*), 1943. Reprinted in *Mei Niang xiaoshuo sanwen ji* (*Mei Niang's Collected Novels and Essays*), ed. Zhang Quan, 394-508. Beijing: Beijing chubanshe, 1997.

–. "Yi ge chaqu" (A Sideline). In *Dongbei lunxian shiqi wenxue* (*Literature of the Northeast Enemy-Occupation Period*), ed. Feng Weiqun, Wang Jianzhong, Li Chunyan, Li Shuquan, 414-16. Shenyang: Shenyang chubanshe, 1992.

–. "Yu" (Fish). In Mei Niang. *Yu* (*Fish*). Beijing: Xinmin yinshuguan, 1943, 27-74. Reprinted in *Mei Niang xiaoshuo sanwen ji* (*Mei Niang's Collected Novels and Essays*), ed. Zhang Quan, 75-110. Beijing: Beijing chubanshe, 1997.

Mochizuki Yuriko. "Zai Man-Ri xi nüxing tan" (Discussion of Feminism in Japan and Manzhouguo). *Qingnian wenhua* (*Youth Culture*) 1, no. 3 (1943): 35-6.

"Nimen zhidao ma? Qingnian nüxing de lixiang huoban shi jianchuan nüxing de xin keti" (Do You Know? Women's Ideal Partner Is a Healthy Women's New Topic). *Xin Manzhou* (*New Manchukuo*) 3, no. 10 (1941): 54-7.

Qian Liqun, ed. *Zhongguo lunxianqu wenxue daxi. Shiliao juan* (*Compendium of the Literature of China's Enemy-Occupied Territories. Volume of Historical Data*). Nanling, Guangxi: Guangxi jiaoyu chubanshe, 2000.

Shan Ding, ed. [Liang Shanding]. "Cong *Xiaojie ji* dao *Di'er dai*" (From *Young Lady's Collection* to *The Second Generation*). In Mei Niang, *Di'er dai* (*The Second Generation*), 1-4. Xinjing: Wencong han xinghui, 1940.

Shang Qiuhe. "Ji Yang Xu xiaojie" (Notes on Miss Yang Xu). In Yang Xu, *Wo de riji* (*My Diary*), 181-5. Xinjing: Kaiming tushu gongsi, 1944.

Shangguan Ying. "Dongbei lunxian shiqi wenxue ceying" (Profile of the Northeast's Enemy-Occupied Territory's Literature). In Shangguan Ying, *Yiwen luantan* (*Random Notes on Literature and Art*), 101-13. Changchun: Shidai wenyi chubanshe, 1989.

–. "Wo suo zhidao de Mei Niang" (All That I Know about Mei Niang). In Shangguan Yin, *Shu hua* (*Talking about Books*), 33-6. Changchun: Jilin renmin chubanshe, 2001.

Shen Dianhe and Huang Wanhua. *Dongbei lunxian shiqi wenxue shilun* (*Historical Discourses on the Literature of the Enemy Occupation of the Northeast*). Harbin: Beifang wenyi chuabanshe, 1991.

Sheng Ying. *Ershi shiji Zhongguo nüxing wenxueshi* (*History of Twentieth-Century Chinese Women's Literature*). Tianjin: Tianjin renmin chubanshe, 1995.

Shi Xiuwen. "Zhiyu funü yu jiating funü" (Professional Women and Household Women). *Daban Huawen meiri* (*Chinese Osaka Daily*) 9, no. 7 (1942): 29-30.

"Shidai xiaojiemen" (Contemporary Girls). *Datong bao* (*Great Unity Herald*), 5 November 1936, 7.

Sun Zhongtian. "Lishi de jiedu yu shenmei quxiang" (Towards a History of Interpretation and Aesthetics). In *Dongbei lunxian shiqi wenxue xinlun* (*New Discourse on the Literature of the Northeast Occupation Era*), ed. Feng Weiqun and Li Chunyan, 1-11. Changchun: Jilin daxue chubanshe, 1991.

Sun Zhongtian, Feng Zengyu, Huang Wanhua, and Liu Aihua. *Liaokao xia de Miusi: Dongbei lunxian qu wenxue shigang* (*The Shackled Muse: Historical Outline of the Literature of the Northeast Occupied Territories*). Changchun: Jilin daxue chubanshe, 1999.

Takebe Utako. "Dadongya zhanzheng xia qingnian funü de juewu" (Young Women's Consciousness under the Greater East Asia War). *Qingnian wenhua* (*Youth Culture*) 1, no. 3 (1943): 16-18.

Tian Lin [Dan Di]. "Dongbei lunxianqi wenxue zhi wojian" (My Views on the Literature of the Enemy-Occupied Northeast). In *Dongbei lunxian shiqi wenxue* (*Literature of the Enemy-Occupied Northeast*), ed. Feng Weiqun, Wang Jianzhong, Li Chunyan, Li Shuquan, 410-13. Shenyang: Shenyang chubanshe, 1992.

–. "Huiyi *Wutian* yu Ba Lai" (Recollecting *Grassland* and Ba Lai). *Dongbei wenxue yanjiu shiliao* (*Historical Research Materials of Northeastern Literature*), no. 3 (September 1986): 167-9.

–. "San ru lianyu" (Thrice into Purgatory). Unpublished manuscript. Author's collection.

–. "Wei *Changye yinghuo* dansheng er huanhu" (Hailing the Birth of *Fireflies of the Long Night*). *Dongbei wenxue yanjiu shiliao* (*Historical Research Materials of Northeastern Literature*), no. 5 (1987): 55-7, 81.

Wang Jianzhong. "Nüxing wenxue de jiao'ao: Ping *Changye yinghuo* de sixiang yishu chengjiu" (The Pride of Women's Literature: Appraising the Achievements in Ideological Artistry in *Fireflies of the Long Night*). In *Dongbei lunxian shiqi wenxue guoji xueshu yantaohui lunwenji* (*Collection of Papers from the International Symposium on Literature of the Enemy-Occupied Northeast*), ed. Feng Weiqun, Wang Jianzhong, Li Chunyan, Li Shuquan, 263-80. Shenyang: Shenyang chubanshe, 1992.

Wang Jianzhong and Li Shuquan. "Wu cai binfen de nüxing shijie yu shao'er shijie: Ping nüzuojia Luo Mai de *Luo Mai shiwen ji*" (A Riot of Colour in Women's World and Young Men's World: Evaluating Woman Writer Luo Mai's *Collection of Luo Mai's Writings*). In *Dongbei lunxian shiqi wenxue guoji xueshu yantaohui lunwenji* (*Collection of Papers from the International Symposium on Literature of the Enemy-Occupied Northeast*), ed. Feng Weiqun, Wang Jianzhong, Li Chunyan, Li Shuquan, 325-40. Shenyang: Shenyang chubanshe, 1992.

Wang Qiuying. "Wo suo zhidao de dongbei lunxianqi Shengyang wenxue" (All I Know about Shenyang Literature from the Era of the Enemy Occupation of the Northeast). *Dongbei wenxue yanjiu shiliao* (*Historical Research Materials on Northeastern Literature*), no. 6 (December 1987): 21-44.

–. "Yijiusiling nian qian de dongbei wenyi qingkuang" (The Conditions of the Arts in the Northeast before 1940). *Dongbei xiandai wenxue shiliao* (*Historical Materials of Modern Northeastern Literature*), no. 1 (March 1980): 81-6.

–. "Zhide tantao de ji ge wenti" (Several Questions Worthy of Inquiry). *Dongbei wenxue yanjiu shiliao* (*Historical Research Materials of Northeastern Literature*) , no. 3 (September 1986): 182-9.

Wang Yeping, ed. *Dongbei lunxian shisinian jiaoyushi* (*The History of Education in the Northeast's Fourteen Years of Enemy Occupation*). Changchun: Jilin jiaoyu chubanshe, 1989.

Wei Changming [Li Zhengzhong]. "Dongbei nüxing wenxue shisi nian shi" (A History of Fourteen Years of Northeastern Women's Literature). *Dongbei wenxue* (*Northeastern Literature*) 1, no. 4 (March 1946). Reprinted in *Dongbei xiandai wenxue daxi, 1919-1949*. Vol. 1, *Pinglun juan* (*Collection of Modern Northeastern Literature, 1919-1949*. Vol. 1, *Critical Evaluation*), ed. Zhang Yumao, 511-23. Shenyang: Shenyang chubanshe, 1996.

–. "*Dongbei Wenxue* fakan qianhou" (Before and After the Publication of *Northeastern Literature*). *Dongbei wenxue yanjiu shiliao* (*Historical Research Materials of Northeastern Literature*), no. 3 (September 1986): 107-11.

Wei Zhonglan. "Xin Zhongguo nüxing de dongjing" (Sounds of the New Chinese Women's Movement). *Qingnian Wenhua* (*Youth Culture*) 1, no. 3 (1943): 33-5.

Wu Ying. "Chuxi Dadongya wenxuezhe da hui suo gan" (Feelings about Attending the Greater East Asia Writers' Congress). *Qilin* (*Unicorn*) 3, no. 2 (1943): 49-50.

–. "Cui Hong" (Cui Hong). *Wenxuan* (*Literary Selections*), no. 1 (1940): 116-24. Reprinted in *Changye yinghuo* (*Fireflies of the Long Night*), ed. Liang Shanding, 305-12. Shenyang: Chunfeng wenyi chubanshe, 1986.

–. "Fangwen juezhan xia Uda furen de yu'er" (Interviewing Madame Uda about Raising Her Son with War Resolve). *Xin Manzhou* (*New Manchukuo*) 6, no. 10 (1944): 64-6.

–. "Fu Mei Niang shu" (Responding to Mei Niang's Letter). *Funü zazhi* (*Ladies' Journal*) 5, no. 4 (1944): 20-1.

–. "Fuchen de xinyu" (Drifting Words from the Heart). *Qilin* (*Unicorn*) 2, no. 4 (1942): 110.

Reprinted in *Dongbei xiandai wenxue daxi, 1919-1949*. Vol. 10, *Sanwen juan* (*Compendium of Modern Northeastern Literature, 1919-1949*. Vol. 10, *Essays*), ed. Zhang Yumao, 565-6. Shenyang: Shenyang chubanshe, 1996.

–. "Gan miao hui" (Dashing to the Temple Meeting). *Simin* (*This People*), July 1934, 13.

–. "Ji Shan Ding shu" (Mailing Shan Ding a Letter). *Funü zazhi* (*Ladies' Journal*) 5, no. 4 (1944): 21.

–. "Lianzhe de youren" (Missing Friends). *Daban Huawen meiri* (*Chinese Osaka Daily*) 4, no. 3 (1940): 38-9. Reprinted in *Dongbei xiandai wenxue daxi, 1919-1949*. Vol. 10, *Sanwen juan* (*Compendium of Modern Northeastern Literature, 1919-1949*. Vol. 10, *Essays*), ed. Zhang Yumao, 562-5. Shenyang: Shenyang chubanshe, 1996.

–. "Liang ji" (Two Extremes). In Wu Ying, *Liang Ji* (*Two Extremes*) , 117-28. Xinjing: Wenyi conghan hanxinghui, 1939.

–. "Manzhou nüxing wenxue de ren yu zuopin" (Women Writers and Writings of Manchukuo). *Qingnian wenhua* (*Youth Culture*), May 1944, 24-8. Reprinted in *Dongbei xiandai wenxue daxi, 1919-1949*. Vol. 10, *Sanwen juan* (*Compendium of Modern Northeastern Literature, 1919-1949*. Vol. 10, *Essays*), ed. Zhang Yumao, 342-56. Shenyang: Shenyang chubanshe, 1996.

–. "Ming" (Howl). *Qingnian wenhua* (*Youth Culture*) 1, no. 3 (1943): 90-4.

–. "Nü pantu" (Woman Rebel). In Wu Ying, *Liang Ji* (*Two Extremes*), 23-36. Xinjing: Wenyi conghan hanxinghui, 1939.

–. "Qian sipo" (Fourth Sister-in-law Qian). In Wu Ying, *Liang Ji* (*Two Extremes*), 61-8. Xinjing: Wenyi conghan hanxinghui, 1939.

–. "Wang xiang" (Gazing Homeward). In Wu Ying, *Liang Ji* (*Two Extremes*), 129-53. Xinjing: Wenyi conghan hanxinghui, 1939.

–. "Wo zenyang xie de 'Xuyuan'" (How I Wrote "Dilapidation"), *Yiwenzhi* (*Chronicle of the Arts*) 1, no. 1 (1943): 89-93. Reprinted in *Dongbei xiandai wenxue daxi, 1919-1949*. Vol. 10, *Sanwen juan* (*Compendium of Modern Northeastern Literature, 1919-1949*. Vol. 10, *Essays*), ed. Zhang Yumao, 566-9. Shenyang: Shenyang chubanshe, 1996.

–. "Xiao jie" (Mixed-Up Street). *Wenxuan* (*Literary Selections*), no. 2 (1940). Reprinted in *Changye yinghuo* (*Fireflies of the Long Night*), ed. Liang Shanding, 313-21. Shenyang: Chunfeng wenyi chubanshe, 1986.

–. "Xin kundao" (New Female Path). In Wu Ying, *Liang Ji* (*Two Extremes*), 81-92. Xinjing: Wenyi conghan hanxinghui, 1939.

–. "Xin youling" (New Ghost). In Wu Ying, *Liang Ji* (*Two Extremes*), 1-22. Xinjing: Wenyi conghan hanxinghui, 1939.

–. "Xuyuan" (Dilapidation). *Zhongguo wenyi* (*Chinese Arts*) 6, no. 5 (1942): 56-69. Reprinted in *Changye yinghuo* (*Fireflies of the Long Night*), ed. Liang Shanding, 322-45. Shenyang: Chunfeng wenyi chubanshe, 1986.

–. "Yu" (Lust). *Qilin* (*Unicorn*) 2, no. 10 (1942): 88-92.

Wu Yuying [Wu Ying]. "Furen qianghou huodong zhi chengzhi" (Accomplishments of Women behind the Gun). *Xin Manzhou* (*New Manchukuo*) 2, no. 5 (1940): 61-6.

–. "Zhangfu fushi" (The Matter of Serving Husbands). *Xin Manzhou* (*New Manchukuo*) 2, no. 2 (1940): 70-2.

Xi Yi. "Manzhou funü suixiang" (Casual Thoughts on Women in Manchukuo). *Qingnian wenhua* (*Youth Culture*) 1, no. 3 (1943): 36-8.

"Xiandai jiatingzhong" (In Today's Households). *Datong bao* (*Great Unity Herald*), 5 November 1936, 7.

Xu Naixiang and Huang Wanhua. *Zhongguo kangzhan shiqi lunxianqu wenxue shi* (*History of the Literature of the Enemy-Occupied Territories during China's War of Resistance*). Fuzhou: Fujian jiaoyu chubanshe, 1995.

Yang Xu. "Dang wo tai xinkao pengyou de shihou" (When I Trusted My Friend Too Much). In Yang Xu, *Luoying ji* (*Collection of Fallen Petals*), 107-9. Xinjing: Kaiming tushu gongsi, 1943.

–. "Fangfu shi yi chang wennuan de meng" (As If It's a Warm Dream). In Yang Xu, *Luoying ji* (*Collection of Fallen Petals*), 17-20. Xinjing: Kaiming tushu gongsi, 1943.

–. "Fu Xian shi yan zaji" (Jottings on the Facts of the Performance in Korea). In Yang Xu, *Luoying ji* (*Collection of Fallen Petals*), 90-8. Xinjing: Kaiming tushu gongsi, 1943.

–. "Gechang" (Singing). *Xin Manzhou* (*New Manchukuo*) 5, no. 1 (1943): 54-5.

–. "Gongkai de zuizhuang" (Open Indictment). In Yang Xu, *Wo de riji* (*My Diary*), 89-113. Xinjing: Kaiming tushu gongsi, 1944.

–. "Huainian" (Missing). In Yang Xu, *Wo de riji* (*My Diary*), 49-63. Xinjing: Kaiming tushu gongsi, 1944.

–. "Ji" (Mail). In Yang Xu, *Luoying ji* (*Collection of Fallen Petals*), 129-30. Xinjing: Kaiming tushu gongsi, 1943.

–. "Ji yu fu" (Mail and Response). In Yang Xu, *Luoying ji* (*Collection of Fallen Petals*), 82-9. Xinjing: Kaiming tushu gongsi, 1943.

–. "Jimo de shengyin" (The Sound of Loneliness). In Yang Xu, *Luoying ji* (*Collection of Fallen Petals*), 3-5. Xinjing: Kaiming tushu gongsi, 1943.

–. "Jiyi shi ge canren de du chong" (Memory Is a Cruel Poisonous Insect). In Yang Xu, *Luoying ji* (*Collection of Fallen Petals*), 30-2. Xinjing: Kaiming tushu gongsi, 1943.

–. "Luo hua shijie" (The Season of Fallen Flowers). In Yang Xu, *Luoying ji* (*Collection of Fallen Petals*), 58-66. Xinjing: Kaiming tushu gongsi, 1943.

–. "Luoying ji" (Collection of Fallen Petals). In Yang Xu, *Luoying ji* (*Collection of Fallen Petals*), 153-66. Xinjing: Kaiming tushu gongsi, 1943.

–. "Piaoling de xin" (Forsaken Heart). *Xin Manzhou* (*New Manchukuo*), July 1940, 39. Reprinted in Yang Xu, *Luoying ji* (*Collection of Fallen Petals*), 122-3. Xinjing: Kaiming tushu gongsi, 1943.

–. "Tu yao ou'ji" (Casual Notes Illuminating the Land). In Yang Xu, *Luoying ji* (*Collection of Fallen Petals*), 102-6. Xinjing: Kaiming tushu gongsi, 1943.

–. *Wo de riji* (*My Diary*). Xinjing: Kaiming tushu gongsi, 1944. Excerpts published in *Xin Manzhou* (*New Manchukuo*) 5, no. 5 (1943): 62-6.

–. "Wo he huaju" (Me and Drama). *Manzhou yinghua* (*Manchukuo Movies*) 5, no. 2 (1941): 46-7. Reprinted in Yang Xu, *Luoying ji* (*Collection of Fallen Petals*), 71-8. Xinjing: Kaiming tushu gongsi, 1943.

–. "Wo yu gechang" (Me and Singing). *Manzhou yinghua* (*Manchukuo Movies*) 5, no. 1 (1941): 46-7.

–. "Xiangfeng xin yi jiu" (Meeting Again, the Heart Is as Before). *Qilin* (*Unicorn*) 2, no. 10 (1942): 70-4.

–. "Xin de tiaodong" (Fluttering of the Heart). *Xin Manzhou* (*New Manchukuo*) 3, no. 3 (1941): 106. Reprinted in Yang Xu, *Luoying ji* (*Collection of Fallen Petals*), 151-2. Xinjing: Kaiming tushu gongsi, 1943.

–. "Ye zhi ge" (Song of the Night). In Yang Xu, *Luoying ji* (*Collection of Fallen Petals*), 45-7. Xinjing: Kaiming tushu gongsi, 1943.

–. "Yi di shu" (Letters from Different Places). In Yang Xu, *Wo de riji* (*My Diary*), 1-25. Xinjing: Kaiming tushu gongsi, 1944.

–. "Yidian chunzhen ji guren" (A Little Sincerity Mailed to an Old Friend). In Yang Xu, *Luoying ji* (*Collection of Fallen Petals*), 6-9. Xinjing: Kaiming tushu gongsi, 1943.

–. "Yiqi Zhaoling" (Recalling the Zhao Mausoleum). *Qilin* (*Unicorn*) 2, no. 10 (1942). Reprinted in *Dongbei xiandai wenxue daxi, 1919-1949*. Vol. 10, *Sanwen juan* (*Compendium of Modern Northeastern Literature, 1919-1949*. Vol. 10, *Essays*), ed. Zhang Yumao, 542-4. Shenyang: Shenyang chubanshe, 1996.

–. "Yi qie dou shi yan" (Everything Is Smoke). In Yang Xu, *Luoying ji* (*Collection of Fallen Petals*), 132-3. Xinjing: Kaiming tushu gongsi, 1943.

–. "Zixu" (Author's Preface). In Yang Xu, *Wo de riji* (*My Diary*), 1-4. Xinjing: Kaiming tushu gongsi, 1944.

Yang Yi. "Dongbei lunxianqu xiaoshuo" (Novels of the Northeastern Enemy-Occupied Territory). *Dongbei wenxue yanjiu shiliao* (*Historical Research Materials on Northeastern Literature*), no. 6 (December 1987): 3-20.

Yang Yong. "Caifang Mei Niang" (Interview with Mei Niang). In *Xunzhao Mei Niang*

(*Searching for the World of Mei Niang*), ed. Zhang Quan, 68-72. Brampton, ON: Mirror Books, 1998.

Yi Bing. "Nü zuojia Wu Ying shi fangwen ji" (Notes from an Interview with Female Writer Wu Ying), *Qilin* (*Unicorn*), no. 8 (1943): 136-9.

Yin Tiefen. "Wei nüren er zuo aishang zhi ge: Shilun Dongbei lunxian shiqi nüzuojia Wu Ying de xiaoshuo chuangzuo" (A Song of Sadness for Women: Tentative Views on the Fictional Works of Northeast Enemy-Occupation Era Woman Writer Wu Ying). In *Dongbei lunxian shiqi wenxue guoji xueshu yantaohui lunwenji* (*Collection of Papers from the International Symposium on Literature of the Enemy-Occupied Northeast*), ed. Feng Weiqun, Wang Jianzhong, Li Chunyan, Li Shuquan, 316-32. Shenyang: Shenyang chubanshe, 1992.

Yu Lei, trans. "Diwei mijian" (Secret Documents of the Enemy and Puppet Regime). *Dongbei wenxue yanjiu shiliao* (*Historical Research Materials of Northeastern Literature*), no. 6 (December 1987): 153-9.

–. "Ziliao" (Data). In *Dongbei lunxian shiqi wenxue guoji xueshu yantaohui lunwenji* (*Collection of Papers from the International Symposium on Literature of the Enemy-Occupied Northeast*), ed. Feng Weiqun, Wang Jianzhong, Li Chunyan, Li Shuquan, 171-81. Shenyang: Shenyang chubanshe, 1992.

Yu Yanbin. "Wo liuxiale beishang he xiyue: Shenqie huainian Luo Mai tongzhi" (I Cry Tears of Sadness and Joy: Heartfelt Memories of Comrade Luo Mai). In *Luo Mai xiaoshuo sanwen ji* (*Luo Mai's Collected Essays and Short Stories*), ed. Liang Shanding, 187-91. Shenyang: Shenyang renmin chubanshe, 1990.

Zhang Quan. "Mei Niang: Ta de lijing he ta de zuopin shijie" (Mei Niang: Her Place in History and the World of Her Writings). In *Xun zhao Mei Niang* (*Searching the World of Mei Niang*), ed. Zhang Quan, 3-25. Brampton, ON: Mirror Books, 1998.

–. "Wei wanjie de huati: Luxianqu wenxue de zhengzhi pingjia" (Unfinished Conversation: Political Evaluation of Enemy-Occupied Territory Literature). In *Mei Niang xiaoshuo sanwen ji* (*Mei Niang's Collected Novels and Essays*), ed. Zhang Quan, 493-6. Beijing: Beijing chubanshe, 1997.

–, ed. *Mei Niang xiaoshuo sanwen ji* (*Mei Niang's Collected Novels and Essays*). Beijing: Beijing chubanshe, 1997.

–. *Xunzhao Mei Niang* (*Searching for the World of Mei Niang*). Brampton, ON: Mirror Books, 1998.

Zhang Yumao. "Ping *Changye yinghuo*" (A Critique of *Fireflies of the Long Night*). In Zhang Yumao, *Zhe tuan huo, zhe zhen feng* (*This Ball of Fire, This Gust of Wind*), 466-77. Shenyang: Shenyang chubanshe, 2000.

–, ed. *Dongbei xiandai wenxue daxi, 1919-1949* (*Compendium of Modern Northeastern Literature, 1919-1949*). 14 vols. Shenyang: Shenyang chubanshe, 1996.

Zhang Yumao and Yan Zhihong. "Lun Dongbei lunxian shiqi xiaoshuo" (Discussing Novels of the Northeast Enemy-Occupation Era). In *Dongbei lunxian shiqi wenxue guoji xueshu yantaohui lunwenji* (*Collection of Papers from the International Symposium on Literature of the Enemy-Occupied Northeast*), ed. Feng Weiqun, Wang Jianzhong, Li Chunyan, Li Shuquan, 1-27. Shenyang: Shenyang chubanshe, 1992.

Zhong Dazhong. "'Nan Ling Bei Mei' de 'Mei'" (The "Mei" of "The South Has Zhang Ailing, the North Has Mei Niang"). In *Xunzhao Mei Niang* (*Searching for the World of Mei Niang*), ed. Zhang Quan, 60-3. Brampton, ON: Mirror Books, 1998.

Zhou Qinghe. "Tian Lin de wenxue chuangzuo qingxiong he yishu tese" (The Production Tendencies and Artistic Characteristics of Tian Lin's Literature). *Dongbei wenxue yanjiu shiliao* (*Historical Research Materials on Northeastern Literature*), no. 6 (December 1987): 105-9.

Zhu Ti. "Bangwan de shiye" (Dusk Field of Vision). *Daban Huawen meiri* (*Chinese Osaka Daily*) 11, no. 12 (1944): 31.

–. "Da Heilongjiang de youyu" (The Melancholy of the Mighty Black Dragon River). *Funü*

huabao (*Ladies Pictorial*), 1943. Reprinted in *Changye yinghuo* (*Fireflies of the Long Night*), ed. Liang Shanding, 459-77. Shenyang: Chunfeng wenyi chubanshe, 1986.
–. "Du Bohai" (Crossing the Bohai Sea). In Zhu Ti, *Ying* (*Cherry*). Xinjing: Guomin tushu zhushi huishe, 1945. Reprinted in *Changye yinghuo* (*Fireflies of the Long Night*), ed. Liang Shanding, 492-512. Shenyang: Chunfeng wenyi chubanshe, 1986.
–. "Kugao de xinyuan shang saxia yipian yangguang" (Casting a Layer of Sunlight on Withered Dreams). *Dongbei wenxue yanjiu shiliao* (*Historical Research Materials of Northeastern Literature*), no. 3 (September 1986): 171-2.
–. "Meng yu qingchun" (Dreams and Youth). *Daban Huawen meiri* (*Chinese Osaka Daily*) 10, no. 7 (1943): 42-3.
–. "Shengming zhi xiyue" (The Joy of Life). In Zhu Ti, *Ying* (*Cherry*), 40-55. Xinjing: Guomin tushu zhushi huishe, 1945.
–. "Wo he wo de haizimen" (Me and My Children). In Zhu Ti, *Ying* (*Cherry*), 69-82. Xinjing: Guomin tushu zhushi huishe, 1945.
–. "Xiao Yinzi he ta de jiazu" (Little Yinzi and Her Relations). *Dongbei wenxue* (*Northeastern Literature*) 1, no. 1 (1945): 39-47. Reprinted in *Changye yinghuo* (*Fireflies of the Long Night*), ed. Liang Shanding, 478-91. Shenyang: Chunfeng wenyi chubanshe, 1986.
–. "Xu" (Author's preface). In Zhu Ti, *Ying* (*Cherry*), 1-5. Xinjing: Guomin tushu zhushi huishe, 1945.
–. "Ying" (Cherry). In Zhu Ti, *Ying* (*Cherry*), 153-61. Xinjing: Guomin tushu zhushi huishe, 1945.
–. "Yuantian de Liuxing" (A Shooting Star in a Faraway Sky). *Xin chao* (*New Tide*) 1, no. 7 (March 1943). Reprinted in Zhu Ti, *Ying* (*Cherry*), 82-98. Xinjing: Guomin tushu zhushi huishe, 1945.
–. "Ziji de geying, ziji de ganqing" (My Song, My Feelings). In Zhu Ti, *Ying* (*Cherry*), 1. Xinjing: Guomin tushu zhushi huishe, 1945.
Zhu Ti and Li Keju. "1942 yu 1945 nian Dongbei wenyijie" (The Northeast's Literary World, 1942 to 1945). In *Dongbei lunxian shiqi wenxue guoji xueshu yantaohui lunwenji* (*Collection of Papers from the International Symposium on Literature of the Enemy-Occupied Northeast*), ed. Feng Weiqun, Wang Jianzhong, Li Chunyan, Li Shuquan, 405-9. Shenyang: Shenyang chubanshe, 1992.
Zhu Zhenhua [Lan Ling]. "Dong yi dao jie wu hao" (Number Five on East Number One Road). In *Qiqihaar ribao: Chuanghan* (*The Qiqihaar Daily: Achievements in Publication*), 96-100. Qiqihaar: Qiqihaar ribao, 1985.
–. "Nan wang de baojia hutong yi hao" (Unforgettable Baojia Hutong Number One). *Qiqihaar ribao: Chuanghan* (*The Qiqihaar Daily: Achievements in Publication*), 70-2. Qiqihaar: Qiqihaar ribao, 1985.
–. "Xi er dao jie shi hao de dong xiangfang" (The East Wing of Number Ten on West Second Street). In *Qiqihaar ribao: Chuanghan* (*The Qiqihaar Daily: Achievements in Publication*), 89-92. Qiqihaar: Qiqihaar ribao, 1985.
Zuo Di. "Buqu de renmin" (Indomitable People). *Dongbei minbao* (*Northeast People's Herald*), no. 1 (1946). Reprinted in *Changye yinghuo* (*Fireflies of the Long Night*), ed. Liang Shanding, 427-35. Shenyang: Chunfeng wenyi chubanshe, 1986.
–. "Liu Qi" (Liu Qi). *Qilin* (*Unicorn*) 2, no. 10 (1942): 75-8. Reprinted in *Changye yinghuo* (*Fireflies of the Long Night*), ed. Liang Shanding, 391-9. Shenyang: Chunfeng wenyi chubanshe, 1986.
–. "Meiyou guang de xing" (A Lustreless Star). *Funü shenghuo* (*Ladies' Life*), 1943. Reprinted in *Changye yinghuo* (*Fireflies of the Long Night*), ed. Liang Shanding, 436-56. Shenyang: Chunfeng wenyi chubanshe, 1986.
–. "Nü nan" (Women's Difficulty). *Qingnian wenhua* (*Youth Culture*) 1, no. 3 (1943): 86-7.
–. "Xu" (Preface). In *Nüzuojia chuangzuoxuan* (*Selected Writings of Women Writers*), ed. Zuo Di, 1-3. (Xinjing: Wenhuashe, 1943). Reprinted in *Luo Mai xiaoshuo sanwen ji* (*Luo Mai's Collected Short Stories and Essays*), ed. Liang Shanding, 30-1. Shenyang: Shenyang renmin chubanshe, 1990.

–. "Yi ge huise de meng" (A Grey-Coloured Dream). *Qilin* (*Unicorn*) 2, no. 4 (1942): 112-13. Reprinted in *Dongbei xiandai wenxue daxi, 1919-1949*. Vol. 10, *Sanwen juan* (*Compendium of Modern Northeastern Literature, 1919-1949*. Vol. 10, *Essays*), ed. Zhang Yumao, 374-5. Shenyang: Shenyang chubanshe, 1996.

–. "Yi ge nüpanni" (A Woman Rebel). In *Funü Shenghua* (October 1945). Reprinted in *Luo Mai xiaoshuo sanwen ji* (*Luo Mai's Collected Short Stories and Essays*), ed. Liang Shanding, 67-70. Shenyang: Shenyang renmin chubanshe, 1990.

–. "Zhai xiang" (Narrow Alley). *Dongbei minbao* (*Northeast People*), no. 1 (1946). Reprinted in *Changye yinghuo* (*Fireflies of the Long Night*), ed. Liang Shanding, 400-13. Shenyang: Chunfeng wenyi chubanshe, 1986.

English-Language Sources

Adas, Michael. "From Avoidance to Confrontation: Peasant Protest in Pre-Colonial and Colonial South-East Asia." In *Colonialism and Culture*, ed. Nicholas Dirks, 89-126. Ann Arbor: University of Michigan Press, 1992.

Adereth, Max. *Elsa Triolet and Louis Aragon: An Introduction to Their Interwoven Lives and Works*. Lampeter, UK: Edwin Mellen Press, 1994.

Atack, Margaret. *Literature and the French Resistance*. Manchester: Manchester University Press, 1989.

Atwood, Margaret. *Survival: A Thematic Guide to Canadian Literature*. Toronto: Anansi, 1972.

Barrett, David P. "Introduction: Occupied China and the Limits of Accomodation." In *Chinese Collaboration with Japan, 1937-45: The Limits of Accommodation*, ed. David P. Barrett and Larry N. Shyu, 1-17. Stanford: Stanford University Press, 2001.

Borthwick, Sally. "Changing Concepts of the Role of Women from the Late Qing to the May Fourth Period." In *Ideal and Reality: Social and Political Change in Modern China, 1860-1949*, ed. David Pong and Edmund Fung, 63-91. Lanham, MD: University Press of America, 1985.

Boyle, John Hunter. *China and Japan at War, 1937-1945: The Politics of Collaboration*. Stanford: Stanford University Press, 1972.

Brook, Timothy. *Collaboration: Japanese Agents and Local Elites in Wartime China*. Cambridge, MA: Harvard University Press, 2005.

Buck, David D. "Railway City and National Capital: Two Faces of the Modern in Changchun." In *Remaking the Chinese City: Modernity and National Identity, 1900-1950*, ed. Joseph W. Esherick, 65-89. Honolulu: University of Hawai'i Press, 2000.

Ching, Leo T.S. *Becoming Japanese: Colonial Taiwan and the Politics of Identity Formation*. Berkeley: University of California Press, 2001.

Chow, Rey. *Woman and Chinese Modernity: The Politics of Reading between West and East*. Minneapolis: University of Minnesota Press, 1991.

"Concordia Association, A Unique Organ." *Japan Today and Tomorrow*, 190-1. Osaka: Osaka Mainichi, 1939.

Crossley, Pamela Kyle. *The Manchus*. Cambridge, MA: Blackwell, 1997.

Dirks, Nicholas B. "Introduction." In *Colonialism and Culture*, ed Nicholas Dirks. Ann Arbor: University of Michigan Press, 1992.

Duara, Prasenjit. "Of Authenticity and Woman: Personal Narratives of Middle-Class Women in Modern China." In *Becoming Chinese: Passages to Modernity and Beyond*, ed. Wen-hsin Yeh, 342-64. Berkeley: University of California Press, 2000.

–. "Local Worlds: The Poetics and Politics of Native Place in Modern China." *South Atlantic Quarterly* 99, 1 (2000): 13-45.

–. *Sovereignty and Authenticity: Manchukuo and the East Asian Modern*. Oxford: Rowman and Littlefield, 2003.

Fu Poshek. *Passivity, Resistance, and Collaboration: Intellectual Choices in Occupied Shanghai, 1937-45*. Stanford: Stanford University Press, 1993.

–. "Resistance in Collaboration: Chinese Cinema in Occupied Shanghai, 1941-1945" in *Chinese Collaboration with Japan, 1937-45:*

The Limits of Accommodation, ed. David P. Barrett and Larry N. Shyu, 180-98. Stanford: Stanford University Press, 2001.

Fulton, Austin. *Through Earthquake, Wind and Fire.* Edinburgh: Saint Andrew Press, 1967.

Gilmartin, Christina Kelley. *Engendering the Chinese Revolution: Radical Women, Communist Politics, and Mass Movements in the 1920s.* Berkeley: University of California Press, 1995.

Goldblatt, Howard. *Hsiao Hung.* Boston: Twayne, 1976.

Gordon, Andrew. *Labor and Imperial Democracy in Pre-War Japan.* Berkeley: University of California Press, 1991.

Gunn, Edward M., Jr. *Unwelcome Muse: Chinese Literature in Shanghai and Peking, 1937-45.* New York: Columbia University Press, 1980.

Higonnet, Margaret, et al., eds. *Behind the Lines: Gender and the Two World Wars.* New Haven, CT: Yale University Press, 1987.

Hiroshi Takama. "New Culture in Manchoukuo." *Manchoukuo Today*, no. 6 (1940): 37-41.

Hsinking, Bureau of Information, ed. *An Outline of the Manchoukuo Empire, 1939.* Dairen: Manchoukuo Daily News, 1939.

Huang, Nicole. *Women, War, Domesticity: Shanghai Literature and Popular Culture of the 1940s.* Leiden: Brill, 2005.

Iriye Akira, ed. *The Chinese and the Japanese: Essays in Political and Cultural Interactions.* Princeton, NJ: Princeton University Press, 1980.

Japan Today and Tomorrow. Osaka: Osaka Mainichi, 1939.

Kasza, Gregory. *The State and Mass Media in Japan, 1918-45.* Berkeley: University of California Press, 1988.

Kawakami, K.K. *Manchoukuo: Child of Conflict.* New York: Macmillan, 1933.

Kinney, Ann Rasmussen. *Japanese Investment in Manchuria, 1931-45.* New York: Garland Publishing, 1982.

Larson, Wendy. "The End of *Funü Wenxue*: Women's Literature from 1925 to 1935." In *Gender Politics in Modern China: Writing and Feminism*, ed. Tani Barlow, 58-73. Durham, NC, and London: Duke University Press, 1993.

Lary, Diana, and Thomas Gottschang. *Swallows and Settlers: The Great Migration from North China to Manchuria.* Ann Arbor: University of Michigan, 2000.

Lattimore, Owen. *Manchuria: Cradle of Conflict.* New York: Macmillan, 1935.

Lee, Leo Oufan. "Modernity and Its Discontents: The Cultural Agenda of the May Four Movement." In *Perspectives on Modern China: Four Anniversaries*, ed. Kenneth Lieberthal, Joyce Kallgren, Roderick MacFarquhar, and Frederic Wakeman Jr., 158-77. Armonk, NY: M.E. Sharpe, 1991.

Liu, Lydia. "The Female Body and Nationalist Discourse: Manchuria in Xiao Hong's Field of Life and Death." In *Body, Subject and Power*, ed. Angela Zito and Tani E. Barlow, 157-77. Chicago: University of Chicago Press, 1994.

–. *Translingual Practice: Literature, National Culture, and Translated Modernity – China, 1900-1937.* Stanford: Stanford University Press, 1995.

Lo Jiu-Jung. "Survival as Justification for Collaboration, 1937-1945." In *Chinese Collaboration with Japan, 1937-45: The Limits of Accommodation*, ed. David P. Barrett and Larry N. Shyu, 116-32. Stanford: Stanford University Press, 2001.

Mackie, Vera. *Creating Socialist Women in Japan: Gender, Labour, and Activism, 1900-1937.* Cambridge: Cambridge University Press, 1997.

Manchoukuo Yearbook: 1941. Hsinking: Manchoukuo Yearbook Company, 1942.

McCormack, Gavan. *Chang Tso-lin in Northeast China, 1911-1928.* Stanford: Stanford University Press, 1977.

Milligan, Jennifer. *The Forgotten Generation: French Women Writers of the Inter-War Period.* Oxford: Berg, 1996.

Mitter, Rana. *The Manchurian Myth: Nationalism, Resistance, and Collaboration in Modern China.* Berkeley: University of California Press, 2000.

Muel-Dreyfus, Francine. *Vichy and the Eternal Feminine: A Contribution to a Political*

Sociology of Enemy Occupation. Trans. Kathleen A. Johnson. Durham, NC, and London: Duke University Press, 2001.

Myers, Ramon H. "Creating a Modern Enclave Economy: The Economic Integration of Japan, Manchuria, and North China, 1932-45." In *The Japanese Wartime Empire, 1931-45*, ed. Peter Duus, Ramon H. Myers, and Mark R. Peattie, 136-70. Princeton, NJ: Princeton University Press, 1996.

Oka Yoshitake. *Konoe Fumimaro: A Political Biography.* Tokyo: University of Tokyo Press, 1983.

Peattie, Mark. *Ishiwara Kanji and Japan's Confrontation with the West.* Princeton, NJ: Princeton University Press, 1975.

Pollard, Miranda. *Reign of Virtue: Mobilizing Gender in Vichy France.* Chicago: University of Chicago Press, 1998.

Rings, Werner. *Life with the Enemy: Collaboration and Resistance in Hitler's Europe, 1939-1945*, trans. J. Maxwell Brownjohn. London: Weidenfeld and Nicolson, 1979.

Rossiter, Margaret. *Women in the Resistance.* New York: Praeger, 1986.

Scherer, James A.B. *Manchukuo: A Bird's Eye View.* Tokyo: Hokuseido Press, 1933.

Schoppa, Keith R. "Patterns and Dynamics of Elite Collaboration in Occupied Shaoxing County." In *Chinese Collaboration with Japan, 1937-45: The Limits of Accommodation*, ed. David P. Barrett and Larry N. Shyu, 156-79. Stanford: Stanford University Press, 2001.

Schwarcz, Vera. *The Chinese Enlightenment: Intellectuals and the Legacy of the May Fourth Movement of 1919.* Berkeley: University of California Press, 1986.

Sewell, William. "Japanese Imperialism and Civic Construction in Manchuria: Changchun, 1905-45." PhD diss., University of British Columbia, 2000.

Shinichi Yamaguchi. "Contemporary Literature in Manchuria." *Concordia and Culture in Manchoukuo*, 27-29. Xinjing: Manchuria Daily News, 1938.

Sixth Report on Progress in Manchuria to 1939. Dairen: South Manchuria Railway Company, 1939.

Suleski, Ronald. *The Modernisation of Manchuria: An Annotated Bibliography.* Hong Kong: Chinese University Press, 1994.

Tagore, Rabindranath. *Fireflies.* New York: Macmillan, 1928.

Tamanoi, Mariko Asano. "Introduction." In *Crossed Histories: Manchuria in the Age of Empire*, ed. Mariko Asano Tamanoi, 1-24. Honolulu: University of Hawai'i Press, 2005.

Toshio Tamura. "On Cultural Administration." *Manchoukuo Today*, no. 6 (1940): 1-3.

Tsurumi, Patricia. "Visions of Women and the New Society in Conflict: Yamakawa Kikue versus Takamure Itsue." In *Japan's Competing Modernities: Issues in Culture and Democracy, 1900-1930.* Ed. Sharon A. Minichiello, 335-57. Honolulu: University of Hawai'i Press, 1998.

Wang Zheng. *Women in the Chinese Enlightenment: Oral and Textual Histories.* Berkeley: University of California Press, 1999.

Weitz, Margaret. *Sisters in the Resistance: How Women Fought to Free France.* New York: J. Wiley, 1995.

Woodhead, H.G.W. *A Visit to Manchukuo.* Shanghai: Mercury Press, 1932.

Yamamuro Shin'ichi. *Manchuria under Japanese Dominion.* Trans. Joshua A. Fogel. Philadelphia: University of Pennsylvania Press, 2006.

Young, Louise. "Imagined Empire: The Cultural Construction of Manchukuo." In *The Japanese Wartime Empire, 1931-45*, ed. Peter Duus, Ramon H. Myers, and Mark R. Peattie, 71-96. Princeton, NJ: Princeton University Press, 1996.

–. *Japan's Total Empire: Manchuria and the Culture of Wartime Imperialism.* Berkeley: University of California Press, 1998.

Yü Ying-shih. "Neither Renaissance nor Enlightenment: A Historian's Reflections on the May Fourth Movement." In *The Appropriation of Cultural Capital: China's May Fourth Project*, ed. Milena Dolezelova-Velingerova and Oldrich Kral, 299-324. Cambridge, MA: Harvard University Press, 2001.

Index

Printed and bound in Canada by Friesens

Set in News Gothic and Walbaum by Artegraphica Design Ltd.

Text design: Blakeley

Copy editor: Barbara Tessman

Proofreader: Gail Copeland